ANXIETY OF ERASURE

Gender, Culture, and Politics in the Middle East
miriam cooke, Simona Sharoni, and Suad Joseph, *Series Editors*

Other titles in Gender, Culture, and Politics in the Middle East

Arab and Arab American Feminisms: Gender, Violence, and Belonging
Rabab Abdulhadi, Evelyn Alsultany, and Nadine Naber, eds.

Arab Women's Lives Retold: Exploring Identity through Writing
Nawar Al-Hassan Golley, ed.

The Female Suffering Body: Illness and Disability in Modern Arabic Literature
Abir Hamdar

Intersections: Gender, Nation, and Community in Arab Women's Novels
Lisa Suhair Majaj, Paula W. Sunderman, and Therese Saliba, eds.

Masculine Identity in the Fiction of the Arab East since 1967
Samira Aghacy

Palestinian Women's Activism: Nationalism, Secularism, Islamism
Islah Jad

Rituals of Memory in Contemporary Arab Women's Writing
Brinda Mehta

Words, Not Swords: Iranian Women Writers and the Freedom of Movement
Farzaneh Milani

For a full list of titles in this series,
visit https://press.syr.edu/supressbook-series/
gender-culture-and-politics-in-the-middle-east/.

ANXIETY
OF ERASURE

Trauma, Authorship, and the Diaspora in Arab Women's Writings

HANADI AL-SAMMAN

Syracuse University Press

Copyright © 2015 by Syracuse University Press
Syracuse, New York 13244-5290

All Rights Reserved

First Paperback Edition 2019

19 20 21 22 23 24   6 5 4 3 2 1

∞ The paper used in this publication meets the minimum requirements
of the American National Standard for Information Sciences—Permanence
of Paper for Printed Library Materials, ANSI Z39.48-1992.

For a listing of books published and distributed by Syracuse University Press,
visit https://press.syr.edu.

ISBN: 978-0-8156-3402-7 (cloth)   978-0-8156-3662-5 (paperback)   978-0-8156-5329-5 (e-book)

Library of Congress has cataloged the hardcover edition as follows:

Names: Al-Samman, Hanadi.
   Title: Anxiety of erasure : trauma, authorship, and the diaspora in Arab
women's writings / Hanadi Al-Samman.
   Description: First edition. | Syracuse : Syracuse University Press, 2015. |
   Series: Gender, culture, and politics in the Middle East | "Covers [Arabic] literature
produced by women writers in Europe and in North and South America from 1920 to
2011"—Introduction. | Includes bibliographical references and index.
   Identifiers: LCCN 2015035801| ISBN 9780815634027 (cloth : alk. paper) |
ISBN 9780815653295 (e-book)
   Subjects: LCSH: Arabic literature—America—History and criticism. | Arabic literature—
Europe—History and criticism. | Arabic literature—Women authors—History and criticism. |
Autobiographical fiction, Arabic—History and criticism. | Psychic trauma in literature. |
Identity (Psychology) in literature. | Liberty in literature. | Emigration and immigration
in literature. | Women in literature. | Culture in literature.
Classification: LCC PJ8502 .A47 2015 | DDC 892.7/099287—dc23
LC record available at http://lccn.loc.gov/2015035801

Manufactured in the United States of America

To Kinan and Tamim,
my light and my compass

Contents

Acknowledgments

This book is the culmination of an arduous journey that mirrored the trials and tribulations of the Arab women writers it examines, the trauma of their displacement, and the exuberance of their triumphant message. Along the way I was blessed with the support of colleagues and mentors, and the unconditional love of family and friends who cheered me on with undying conviction.

I am indebted to a Woodrow Wilson Career Enhancement Fellowship (2009) and to a Virginia Foundation for the Humanities Residential Fellowship (2010), which availed me of the time and space needed to complete my book manuscript. At the University of Virginia, I am grateful for the College and Graduate School of Arts and Sciences Summer Stipend Award (2011) and the Teaching Resource Center's Book Manuscript Grant (2012), which allowed me to seek external, editorial feedback on the final manuscript.

I thank miriam cooke for her incredible generosity and mentorship, and for believing in my project, every step of the way. I am grateful to Muhsin al-Musawi for his gracious invitation to present aspects of this book at Columbia University's Arabic Seminar Series, and for providing insightful comments on earlier versions of the manuscript. The book has benefited tremendously from the thoughtful and generous feedback of Roger Allen, Samer Ali, Sahar Amer, Marilyn Booth, Rasheed El-Enany, Adel Gamal, Ferial Ghazoul, William Hutchins, Suad Joseph, Mohja Kahf, and Suzanne Stetkevych. Their astute comments informed the book's arguments on various levels, it goes without saying; I am solely responsible for all remaining imperfections.

My colleagues at the University of Virginia provided the ideal haven for cultivating and enriching my thoughts as the book progressed. I am immensely grateful for Farzaneh Milani's insightful comments and superb mentorship, for Mohammed Sawaie's guidance, and for Zjaleh Hajibashi's thoughtful editing of some parts of my manuscript. Marva Barnett, Alison Booth, Cristina Della Coletta, Corinne Field, Robert Hueckstedt, María-Inés Lagos, Maurie McInnis, Geeta Patel, Elizabeth Thompson, Rina Williams, and Lisa Woolfork were ideal interlocutors who kept the inspiration's flame going. At the Virginia Foundation for the Humanities, Roberta Culbertson, Nancy Damon, Theodore DeLaney, William Freehling, Hilary Holladay, Sarah McConnell, Kevin McFadden, Judy Moody, and Robert Vaughan nourished my body and soul with delightful food and conversation.

I am extremely fortunate to have had the friendship and support of Salwa al-Neimi, Ghada al-Samman, and Hoda Barakat throughout the writing process. They generously read and commented on their respective chapters, shared unpublished work with me, and were truly inspirational during our personal interviews, correspondence, and beyond.

At Syracuse University Press, I thank the vision and the resolve of my current editor, Suzanne Guiod, in seeing this project through as well as the support of my previous editor, Mary Selden Evans, for her selection of my book for this series. Special thanks goes to my editor, Kenny Morata, for his exacting, yet light-handed, editing of my manuscript.

To my mother, Daad Chaker, goes my undying gratitude. She read and critiqued all the primary works and was the Muse behind my inspiration. The spirit of my aunt, Najdat Chaker, guided me through difficult terrains. My father, Walid al-Samman, supported me in manifold ways. My cousin, Waed Attar, always reminded me of the light at the end of the tunnel. I owe a great deal to Wayne Martin for being the ideal companion on this journey, and for his unwavering confidence in my success. My sons, Kinan and Tamim, were always there inspiring and cheering me on every step of the way. I am grateful for their love, patience, and ever-cheerful smiles. It is to them that I dedicate this book, hoping that their wondrous journeys will always bring them back home.

Note on Translation and Transcription

I have used English translations for the fictional works in question. In the absence of known English translations, I have used my own translation and indicated that both in the text and in the notes. All translations of Arabic poetry and primary critical texts are mine unless stated otherwise.

For the convenience of the general reader, I opted not to use the lengtheners to indicate special Arabic letters, but represented the *'ayn* (') and the *hamza* (') by their conventional symbols. Specialists should be able to easily identify the Arabic words. Because some authors anglicized their name, I use the anglicized form in the text. I have, however, transcribed their names in the notes and bibliography when referring to the Arabic originals of their works.

ANXIETY OF ERASURE

Introduction

Al-Maw'udah/Shahrazad, Icons of Erasure and Revolutionary Resurrection

> When the female (infant), buried alive, is questioned
> For what crime she was killed (*wa-idha al-maw'udatu su'ilat bi-ayyi dhanbin qutilat*).
> —The Holy Qur'an, *Surat al-Takwir* 81:8

> Silence, Shahrazad
> Silence, Shahrazad
> You're in a whole different world
> from my world of sad
> Looking for love
> isn't like looking for a homeland
> under the ash
> you didn't lose much
> But I lost my history,
> my family, and my land.
> —Nizar Qabbani, "A Chat with a Noncommittal Woman"

During the uprisings that swept several Arab countries after Tunisia's Mohamed Bouazizi first ignited the fires of people's indignation at authoritarian regimes by his self-immolation on December 17, 2010, a common motto repeated by the rebellious masses in Tunisia, Egypt, Libya, Syria, and Yemen was "people want to topple the regime" (*al-sha'b yurid isqat al-nitham*). Yet another less known motto went hand in hand with that first iconic one, particularly when peaceful demonstrations were faced with live ammunition in the case of Bashar al-Assad's Syria: banners and social media demanded "Don't bury our revolution" (*la ta'idu thawratana*). In the ensuing four-year reign of terror that engulfed the Syrian revolution after its inception on March 15, 2011, because of the Assad regime's massacres and continued shelling of innocent civilians with tanks, mortars, scud missiles, and military bombers, the tropes of *wa'd al-banat* (female infant burial) and its traditional victim *al-maw'udah* (the buried infant girl) have become representative of the innocent children massacred by Assad's ruthless militias, thereby uniting gender and politics in an inseparable bond. The Syrian revolution is the only revolution in the Arab Spring that was inspired by the thirteen-year-old children of Dar'a whose nails were pulled by the regime's security forces as a punishment for writing on their school walls "people want to topple the regime." It was Hamza al-Khatib who would, three months later, be the iconic image of this revolution when his tortured body was returned to his parents lifeless, and emasculated.

After the killing of ten thousand children, some in brutal massacres as in al-Hola (May 25, 2012), al-Qubair in Homs, Douma, and countless others in the infamous chemical attack on Ghouta (a suburb of Damascus) on August 21, 2013, another motto surfaced directly reflecting the female infant burial motif (*wa'd*). "*Bi-ayyi dhanbin Qutilna?*" (For what crime were we killed?) was and still remains a dominant motto in demonstrations and Syrian revolution Facebook pages. The activation of the pre-Islamic, *jahiliyyah* ritual of burying female infants alive in the sand (wa'd al-banat) in the context of the Arab Spring's demands for freedom and justice denotes the survivability of wa'd as a cultural myth, in Roland Barthes's sense, embodying the epitome of personal and political erasure. Barthes defines mythology as a mixture of semiology (formal science) and ideology (historical science) bent on studying what he calls "ideas-in-form" (Barthes 2012, 221). Mythology alerts us to the presence of cultural narratives, points out their repetitions as it explains their omnipresent imposition. However, mythological concepts do not resurface in the same fixed attire; rather they "alter, disintegrate, disappear completely . . . and can very easily [be] suppress[ed]," and then restored in a different fashion (Barthes 2012, 230). This explains the resurfacing of wa'd at this critical juncture during the Arab Spring's demonstrations, for it alerts contemporary Arab citizens to the return of the unjust era of the jahiliyyah, and foregrounds the need to eradicate despotism. As a cultural trope, wa'd is utilized to access the political turmoil of the nation. It denotes the political erasure of the voices of the Arab masses just as its historical use came to represent the personal erasure of female selfhood. Just as "myth is speech stolen and restored," in Barthes's estimation, so when the restoration of the wa'd trope as myth enrolls the latter in the service of the political, its connotations and manifestations are never the same (Barthes 2012, 236).

However, this was not the only time the wa'd motif resurfaced in contemporary Arab cultural history, for it appeared conspicuously in Syrian and Lebanese (*mashriq*) diaspora women writers' literature, the subjects of this study. The experiences of these writers (Salwa al-Neimi [b. 195?], Hanan al-Shaykh [b. 1945], Hoda Barakat [b. 1952], Hamida Na'na' [b. 194?], Ghada al-Samman [b. 1942], and Samar Yazbek [b. 1970]) with authoritarian regimes and the prolonged sixteen-year Lebanese Civil War, coupled with their diaspora experience, positioned them in a unique place to access the political traumas of the nation and the personal ones of its dispossessed, diasporic citizens. With these authors the wa'd trope is fabricated as a cultural myth, iconized, and deployed to interrogate cultural discourses pertinent to women's bodies, identity, and subjectivity; to their role as literary women and voice; to nation as a woman; and to tradition as a woman. Along with wa'd, an equally poignant, though less threatening, cultural icon is invoked in their writings, that of the masterful narrator Shahrazad. Both icons activate the corporal (al-maw'udah) and the literary (Shahrazad), thereby reuniting body and voice to heal the nation. Just as wa'd's incarnation moves the trope from the realm of feminine suffocation to that of the political suppression of freedoms, so does Shahrazad's. At the hands of Arab diaspora women writers, Shahrazad's trope moves from the purview of feminist and postmodernist context to that of the political. This is the unique contribution of these writers, and it is at this juncture that Shahrazad's trope joins with the political engagement achieved through the activation of the wa'd trope in recent literary and political articulations. By reengaging these cultural myths and recurrent traumas, diaspora women writers defy conventional narratives of personal and national erasure.

Anxiety of Erasure explores the transformation of these two iconic cultural motifs in diasporic, contemporary Arabic literature, the wa'd and Shahrazad, from the purely feminist signification to political engagement. The resurrection of these myths and traumatic memories is pivotal to the healing of both individuals and nations. This book articulates the therapeutic effects resulting from revisiting forgotten history(ies) as well as the collective, cultural memories of the maw'udah and of Shahrazad. The journeys in time and space undertaken by Muslim and Christian diaspora women writers take them beyond Shahrazad's conventional fixed locale and into multiple locations from whence they assert the value of maintaining mobility, fluidity, and nonfixity of roots/routes, and of multiaxial sociopolitical critique. The result is a nuanced Arab women's poetics that at once celebrates rootlessness and rootedness, autonomy and belonging.

Beyond Shahrazad

In his *Freedom, I Married You* (1988), the Arab world's most celebrated contemporary Syrian poet, Nizar Qabbani, begs a modern-day Shahrazad, whom he dubs a "noncommittal woman," to cease narrating stories from distant fantasyland and to feel the pain of the dispossessed Arab masses, deprived of their homelands and estranged from their history. His poem "A Chat with a Noncommittal Woman," quoted in the introductory epigraph above, articulates the catastrophe of the Arab citizen's alienation, and cries for political change akin to the one demanded by the Arab Spring's demonstrators in Tunisia, Egypt, Libya, Syria, and Yemen. The necessity to question Shahrazad's traditional role, to modernize her narrative so that her tales indict all the contemporary Shahrayars of the Arab world, is of paramount importance. Interestingly, Qabbani's appeal was also echoed in the early nineties by the Palestinian female writer Liana Badr. Her moving plea in *The Eye of the Mirror* (1991 [1994]) articulates the plight of the female narrator who needs to disseminate the stories of her homeland's colonial dismemberment, yet is unable to cross the borders into her country owing to checkpoints, barriers, and walls erected by the occupying Israeli forces to hinder her mobility. In the opening scene of her novel, her female narrator distinguishes her politically charged narrative from the fantasy tales of Shahrazad, her diasporic locale from Shahrazad's fixed positioning:

> You are insistent, calling again. You want me to tell you the story of Scheherazade, who rocks the sad king on her knees as she sings him tales from wonderland. Yet you know that I am not Scheherazade, and that one of the world's greatest wonders is that I am unable to enter my country or pass through the regions around it. Do not be surprised. Let us count them country by country. (Badr 1994, 1)

At issue for Arab women diaspora writers is the need to redefine Shahrazad's role, and to circumvent local, global, and colonial borders that restrict their access to their homelands and forget their lifesaving stories. In today's world, Shahrazad's role is no longer to heal the possessed Shahrayar or to be liberated from real or imaginary veils. Rather she is intent on exposing the dictatorial practices of Arab contemporary leaders—the Shahrayars of the Arab world—and on transforming the dispossessed Arab nation.

Shahrazad in Contemporary Arabic Literature

A survey of the ways in which Arab writers have used the iconic Shahrazad in the literature of the early twentieth century is necessary if we are to gauge the extent of the innovation undertaken by Arab diaspora women writers regarding the Shahrazad trope. In his *Shahrazad fi al-Fikr al-'Arabi al-Hadith* (1985) (Shahrazad in Contemporary Arab Thought), Mustafa 'Abd al-Ghani argues that the use of Shahrazad as an archetype in the writings of prominent writers such as Taha Husayn (1889–1973), Tawfiq al-Hakim (1898–1987), Naguib Mahfouz (1911–2006), and others is influenced by a romantic and exotic view derived from Shahrazad's portrayal in Western writings of the eighteenth and nineteenth century. Similarly, in his discussion of the Shahrazad trope in postcolonial Arab narratives in *The Postcolonial Arabic Novel: Debating Ambivalence*, Muhsin al-Musawi affirms that "[t]he colonizer who feminizes the land to be conquered and exploited has already appropriated the Arabian tales in the receiving Western culture" to the extent that this "exoticizing tendency" has forced Shahrazad to "almost [lose] identity in the West" (al-Musawi 2003, 15). Certainly at the hands of Western translators such as the eighteenth-century translation of the French Antoine Galland (1646–1715), which appeared in twelve volumes between 1704 and 1717, and later the English translations of Jonathan Scott (1754–1829), Edward William Lane (1801–1876), Richard Burton (1821–1890), and John Payne (1842–1916), Shahrazad was cloaked in romantic and exotic portrayals that fit the stereotypical mold of an outlandish Orient.[1] Her nineteenth and twentieth centuries' incarnation at the hands of American writers Edgar Allan Poe (1809–1849) and John Barth (b. 1930) stripped Shahrazad of her narrative mastery as it portrayed her at a loss for creative inspiration, willing to trade her body for access to stories in Barth's version,[2] and deserving of death for failing to impress the king with her narration in Poe's rendition.[3] Other contemporary Western portrayals such as Ethel Johnston Phelps's "Scheherazade Retold" took the opposite direction as it enrolled Shahrazad in a zealous, feminist project that was never her sole trademark.[4]

Yet for all the fame that *A Thousand and One Nights* garnered in the West, Husain Haddawy remarks that in the Arabic literary canon it was "regarded with condescension and contempt by the Arab literati of the eighteenth and nineteenth centuries" (Haddawy 1990, xxii). This demeaned status is attributed to its origination in the oral tradition as well as its association with folk tales and the populace of the coffeehouses. When Shahrazad finally makes her debut in adaptations of contemporary Arabic literature in the early twentieth century, she has been estranged from her Middle Eastern tradition, forced to exhibit foreign sensibilities borrowed from these exotic translations. 'Abd al-Ghani contends that the Shahrazad whom we encounter in Tawfiq al-Hakim's play *Shahrazad* (1934) and in

1. See Galland 1941, Scott 1811, Lane 1877, Burton n.d., and Payne 1901. For more on the *Nights* reception in English criticism, see Al-Musawi 1981.

2. See Barth 1972, 9–64, specifically 23, 26, and 29.

3. See Poe 1981, 491–502.

4. See Phelps 1981, 167–73.

Taha Husayn's and al-Hakim's jointly authored novel *Al-Qasr al-Mashur* (1932) (The Enchanted Palace) as well as Husayn's *Ahlam Shahrazad* (1951) (Shahrazad's Dreams) is greatly influenced by the romantic bent of the thirties that the Egyptian writers imported from the West. The 1798 French Expedition, Muhammad 'Ali's project to westernize Egypt, and the writers' exposure to European fiction during their study abroad brought about an acculturation process resulting in distancing Shahrazad's archetype from its Arabic milieu ('Abd al-Ghani 1985, 40). Along with romanticism, Arabic plays and novels of the forties and fifties that invoked the *Nights* were influenced by the symbolist movement. However, the activation of Shahrazad as an archetype mimicked the West's interest only in the frame story, and did not benefit from the plethora of Eastern symbols (magic, genies, Sinbad, animals allegory) specific to other *Nights* tales that could have been employed for social and political satire. With the exception of Husayn's *Ahlam Shahrazad* that critiqued Egypt's political conditions during World War II and a handful of poets who employed the Shahrazad trope to explain reasons and reverberations of the 1967 *naksa*, 'Abd al-Ghani argues, "the use of the trope in fifty writers of Arabic proved their failure in invoking Shahrazad's true heritage, for they portrayed her as the daughter of the European renaissance and they ignored the rich potential of the rest of the *Nights* stories" ('Abd al-Ghani 1985, 59, my translation).

Influenced by global feminist movements, the Arabic playwrights who employed Shahrazad's trope in the sixties, such as Ahmad Othman and Sabah Muhi al-Din, highlighted the idea of women's personal freedoms (al-Ghani, 140). Other feminist recasting includes fiction written by Arab women writers, though not always in Arabic, such as Assia Djebar's *Ombre Sultane* (1987a),[5] Leïla Sebbar's *Shérazade* (1982),[6] and Nawal El Saadawi's *Suqut al-Imam* (1987) (*The Fall of the Imam*, 1988).[7] However, not all of these representations are equal, for they range from the exotic in Djebar,

5. For the English translation, see Djebar 1987b.
6. For the English translation, see Sebbar 1991.
7. For the English translation, see El Saadawi 1988.

to addressing issues of Beur (French citizens of Arab descent) identity in Sabbar, until they reach full political and cultural engagement in El Saadawi. Furthermore, critical studies produced in the West and in the Arab world affirmed Shahrazad's feminist role while downplaying the political aspect of the trope in its cultural context (Malti-Douglas 1991, 2006; Sakakini 1950). In the eighties, Nu'man 'Ashour and Ahmad Suaylim present politically engaged representations of Shahrazad's archetype in which the dialectic of a sultan's tyranny and people's silence is addressed. Still, al-Ghani contends, this abstract vision did not benefit fully from the *Nights* model in which the archetype develops intrinsically from the *turath* (heritage), thereby establishing a futuristic, socially engaged vision representing, and embraced by, the collective.

Despite the fact that Arabic fiction and plays of the period did not cast Shahrazad in a revolutionary light, owing to the writers' desire to make amends with the powers that be instead of revolutions, poets of the free-verse movement resurrected the archetype in such a way as to call attention to its ambivalence. Indeed, this vacillation between attraction and aversion is what characterizes most of the poetry that evoked Shahrazad. She is at once a savior and a slave, a deliverer and a death trap. In his collection *Al-Mawt fi al-Hayat* (1968) (The Living Dead) one of the pioneers of the free verse movement in Arabic poetry, the Iraqi poet 'Abd al-Wahhab al-Bayati (1926–2001) revives the Shahrazad trope only to negate the importance of her role. He is suspicious of the traditional narrative that sings the praises of her masterful narration, thereby anointing her as the giver of life. He states, "I saw Shahrazad / a slave girl sold in the auction." To al-Bayati, she is the epitome of the "living dead / in eternal slumber without resurrection or serenity." In her acquiescence to the shah's tyranny, al-Bayati views her role as maintaining the status quo as she becomes one with "those buried alive in caverns" (al-Bayati 1968, 112–16). Al-Bayati's image unites Shahrazad's archetype with that of the maw'udah, thereby foreshadowing their future fusion in contemporary diaspora women's writings. Similarly, to the Jordanian Tayseer al-Saboul (1939–1973) Shahrazad's legendary skill in facing the tyrannical Shahrayar is just a myth, for she is an "imposter" (*Khid'a*), incapable of changing the state of constant fear that continues to engulf her and the Arab nation. His poem "What Has Not Been Said about

Shahrazad?" expresses his frustration: "My Shahrazad is a ruse who, for eternity, casts a veil of deafness in our ears" (al-Saboul 1998, 162). Furthermore, in the poetry of his compatriot ʿAbd al-Rahim Omar (1929–1993), Shahrazad is the defeated Arab nation, for both sell their honor for the sake of another night of enslavement. In his poem "How Did Shahrazad Die?" Shahrazad is at once "an honored idol and a concubine," representing fear and nation's death (Omar 1989, 184–85). Indeed, death is all that endures in the Syrian/Lebanese Yousef al-Khal's (1917–1987) poetic renditions of the archetype. When Shahrazad's tales become void of their moral compass and Eastern soul, he asserts that nothing is left but "Shahrazad's body / falling like leaves, a body / but the secret lies in the roots." The soil becomes at once "a womb and a tomb / Only death prevails" (al-Khal 1979, 210). Shahrazad and the maw'udah unite, yet again, when the former's disengaged tales, in Yousef al-Khal's recasting, lead to the symbolic death of the nation. It is the intertwining of these two cultural myths that I find most intriguing, most promising, for only a return to the "roots" of the trauma of political alienation and exclusion of the Arab masses, to the "tombs" of forgetfulness, can deliver the resurrection of women's narration and their nation from despotic regimes. An examination of how diaspora Arab women writers activate these two tropes to reflect the endless possibilities of death and rebirth, of social and political engagement, in order to ignite a revolution on the personal and political levels is my paramount goal in *Anxiety of Erasure*. This study deals with contemporary Arab women writers who, like their legendary foremother Shahrazad, decided to tell their stories in order to defy oblivion and symbolic death. However, unlike Shahrazad's fixed location, they have spun their stories from diasporic sites, woven from their experience with dislocation and decentralization. In other words, as they redefine the meaning of Shahrazad as NOT "born of the city" (Ouyang 2003, 405) but of the world, they remain committed to issues pertaining to home, albeit now recast from global perspectives. Moreover, departing from Shahrazad's devotion to storytelling, they have left behind the tradition of orality that kept their literary foremothers' legacy locked away, in Fadia Faqir's words, within "the house of silence" (1998) by male co-optation of their literary corpus and dominance of the written as well as the public and published form of the spoken word.

Most of the Arab women diaspora writers addressed in this study (Salwa al-Neimi, Hanan al-Shaykh, Hoda Barakat, Hamida Na'na', Ghada Samman, and Samar Yazbek) subscribe to the literary heritage of the queen of narrative, but not to the tradition of her subsequent co-optation. At the end of *A Thousand and One Nights*, Shahrazad is relegated to the traditional role of wife and mother. In essence, she is doomed to reside eternally within the walls of orality, for despite the *Nights'* acknowledgment of her role as the narrator of the embedded stories, she is nevertheless placed in the written version exactly as Shah Shahrayar willed it, within the appropriative prologue and epilogue of a male narrator.[8] Consequently, the writers in question realize the need to move beyond the realm of orality so as to avoid men's co-optation of their stories and lives. They also realize the value of their commitment to their Arabic language and the embattled countries they left behind. Their literary corpus bespeaks admiration for Shahrazad's narrative mastery, her resourcefulness, and her genuine interest in transforming the disturbed psyche of the unhappy king, and through him curing an ailing nation. However, unlike her, they redefine their roles not as "ministering angels" but as social agents with full authority over their written/published texts and complete involvement in their countries' political climates.[9] This means, of course, learning how to go beyond the confines of the private/oral world and to inscribe an everlasting public/written word. What Shahrazad could not

8. The original fourteenth-century Syrian manuscript only mentions Shahrazad's role as wife and mother at the end, but not how her stories were transmitted. However, the Bulaq Egyptian edition, written at a much later date in the eighteenth and nineteenth centuries, elaborates in its epilogue on the role of the male narrator who recorded Shahrazad's stories and placed them in the shah's safe. Furthermore, it is not clear whether Shahrazad's diminished role is intrinsic to the original text or an alteration enacted by the *Nights'* first French translator, Antoine Galland, in the early eighteenth century. See Haddawy 1990, 428, xvii, xx. Also see *Alf Layla wa-Layla* (1252 AH).

9. For more on the role of Victorian and nineteenth-century women as "ministering angels," see Gilbert and Gubar 1979, 45–92.

achieve in the limited, traditional world of the ninth century (the date of the first recorded manuscript of the *Nights*), these female writers have vowed to pursue with zeal and conviction. At stake here is physical and literary presence, the importance of leaving a literary trace that is truly one's own and not subject to erasure. The spirit of Shahrazad is forever present in the literature of Arab diaspora women; she makes sudden appearances in the folds of their narratives and is always in the background. Her presence invigorates their narratives with the message of commitment to their compatriots, men and women alike, as well as to the nation. More important, she always warns them against the dangers of male appropriation of their literature, which inevitably leads to female literary dispossession and a marginal existence threatened with erasure.

By activating the Shahrazad motif in contemporary diasporic and revolutionary literature, "[t]he medieval element is recalled to join force[s] with new historicism, too, to reassess the past and use it to criticize the present . . . the medieval intensifies narrativity, the practice of narrative, while paving the way for oblique criticism" (al-Musawi 2003, 115)—a criticism made more poignant by entwining the queen of medieval narrative with her pre-Islamic maw'udah counterpart. The pairing of such distant yet powerfully charged cultural icons in contemporary Arabic literature and culture has been staged remarkably well in the digital art of the Syrian revolution, in which Shahrazad and maw'udah resurface and mysteriously unite. Take, for example, episode 15, entitled "Hakawati," of the *Top Goon: Diaries of a Little Dictator* (a YouTube puppet show production filmed in Beirut) featuring a modern-day Shahrazad.[10] She tells the story of an ogre "ghoul" who ruled a magnificent kingdom with terror until fear and darkness engulfed all the citizens. Tyranny prevailed until the children wrote "hope" and "freedom" on the walls of their school. The show interfaces the story of Darʿa's children that we encountered in the context of waʾd at the outset of this introduction with the Shahrazad story. In this modern

---

10. See the "Hakawati" episode 15 published on Oct. 23, 2012, and dedicated to the children of Syria on this link: https://www.youtube.com/watch?v=vPS9sJvBUTk (accessed Aug. 22, 2015).

revolutionary narrative, the schoolchildren perform Shahrazad's role of the nation's savior with a contemporary twist. They inscribe, rather than tell, the conditions of honorable, free existence. In turn, they also pay with their lives the price of their courage as their little bodies, tortured and left to bear the brunt of the tyrant's wrath, stand as a trace reminding us of the maw'udah's body as well. Paring these two icons together, the maw'udah and the politicized Shahrazad, fuses these traditional cultural tropes in a most unusual symbiotic relationship characterized by an energized, contemporary revolutionary commitment—a commitment endorsed and activated in the literature of Arab diaspora women writers discussed in this study.

Conceptual Framework

Anxiety of Erasure uniquely examines the manifestations of Shahrazad's and the maw'udah's tropes in the literature of both Muslim and Christian mashriq diaspora women writers. Most of the writers in question engage in their own cultural remembrance of these two tropes in their writings. They materialize Shahrazad's literary erasure and the historical nightmare of wa'd in their narratives, thereby bringing these traumas to the surface and using them as a distant memory that propels the writing of their literature and inspires, above all, their survival.

The literature covered is of necessity transnational, since the diasporic site operates as a catalyst for this artistic canon. My research covers literature produced by women writers in Europe and in North and South America from 1920 to 2011. My book relies on the principle of cultural conflict and resolution to produce an understanding of the lost traumatic knowledge of Arab women's erasure and of diasporic Arab women's perception of themselves in both Western and Eastern mirrors. The book's scope is also multigenerational, often dealing with the literary productions of both first- and second-generation emigrants, engendering in the process an intergenerational dialogic and traumatic haunting. For example, the issues raised by the South American diaspora female writers in the 1920s (discussed in chapter 1) find their echo in the scathing critiques that their literary successors—contemporary European diaspora writers—have leveled against the Lebanese Civil War, the Gulf War, and the war in Iraq in the latter half of the twentieth century. The connection between these literary foremothers and contemporary diaspora writers intensifies the urgency of locating Shahrazad's literary trace in the traumatic past of the maw'udah tradition so as to resurrect women's body and word to ensure feminine agency in reconstructing cultural and national narratives. What this book offers is a deeply imbedded, culturally specific basis for reading Arab women's narratives. Their works act as incentives to memory, as a way to speak to and for the lost, forgotten, or erased selves, encouraging readers to listen to the archives, to keep Shahrazad's literary legacy and the buried voice of the maw'udah ever present.

Anxiety of Erasure proposes a transnational, intergenerational, mosaic framework for studying authorship and identity construction in Arab women's literature. It seeks to rectify the state of female literary erasure, by broadening the scope of gender and geographic definitions of *adab al-mahjar* proper and by shifting its focus from predominantly male writers residing in North and South American sites to women writers located in the European continent instead. Unlike previous scholarship, which addressed Arab women's authorship from the standpoint of harem walls, veiling, and imposed silence, my study examines the liberating, recentering role of diaspora in creating a reciprocated conversation with the foreign Other combined with an impact both on the streets of every Arab city (the women continue to publish in Arabic) and in the West that hosts them. My intention in amplifying their voices is to bring forward the writers' urgent message of transforming orality into print, and of reclaiming the corpus of their foremother Shahrazad through revisiting the traumatic sites of the pre-Islamic wa'd tradition. The writers' diasporic locales offer them a safe haven to challenge authoritarian states and censorship rules, and the fixity of essentialist concepts of nationhood. Their journey of national reconstruction is a transnational, interdisciplinary, and transformative project encompassing a broad spectrum of fictional genres: fantasy, autobiography, and war narratives expressed in novels, memoirs, journals, revolutionary diaries, and political commentary.

In *Anxiety of Erasure* I propose a theory for understanding the narrative strategies of Arab women writers in diaspora, and a framework within which to decipher the perplexing persistence of female infant burial and Shahrazad motifs in literature penned by these writers during the last century. This project further questions literary trauma theory's claims that traumatic knowledge can only be gained in ephemeral, oblique references, owing to what Freud and later Cathy Caruth called the "incomprehensibility" and the "irretrievability" of traumatic events (Caruth 1996, 18). My book disrupts this prevailing view of traumatic knowledge by arguing that, through the process of intergenerational insidious trauma, the reenactments of the wa'd trauma in diasporic women's literature do, indeed, make the traumatic event more "accessible," thus engendering a corporeality that allows healing and an understanding of the traumatic past. In employing the two tropes of Shahrazad and the maw'udah, Arab women writers materialize the site of the traumatic past, making it retrievable to the diasporic granddaughters of these female figures whose awakening engenders a survival project for two entities: diaspora women and their embattled countries.

In the literature of diaspora Arab women writers, the diasporic site itself is recreated as a synthesizing force that propels Arabs from different backgrounds to revitalize Shahrazad's literary image and to expand its reach in order to open up not just linguistic personal spaces, but political and cultural spaces as well. The book builds on Middle Eastern scholarship that has invoked Shahrazad as an inspiring or debilitating figure. However, unlike other studies that celebrated Shahrazad's orality, my project focuses on the moment of traumatic leap that women writers have to make in the process of moving beyond the oral and into the written embodiment of their literature. *Anxiety of Erasure* introduces the new politicized Shahrazad who has moved beyond her fixed locality and orality as she celebrates new definitions of self and state from multiple diasporic locales. To my knowledge, no other book in the fields of Middle Eastern, gender, and literary studies locates the dilemma of Arab female authorship in the anxiety generated by the double jeopardy of Shahrazad's orality and the wa'd trauma of erasure. Nor does any other book root this anxiety in the pre-Islamic female infant burial ritual and document the transformation of its ramifications by examining the literary works of Christian and Muslim Arab women during the last century.

In chapter 1, "Arab Women and the Experience of Diaspora," I explore the ways in which Arab diaspora women writers, both early and modern, have managed to redefine Shahrazad's role so as to simultaneously recall her trace, but situate themselves beyond her orality and fixed locality. Their diasporic locales help them articulate a multiaxial critique of the local, global, and colonial powers that restrict their access to their homelands. This chapter explores the contribution of early North American and South American women diaspora writers, and locates their literary corpus within Arab diasporic studies (*adab al-mahjar*). Furthermore, the chapter introduces the six contemporary diaspora women writers who are the focus of this research. I also articulate their practice of "living life as a nomad"—a practice that celebrates through the interplay of roots, routes and rhizomes, filiation/affiliation, deterritorialization/reterritorialization, departure/return, and loss/retrieval the creation of alternate, multilocal public spheres from which to engender a sociopolitical critique of the homeland.

Chapter 2, "Anxiety of Erasure: Arab Women's Authorship as Trauma," isolates two significant tropes in Arab women's narrative: Shahrazad and the maw'udah. These traditional foremothers are pivotal in vigorously resisting an Arab feminine poetics of erasure. The persistent traumatic erasure of these two figures, both literarily and physically, demands an immediate reinscription of female agency in the national and personal narratives. Despite the spatial and temporal distance that separates the early wa'd victims from these contemporary women writers, the various personal and political persecutions they endured or witnessed in the homeland, in times of both peace and war, have led to the survivability of the wa'd motif in their literary output, thereby attesting to the ability of intergenerational trauma to cross spatial and temporal boundaries. My application of the trauma examined in this literature follows the model of the posttraumatic stress disorder (PTSD), advanced in 1980, in which traumatic awareness surpasses the immediacy of the traumatic event experienced by the victim, and survives in the reenactment of said trauma in the individual's successors of the same gender or ethnic group. As such, the literature of contemporary diaspora Arab writers is riddled with apparitions of such historical, traumatic recollections. The reenactment of the traumatic event of the wa'd highlights Arab writers' contribution to the field of trauma theory and to Arab poetics, in which an awakening to the reality of this traumatic past alerts Arab citizens to the urgency of addressing the despotic present and enacting a national survival project. I argue that early diasporic women writers have internalized the trauma of Shahrazad's and al-maw'udah's erasure on an intergenerational level, and have, as a result, established certain landmarks for their successors to follow on the road to female literary self-assertion and resurrection.

By focusing on Ghada Samman's autobiographical novel *The Impossible Novel: A Damascene Mosaic* (1997a) and Hanan al-Shaykh's *The Locust and the Bird: My Mother's Story* (2009), chapter 3, "Mosaic Autobiography," traces the resurrection of the maternal stories through the autobiographies of the daughters. In this context, the matriarch's buried body is transformed into the written narrative of the daughter as orality is transcribed into print. This chapter proposes a transnational, intergenerational, mosaic framework for studying identity construction in Arab women's autobiographies. It further locates the origin of a new kind of collective, mosaic autobiography in diasporic experiences. By insisting on adding their female inscription to history and to the autobiography genre, Arab women writers risk conjuring up the demonic infant burial metaphor, often resurrected in Samman's and al-Shaykh's narratives. This traumatic metaphor cements the double jeopardy Arab women endure as they defy their physical and literary erasure. It is therefore significant that the diasporic site allows for the distancing needed to recast this haunting memory in the survival project. This chapter argues that the authors' way of circumventing autobiography's restrictive taboos is to pen a mosaic-like autobiography from the standpoint of a collective "We" rather than a subjective, individual "I." The mosaic autobiography departs from unitary subjectivity, individual accomplishments, and linear chronology. It subverts the illusory unity of the individual "I"; relishes tension and narrative gaps; acknowledges the tiny tesserae that eventually form the whole story, not just of the female narrator but also of her male characters; and captures the temporal and spatial properties of her distant homeland. In this vein, I contend that mosaic autobiography becomes a catalyst for enacting social change by incorporating the hauntingly discordant and collective voices of humans, animals, nature, and even the homeland itself in a final homogeneous, reconciling tune.

Heeding the forgotten voices of the masses leads to exorcizing the sins of the past on the way to reclaiming the future. In chapter 4, "Diasporic Haunting," Ghada Samman's experimentation with this past takes the form of fantasy fiction: a collection of short stories, *The Square Moon* (1994), and a novel, *A Masquerade for the Dead* (2003b). Fantasy for Samman is not the creation of a utopian frontier; rather, it is an avenue for traveling back in time to the virtual dimensions of the homeland, back to the hybrid and painful realities of the traditional Middle East. She conjures up characters from the past who embody the heart of Arabic myths and traditions: Sorcerers and matchmakers, ghosts of buried female infants, forgotten forefathers, political and religious apparitions, and even Shahrazad herself are all beamed up to the Paris of the 1990s to encounter the tormented souls and minds of their lost and dispossessed Lebanese compatriots. I argue that this technique allows the traumatic past to be retrieved in its full corporeal intensity, to be examined, criticized, and transformed to facilitate the process of self-interrogation in diaspora, and ultimately to eliminate the sociopolitical, global, and local conditions that caused Arab citizens' initial dispossession. The reenactment of cultural and personal traumas in Samman's fantasy fiction facilitates the process of healing by forcing the characters to revisit the site of forgotten, historical traumas so as to engender a process of remembering and of overcoming unresolved cultural memories

In chapter 5, "Transforming Nationhood from within the Minefield," I examine Hamida Na'na''s *The Homeland* (1995 [1979]) as an example of a war narrative covering the *adab al-naksa* (literature of defeat since 1967) and contesting the forgotten role of women in national construction. Once again, trauma theory unlocks the connection between the atrocities committed on both bodies: that of oppressed women and that of the embattled nation. In Na'na''s narrative, women's bodies and national bodies are fused, so that an assault on the former constitutes an assault on the latter, thereby embodying the traumatic effects on both entities. Na'na' articulates the simultaneous revival of women as icons of revolutions, and the symbolic burial (wa'd) of their agency in national construction. This woman/nation identification proves that the essentialist, military, and war rhetoric that ravaged the nation results from the same patriarchal discourse that persists in violating women. This body of literature highlights the novel ways in which Arab women writers came to be empowered by the decentralizing, marginalizing effect of the immigrant experience, and consequently to critique the masculine ideologies that propel the war machine. In this context, Naʿnaʿ's heroine echoes early diaspora writers such as Mari Yini ʿAtta Allah, offering pronouncements on the necessity of a postwar, humanist rhetoric of citizenship built on the exchange of words rather than gunfire. Challenging patriarchal, dominant ideologies necessitates the systematic deconstruction of institutionalized patterns of violence from within and requires disseminating a gospel of human love instead of religious or political separatism. The text articulates a need for a constant shifting and reshuffling of all centers of power so as to ensure equal participation of all the ousted citizens. Naʿnaʿ asserts that unitary, totalitarian definitions of a nation must also be revisited in order for it to be rebuilt through the constructive, healing dialogue of all the diasporic national selves, with the feminine prominent among them. This goal can only be accomplished if women are active participants in the construction of the new national narrative, and not spectators on the sidelines. Similar to early traumatic recollections of the mawʾudah in diaspora women's writings, the ethical purpose of the war narratives is ultimately the survival of the war-torn country and its tormented citizens.

Building on the need to save the country from the grip of authoritarian dictators, chapter 6, "Paradigms of Dis-ease and Domination," explores the fraternal dynamics of power exposed in Hoda Barakat's *The Stone of Laughter* (1995 [1990]), *Disciples of Passion* (2005 [1993]), *The Tiller of Waters* (2001 [1998]), and *Sayyidi wa Habibi* (2004b) (*My Master and My Lover*). In these novels Barakat articulates a framework for pinpointing the causes of Arab citizens' dispossession and consequent alienation. In the process, she also manages to question the fixity of gender identification along with socially forced and enforced heterosexual norms. Following Hisham Sharabi's seminal work on "neopatriarchy" (1988), I identify a system of fraternal association built on unquestioned obedience to the familial patriarch and the cult of the idolized leader as the major culprit for engendering the Lebanese Civil War, which always forms the backdrop of Hoda Barakat's narratives. It is the discovery of this "patrimonial" pyramidlike system—one built on the arbitrary form of political domination and, in Suad Joseph's words, a "care/control" dynamics (2001) and a Hegelian "master-slave dialectic" (Hegel 1807) between the ruler/the ruled that drives Badiʿ, the protagonist of *Sayyidi wa Habibi*, to exile in Cyprus, to impotence, and finally to suicide. Similarly, the forced homosocial affiliations resulting in "neopatriarchal" governments are the reasons behind the male characters' transformation, in the rest of Hoda Barakat's novels, from peace-loving individuals to violent militia members capable of engaging in arms deals, of committing murder and rape. Neopatriarchy, Hoda Barakat asserts, eliminates any space for alternative sexuality or politics.

Furthermore, I argue that the activation of the maw'udah and Shahrazad tropes in Barakat's *The Tiller of Waters* serves to shift the reader's interest from the personal feminine, to the political, to the communal. The male protagonist is forced to assume Shahrazad's role and vision, is thrust into the underground to learn invaluable lessons from the violent history of the wa'd tradition. In this context, the maw'udah becomes the amphora girl that embodies the buried Arab nation. In an attempt to resurrect premodern national histories and cultural memories of peaceful coexistence, Barakat unearths the buried city of ancient Beirut through the protagonist's exploration of the city's underground tunnels and the history of fabric. His search for the peace-loving voice of the buried Beirut mirrors other female diaspora writers' search for the buried maw'udah's voice. Once again, the national civil war's trauma befalling the nation mirrors the trauma of feminine erasure that afflicted the bodies of both Shahrazad and the maw'udah. Barakat cautions that Arab citizens are doomed to live in a constant state of real or symbolic burial until they topple their oppressive, authoritarian regimes and abandon their deference to the cult of the patriarch.

The absenting of Arab citizens' political agency leads to erasure and a self-imposed denial of their Arab identity. Chapter 7, "Border Crossings: Cultural Collisions and Reconciliation," traces the process of identity renunciation and reclamation in Hanan al-Shaykh's *Only in London* (2002

[2001]). The novel maps out the course of cultural interactions and collisions between the homeland and the diaspora. Al-Shaykh's three Arab
characters set out to redefine women's personal freedoms, class inequi-
ties, and forced heterosexuality. Along the way, they discover that the process of self-affirmation does not necessarily mean a renunciation of their
Arab identity. They learn to negotiate the gains and losses of hyphenated
identities, and to appreciate flexible citizenship, thereby forsaking homeland longings and engendering new belongings articulated through the
"dialogic" relationship between roots and routes. The main protagonist's
discovery of forgotten Arab manuscripts and reclamation of Arabic language and heritage constitute a return to the site of the traumatic past so
as to rewrite her feminine history and to reinvigorate her country with her
intercultural knowledge. Her capacity to move freely through the borders
that separate home from diaspora ultimately transforms them into hybrid
sites of identity regeneration where both attachments and detachments are
acknowledged and cherished. The final message is one of reconciliation, of
the necessity to build bridges of intercultural/intracultural understanding among individuals and nations, and of the value of shifting centers of
identity location to avoid fixed positionalities.

Harkening back to the literary and folkloric tradition signals contemporary diaspora writers' intent to access and listen to the historical
and literary archives. Chapter 8, "Unearthing the Archives, Inscribing
Unspeakable Secrets," focuses on the diasporic writings of the Syrian,
Parisian-based writer Salwa al-Neimi. In one renowned novella, *The Proof
of the Honey* (2009 [2007]); a collection of short stories, *The Book of Secrets*
(1994); and three poetry collections—*Gone Are the Ones I Love* (1999),
My Murderous Ancestors (2001), and *We Bequeathed Unto You* (2004)—
al-Neimi highlights the need to unearth the cultural archives in order to
access unspoken, thereby erased, cultural memory. By reinscribing love
and erotic poetics onto the Arab cultural map, al-Neimi is able to resurrect
the Arabic language and distant banned histories of pleasure that ensure
the celebration of Arab bodies, identity, and heritage. In al-Neimi's poetic
and prosaic literature, unearthing the cultural corpus and resurrecting
the trope of the buried body of the female infant, of the maw'udah and
her erased verbal expression, inevitably leads to the resurrection of a more

secure Arab premodern period. By engaging her Arab local and Western global interlocutors in what Gayatari Spivak calls a "plenary discussion" (2003), al-Neimi manages to dispel Middle Eastern and Western stereotypes that historically contributed to the erasure of Arab women's bodies and discourse. As the Arabic language and libido are resurrected, so is the belief in a more autonomous and secure Arab self.

Arab diaspora women writers' final message is that of triumph over trauma and adversity. In their resurrection of the maw'udah and Shahrazad tropes, they opted to revive but also to go beyond the debilitating history of both figures in order to reclaim women's history and story. In their literature, the maw'udah and Shahrazad are remarkably transformed from the personal, to the political, to the communal so as to engender resurrecting not just female subjectivity, but rather, in light of the ongoing Arab Spring revolutions, the uprising of the oppressed Arab nation. Samar Yazbek's *A Woman in the Crossfire: Diaries of the Syrian Revolution* (2012) is a perfect example of the transformation of these two icons from the buried feminine to the buried cities and nations. Her work, and that of other mashriq compatriots, is a testament that triumph will be the outcome of traumatic recall, recording, and reconciliation. Indeed, the regenerative reverberations associated with the writers' decision to move beyond Shahrazad's orality and fixed locality, beyond the traumatic memory of wa'd, have been heard loud and clear in exhilarating demonstrations in most revolutionary squares of the Arab world, demanding democracy and social justice.

1

Arab Women and the Experience of Diaspora

For Avatar Brah, a diasporic subject herself, the diasporic site is a prime location for the intersection of individual and collective memories, and for transforming traumas into triumphs. In her repertoire, "the word diaspora often invokes the imagery of traumas of separation and dislocation," as well as "the sites of hope and new beginnings" (Brah 1996, 193). Similarly, for Ghada Samman diaspora offers a unique opportunity to rewrite history, to hold it accountable for past crimes. To rewrite diaspora, then, is to "capture a fleeting" narrative, argues Samman in her *I'tiqal Lahzza Hariba* ("To Capture a Fleeting Moment") (al-Samman 1979, 8). According to Samman, being guarded against and accountable for reporting committed crimes lies at the heart of every artist's mission. Contemporary diaspora women writers' resurrection of the cultural myths of Shahrazad's voice, and the maw'udah's body, is a reminder of a traumatic past of erasure—a legacy in dire need of the female rewriting project so as to transcend its hold on contemporary Arab selfhood. For the last five decades contemporary women writers, Western and Middle Eastern alike, gained immensely from the ongoing rewriting project of narratology in various disciplines such as psychology, gender, culture, and literary studies. Relentlessly, women authors continued to rewrite past stories, to recapture the language, and to retell their own sagas—to invoke Virginia Woolf's imagery, from "rooms" (locations and with pens) "of [their] own" (Woolf 1981). Nowhere has this experiment been truer than in the diaspora, and in particular in that of Arab women writers. Diasporic living intensifies their alienation and defines most of their writings. Yet paradoxically, Arab women writers have benefited from the diaspora experience and managed to turn what is supposed to be a negative encounter into a positive one. The marginal position from which they write has been a liberating factor for most, which allows them to revisit, deconstruct, and reconstruct modernist fictions and replace them with their own postmodern narratives. Indeed, the concept of rewriting trauma is a pivotal one in Arab women's writings, and it is achieved through a variety of thematic and stylistic techniques in their narratives. Thematically, it is addressed through activating the wa'd and Shahrazad's tropes, revisiting recurrent motifs of female infant burials, bodily mutilation, imprisonment, and subsequent flights. Stylistically, rewriting is accomplished through the introduction of a feminine narrative poetics characterized by fluidity of diction, disruption of unity of time and place, and the playful mixing of poetry and fiction. Furthermore, it is apparent in the elimination of barriers between the real and the metaphysical in Samman's fantasy writings, in unearthing buried cities, histories, and memories as in Barakat's *The Tiller of Waters* (2001 [1998]), al-Neimi's *The Proof of the Honey* (2009 [2007]), and Samar Yazbek's *A Woman in the Crossfire* (2012 [2011]). The majority of these writings employ multiple narratives and innovative genres, such as war, travel, autobiography, fantasy, and revolutionary diaries. The writers' preference for using the fictive genre, rather than the more accepted poetry, as their medium of expression reflects this literary commitment to polyphony, which in turn displays a political commitment to representing all of the fragmented, marginal voices in their narratives. Furthermore, by mixing formal and vernacular language, as is often the case in the dialogic moments created in the private spheres of female characters, such as the feminine site of the *hammam* in Samman's *Al-Riwayah al-Mustahilah* (1997a, 278–87) and al-Shaykh's *Hikayati Sharhun Yatul* (2005), the writers—reminiscent of Shahrazad—reframe the formal Arabic language (*al-FusHa*) in the image of the feminine so as to affirm a commitment to portraying the hidden, almost exclusively oral women's literature, and to bringing their forgotten voices to the forefront and into print.

Without exception, the diaspora Arab women writers discussed in this book achieve their mastery over literature and the written word by experimenting in postmodern narratology that enables them to redefine the epistolary, travelogue, autobiography, fantasy, and memoir genres through the deconstructive project of rewriting, of trauma recovery. It is through the process of revisiting the debilitating, traumatic past that new reconstructive channels are charted on a daily basis, both literarily and politically, in their work. Their attraction to fiction stems from the urgency of their political message, and from a realization that they cannot afford the luxury of the purely aesthetic, poetry-oriented engagement of the early diaspora male writers. Because political persecution, rather than economic need, is the catalyst of their diasporic experience, it is no surprise that their literary production is fraught with the political and personal engagement characteristic of political dissidents. With two exceptions—Ghada Samman and Salwa al-Neimi—most contemporary Arab diaspora women writers favor prose: short stories, fiction, plays, memoirs, and contemplative essays. These genres, in turn, enhance the immediacy and the authenticity of their social and political commentary on the state of affairs in their homelands, which they represent realistically and in all their complexity. Gone are nostalgia for utopian homelands; commitment to an essentialist, unified form of Arab nationalism; and excessiveness in recalling old Arab glories of times past (al-Naʿuri 1977, 26). The process of homecoming entails dissecting and eliminating the causes of Arab citizens' personal and political alienation.

Remapping Home's Cartographies

For Arab women writers, diaspora (*mahjar*) is a positioning that encapsulates the inherent "perpetual tension" between what Avatar Brah calls the discourse of "home" and "dispersion," at once embodying the idea of scattering and the enactment of "multiple journeys" (Brah 1996, 181). Diaspora is different from exile, which often denotes a forced existence outside of one's homeland and "connot[es] wandering, loss, destruction, and disappearance" (Eisen 1986, 151). By contrast, diaspora implies a chosen, prolonged existence away from one's homeland despite the possibility of return, the intent to live outside the center (home) and in the periphery. This tenuous positioning does not constitute a complete crossing, a total severance of the homeland's attachments, rather a tendency to linger at both sides of the homeland/diaspora borders, to constantly adopt an Orpheus-like posture of looking back. However, the stance of looking back, as the mythological Orpheus story goes, is fraught with conflicting emotions of longing and loss, fear of return to the homeland, as well as anxieties generated from recalling a traumatic past. This in-between positioning defines the very essence of diaspora, which "places the discourse of 'home' and 'dispersion' in creative tension, *inscribing a homing desire while simultaneously critiquing discourse of fixed origins*" (Brah 1996, 193, italics in original). Indeed, adopting a nomadic positioning, in Casey Blanton's opinion, is the only guard against hegemonic ideologies and fixed subjectivities. He asserts, "Unfixing oneself so that place cannot equal truth is to adopt a more nomadic position. Writing as a displaced exile allows one to embark upon a 'two-directional journey examining the realities of both sides of cultural differences so that they may mutually question each other, and thereby generate a realistic image of human possibilities and self-confidence for the explorer grounded in comparative understanding rather than ethnocentrism'" (quoted in Blanton 1997, 111). This technique incorporates the experiences of both travel and dwelling, and allows for constant shifting and reshuffling of the centers of the writers' subjectivity and location. It also recognizes the impossibility of leaving the "home/locale" behind, and acknowledges the writers' role in redefining and expanding the cartographies of home. For Arab diaspora women writers the home trope is not the site of nostalgic longing; rather it is there to remind them of the maladies that plague the homeland's body. Healing the inherent wounds, reconstructing a healthier homeland—one that the authors no longer live *on*, but *with*—is crucial to contemporary diaspora writers' mission. This newly envisioned homeland takes multiple vestiges influenced by the authors' routes and not by their rootedness. As Stuart Hall asserts, "The homeland is not waiting back there for the new ethnics to rediscover it. There is a past to be learned about, but the past is now seen, and it has to be grasped as a history, as something that has to be told. It is narrated. It is grasped through memory. It is grasped through desire. It is grasped through reconstruction. It is not just a fact that has been waiting to ground our identities" (quoted in Kaplan 1996, 159).

For these authors, diasporic living does not engender an identity but a positioning that allows them to simultaneously question the concept of home and the various locales they inhabit. Furthermore, it facilitates the enactment of temporal and spatial journeys to and from the homeland so as to unearth the past. This troubled past of the nation and of women's participation in its construction has to be questioned, traced through memories, resurrected, and reconstructed anew.

Early Diaspora Women Writers

Contemporary Arab women writers of the European diaspora are following a trail blazed by early twentieth-century women writers of adab al-mahjar (diaspora literature). The term encapsulates writers of both genders who contributed to the Arabic literary canon from their North American and South American exilic sites. This unique diasporic experience produced two literary circles: al-Rabitah al-Qalamiyyah (the Pen Circle, 1920–31) in North America and al-'Usbah al-Andalusiyyah (the Andalus Circle, 1932–54) in South America, specifically Brazil and Argentina, both composed of writers who found in the enterprise of writing (mostly poetry) a link to their faraway homelands and an outlet for relieving their sense of alienation.[1] Though the majority of these literary circles were composed of male poets, there were numerous women writers who made a significant contribution to this canon, although not often acknowledged by critics and contemporaries alike. In al-Rabitah al-Qalamiyyah, writers such as Victoria Tanus, Najla Abu al-Lamma' Ma'luf, Linda Karam, and the poet Safiyyah Abu Shadi made an indelible mark on adab al-mahjar. Similarly, Salma Sa'igh, Mari Yini 'Atta Allah, Anjal 'Awun Shlita, and Salwa Salamah Atlas of al-'Usbah al-Andalusiyyah published regularly in the circle's official journal, *al-'Usbah* (al-Na'uri 1977, 36). Despite their

---

1. For a complete history of al-Rabitah al-Qalamiyyah and al-'Usbah al-Andalusiyyah, as well as a listing of their members at different stages of their inception, in addition to their major literary contribution to modern Arabic literature, see al-Na'uri 1976, 17–35; and Khafaji n.d., 82–118. For a survey of the early stages of the Syrian and Lebanese emigration to the American continent, see Saidah 1956, 1–38.

physical existence, the presence of their literary corpus has been consistently ignored and devalued in the annals of adab al-mahjar almost to the point of erasure, of denying that they have ever existed. It is true that early diaspora women writers were fewer in number than their male compatriots because of the cultural and religious restrictions imposed on women's mobility, and possibly for reasons pertinent to issues of class and to women's limited access to literacy in that era. But the quality of their literature is such that these female writers are equally deserving of recognition similar to the male authors who are consistently acknowledged in the chronicles of adab al-mahjar. To take just one example of this systematic obliteration of early female diasporic literature, one need only skim the most thorough bibliography of the field to notice the gender imbalance. This three-year, extended library bibliographic survey conducted at Harvard University by librarian Fawzi 'Abd al-Razzaq, a Middle Eastern specialist, and published in 1981, produced eight thousand entries on adab al-mahjar under three major subheadings: literary works of mahjar authors, critical works in Arabic as well as Romance languages, and Arabic magazines and periodicals ('Abd al-Razzaq 1981). Yet even though the survey covered almost a century (1892–1981), there were only four entries on Arab female writers, and these deal with only Safiyyah Abu Shadi and Salma Sa'igh. A further example illustrating the shortcomings of recent adab al-mahjar studies with regard to the inclusion and investigation of female Arab authors comes from yet another study, by Hatif al-Janabi (1995). As a poet, he remains faithful to the archaic, static conception of poetry as the preferred genre and excludes diasporic Arab women writers' experience.

Indeed the systematic bias against women writers in the diaspora is driven not only by traditional gender biases, but also—ever since the *mu'allaqat* poems of the jahiliyyah times—by the Arabic literary canon's partiality for the poetry genre as the truest embodiment of traditional High Literature.[2] Early diaspora women writers' attraction to fiction, a

---

2. The foundations for this poetic literary canon were established in the 'Ukaz poetry contest—a tradition that dates back to the jahiliyyah times. During an annual poetic contest in Suq 'Ukaz in Mecca, poets of different tribes competed to win the honor

genre not as highly esteemed as poetry in the Arabic canon at that era, compounded the problem of their gender exclusion, as well as the extent to which their contributions were deemed "insignificant" by the most esteemed critics in the field. For example, 'Issa al-Na'uri maintained, in a comprehensive study originally published in 1959 and updated for the third time in 1977, that women's early diasporic literature is "void of value" because it was in the genre of fiction rather than traditional Arabic poetry. He further claims that their literature was mainly "affected" by the male authors' literary production rather than being a major "literary effect" in and of itself:

> As for the woman's role in adab al-mahjar, she was not an effective but only an affected factor. She traced her literary footsteps after the man's own steps. I am only aware of female mahjar novelists, and I did not encounter any mahjar women's poetry, or read any that deserved our concern. As for the North American exiles, I did not know of any woman who served the Arabic canon well to the point worthy of our mention. As for the South American ones, they have contributed mostly in the field of journalism. (Al-Na'uri 1977, 35, my translation)

Statements such as al-Na'uri's are riddled with inaccuracies as well as obvious genre and gender biases. First, Victoria Tanus, Najla Abu al-Lamma' Ma'luf, Linda Karam, and the poet Safiyyah Abu Shadi discredit his claim that the North American mahjar literature did not have any female writers or poets. Furthermore, Abu Shadi's collection of poems entitled *The Immortal Song*, published in Cairo in 1953, is representative of the innovative style of free verse as well as the mystic and philosophical engagement of the poets of al-Rabitah al-Qalamiyyah. In addition, the body of work of the female writers of al-'Usbah al-Andalusiyyah is far from "void of

---

of having their poem recognized for its poetic mastery. The winning poems would be in plain view for days to come, and the public would learn the poems by heart and then disseminate them to their respective tribes, thus adding to the fame of the lucky poets and of their tribes. Only nine poems were selected and thus acknowledged each year. The body of these winning poems is known as *mu'allaqat* (Allen 2000).

value"; rather, it responds to a different set of social and political registers and addresses urgent issues in Arab homelands. The following section is a testament to the significance of the literature produced by women who used their diasporic sites to contest the dominance of patriarchy, colonialism, and the foreign superpowers' intrusion in their home countries. They left a literary trace that awaits uncovering.

Salma Sa'igh and Mari Yini 'Atta Allah: Committed Literature, Women's Imprisonment, and Peace Poetics

Salma Sa'igh's *Suwar wa-Dhikrayat* (1964) (*Pictures and Memories*, not published in English), a collection of essays published originally in al-'Usbah's periodical, addresses topics ranging from the challenges of the Lebanese Women's Association in battling the internal chauvinistic and the external French colonial powers to criticizing the inhumane conditions in the Lebanese women's prison. It offers political assessments and recommendations for dealing with the dilemma of Palestine's occupation. As if already aware of the literary bias against the contemplative essay format that she employs, she warns her readers and her critics that they are about to encounter a different kind of literature—one concerned with the people's "daily bread" rather than literary aesthetics (Sa'igh 1964, 137). Sa'igh's social and political engagement with the problems of the homeland is what separates her work from that of her al-'Usbah al-Andalusiyyah expatriate male counterparts, who poetically recreate a utopian, flawless homeland that exists only in their imaginations.

Sa'igh's concern in Brazil for the deterioration of the political situation in Lebanon stems from her early work on behalf of women prisoners. Until her departure from Lebanon to Brazil only forty days before the outbreak of World War II in 1939, she was committed, through her involvement with the Lebanese Women's Association, to improving the austere social and economic situation in Lebanon that drove frustrated citizens to emigrate in search of their daily bread. In *Suwar wa-Dhikrayat* she recalls her struggle to improve the inhumane treatment of women prisoners and the infant children inside Sijn al-Raml (Sand Prison), the Lebanese women's prison. She criticizes the hypocrisy of a judicial system that imprisons a mother for taking revenge on a man who has killed her only son, while allowing a male murderer to go free after killing his sister for dishonoring the family. She also documents the lack of food and medical supplies, and corrupt prison officials who continuously embezzled from general funds. Additionally, Sa'igh chronicles her numerous attempts to petition the Lebanese minster of the interior and the French chargé d'affaires to rectify these situations, and the challenges of battling reactionary internal as well as external colonial powers. The book further documents the efforts of the Lebanese Women's Association to single-handedly promote and improve the consumption of local products by wearing only Lebanese-made products, and by arranging industrial fairs to increase the local industries' public exposure. After her emigration to Brazil, Sa'igh remained committed to the social and political causes of the Arab world, especially after the loss of Palestine to Israel and the Syrian Iskandarun Gulf to Turkey. She continued to publish politically committed articles despite advice to the contrary by some of her fellow diaspora writers, whom she addresses contemptuously in her book:

> In 1940, when I published my article on the Palestinian question in the *al-'Usbah* journal . . . I felt that my words were "unwelcome" in some literary circles in São Paulo. There is an angered consensus against a female writer who interferes in constructive political criticism. There were also some friends who advised me to write exclusively literature—*adab* proper, only "intoxicating" literature. Well, I thank the "drunkards" for thinking so highly of my potential to write that kind of literature. However, my brand of writing is a truthful one—one that springs from the heart of life, the life of our current generation. (187)

Sa'igh's writings, as well as those of other early Arab women writers of the South American diaspora, evince a commitment to addressing the present, albeit a disappointing and painful one, rather than recalling past "intoxicating" histories and traditional literary models.

Another early female writer from al-'Usbah al-Andalusiyyah, Mari Yini 'Atta Allah, highlights the role of women, especially mothers, in deprogramming their children's minds from the rhetoric of violence and war permeating the modernist, masculine, military-based educational system. In an article entitled "Where Is the Humanist Leader?" published in 1949 in the journal *al-'Usbah*, she calls upon the mothers of the whole world to counter the ideology of violence taught to the new generation and to replace the masculine war rhetoric with peace pedagogy. She insists that children should be taught to value life, not death, that the rhetoric of annihilation created by social violence and the cravings of power-hungry nations eager for war should be eliminated (quoted in al-Na'uri 1977, 39).

All of the early diaspora women writers seem to agree that the role of the Arab woman as mother, political activist, and responsible citizen is crucial to rebuilding Arab nations already demoralized by centuries of colonization and lack of economic empowerment. The key, they suggest, lies in utilizing the "forgotten half" of a newly liberated nation to leverage the empowerment of men, women, and country alike. In her 1949 article "The Forgotten Half," commemorating Huda Sha'rawi and published in *al-'Usbah*,[3] Salma Sa'igh insists that any form of national reconstruction project has to include the forgotten national half: women. At the outset of Lebanese independence Sa'igh warns her male compatriots, "You, sirs, the leaders of Lebanon, Syria, Egypt, Iraq, Hijjaz [Saudi Arabia], and Yemen, will continue to build castles in the sand unless you return to the nation and to the country its lost forgotten half [women]" (quoted in al-Na'uri 1977, 37).

"The Forgotten Half" also exposes the inherent irony in the decision of Lebanon and other Arab countries to join the then newly established United Nations organization, hence agreeing to its charter in its entirety, while denying their women the basic human rights of personal and legal freedoms. Sa'igh writes that it is a sham to allow male criminals the right to vote, while denying the same right to women doctors and lawyers only on account of their gender. Her outrage at women's second-class citizenship expresses a desire to seek female aspirations elsewhere. She writes, "Why am I destined to be the daughter of a country that lacks the basic

---

3. For more on the life of Huda Sha'rawi (1879–1924), the leading Egyptian and Arab feminist, see her autobiography in Arabic (1981) and in English (1986).

conditions of equal national participation, thus becoming, in essence, a nomad—without a country!" (Sa'igh 1964, 114). Sa'igh's rhetorical question highlights the fact that it is not worth belonging to a country that does not recognize basic personal and human rights, and that forces its citizens to emigrate.

Undoubtedly the most important legacy of these early writers is their belief that the body of their writings, if not successful in its entirety, will certainly leave a "trace" for others to follow. As Sa'igh tells one of her male readers, the Women Association's work is "like a piece of mud that we threw against the wall; even if it does not stick it will leave a trace" (78). These authors realized that the social and political problems befalling their homelands were the result not just of external colonial powers, but also of internal reactionary ones benefiting from women's isolation and exclusion. As a result, superpowers' foreign policies as well as the complex geopolitical conditions of the region are as implicated as the local patriarchy in the systematized obliteration of female selfhood. Indeed, past and contemporary diaspora women writers share this critical stance that represents what miriam cooke calls "multiple critique" (cooke 2001, 155), thereby enabling them to articulate the need to acknowledge past feminine traces, and to remember the dismembered nation from their multiple nomadic positioning. For example, Sa'igh argues that the most important role of Arab women is to remind men of their female compatriots' contributions. Perhaps, as Sa'igh puts it cynically, "there are no unbearable traits in a man's character . . . rather, all the harm that he inflicts is an indirect result of his forgetfulness" (37). Women must fight against the "crime of forgetfulness" that erases the authorial trace of their literary mother Shahrazad. The contributions of these forgotten women authors stand as landmarks, as traces of the past, reminding their contemporary successors of the threats to women's selfhood: physical and literary erasure.

Living as a Nomad

Salma Sa'igh's preference to live as "a nomad without a country" rather than endure second-class citizenship in her homeland resonates with contemporary diaspora women writers who, like her, have found in the diaspora a welcoming refuge from personal and political persecution. Almost five decades later, in *Scheherazade Goes West* (2001), Fatema Mernissi would affirm the value of this nomadic belonging as she recalls her grandmother's rendition of the story "The Lady with the Feather Dress" from *A Thousand and One Nights*. The story recounts the adventure of a merchant, Hasan al-Basri, who, while gazing at a pond in one of his travels, witnessed the transformation of a bird into a beautiful lady upon taking off her feather dress. Hasan fell in love with the lady, married her, and buried her feather dress in a secret tomb to prevent her from ever leaving him. However, after she bore him two sons, Hassan relaxed his watch over his wife and started to travel again, only to discover, upon his return one day, that his wife "who had never stopped searching for her feather dress, had finally found it and flown away," taking along her two sons to her native island of Wak Wak (the island of neverland) (Mernissi 2001, 6). Mernissi was later to find out that her grandmother had altered the original *Nights* story in two distinct ways: First, she feminized the title, changing it from "The Tale of Hasan al-Basri" to "The Lady with the Feather Dress," thereby empowering the lady with agency and ownership of her story. Second, she rewrote the traditional happy ending, where Hasan finally finds the elusive Wak Wak and brings his wife and two children back to Baghdad to live happily ever after, and transformed it to an unhappy one (at least for Hasan) where he is doomed to search for them unsuccessfully for eternity.[4] According to Mernissi's grandmother, the "main message [of the story] is that a woman should lead her life as a nomad. She should stay alert and be ready to move, even if she is loved. For, as the tale teaches, love can engulf you and become a prison" (Mernissi 2001, 4). The value of mobility and nonfixity cannot be underestimated for Mernissi's grandmother, and for Arab women diaspora authors who, heeding her call, are determined to leave emotional or

---

4. The location of the island of Wak Wak is a disputed one, thereby adding to the mystery of this enchanted neverland. Mernissi mentions that some "Arab historians such as Mas'udi, the ninth-century author of *Golden Meadows*, situated it in East Africa, beyond Zanzibar, while Marco Polo describes Wak Wak as the land of the Amazons, or the 'female island' of Socotra. Others identify Wak Wak as being the Seychelles, Madagascar, or Malacca, and still others situate it in China or Indonesia (Java)" (Mernissi 2001, 7).

physical fetters behind to embark on routes that, though taking them away from their roots, yet do not completely sever their ties with them.

My analysis of the ways in which contemporary diaspora authors negotiate their attachments and detachments to their home countries is informed by Gilles Deleuze and Félix Guattari's "deterritorialization" and "reterritorialization" process promulgated by the nomadic movement of the rhizome. According to Deleuze and Guattari, the rhizome's potential for transformation lies in its planar movement, in its ability to resist chronology, organization, and historization. Rhizomes transverse several plateaus from "multiple entryways"; they reject beginnings and ends and are prized for inhabiting the "in-between," the "interbeing," the "*intermezzo*" (Deleuze and Guattari 1987, 11–25). In this manner they create "a map [of] multiple entryways, as opposed to the tracing, which always comes back 'to the same'" (12). Although I find the cartographies generated by the women authors' rhizomatic belongings extremely valuable, unlike Deleuze and Guattari I suggest that a return to the idea of the trace in diaspora women's literature does not lead "to the same" fixed positioning. For in tracing the literary steps of Shahrazad and the painful memory of the wa'd, Arab diaspora women writers attempt to place their hands on the root of the problem, rather than affirming its fixity or moral integrity. Following the female ancestral trace is integral as inspiration and as a jumpstart to triggering the retrieval and transformation of these iconic tropes and their traumatic past. In this context, the authors' unique mode of maintaining both the rhizomes and the traces of the roots does not generate an exact decalcomania, but rather a burgeoning of the female author's role in a manner more befitting of her contemporary cultural and political challenges. It is through the interplay of roots, routes and rhizomes, filiation/affiliation, deterritorialization/reterritorialization, departure/return, and loss/retrieval that Arab diaspora women writers rewrite their foremothers' legacy. They articulate a unique discourse that "bends together, both roots *and* routes to construct what [Paul] Gilroy (1987) describes as alternate public spheres, forms of community consciousness and solidarity that maintain identifications outside the national time/space in order to live inside, with a difference" (Clifford 1997, 251). In this manner they are redefining earlier adab al-mahjar's concept of the homeland in which both blind support of their native countries and the nostalgic desire for eventual return to them are challenged. These authors replace the homeland's utopian memories with the dystopian postmemories of personal and national past traumas. For contemporary women diaspora writers, the principle of return is never without ambivalence; nevertheless it is never relinquished, but rather celebrated as part of the impetus for the nonfixity, the back and forth mobility, that guarantees constant rejuvenation.

Contemporary Diaspora Women Writers

Following the same trail that their predecessors charted, contemporary diaspora women writers seem to have an advantage over the early diaspora writers. Their experience differs immensely from that of their late nineteenth- and early-twentieth-century male counterparts, who left their countries primarily because of the economic and/or political constraints imposed upon them by Ottoman colonization and interreligious war in the Lebanese Chouf mountainous region. Although some of the contemporary women's journeys are politically motivated, none is made as a result of dire economic necessity and almost all are ultimately able to return to their homelands once their countries' political havoc is resolved. Most of them fall into the category of either forced or migrant exiles. The former group consists of those women who had to leave their homelands temporarily or on a long-term basis because of civil war or fear of personal and/or political persecution, while the latter group willingly chooses to live a diasporic existence in search of a literary freedom that is often denied them in their homelands.

Despite political persecution, these women are privileged or, at the very least, had the financial power and the educational qualifications that enabled them to engage in meaningful dialogues with the Other, and to sustain their lives in the West. Initially, their diaspora seems to be a chosen one as most of them resided in the West temporarily to pursue higher degrees (Hamida Naʿnaʿ, Salwa al-Neimi, and Ghada Samman), or to work as correspondents for Arabic newspapers, journals, and radio stations based in Europe (Hoda Barakat, Hamida Naʿnaʿ, Salwa al-Neimi, Hanan al-Shaykh, and Ghada Samman). With time, they settled when for various political reasons involving civil wars, denied passports, or political dissidence, they temporarily suspended their return project. Ghada Samman and Hamida Na'na' were refused passports by their native country of Syria, the former for failing to return home to her university teaching position and the latter for belonging to the opposition's political party. Samar Yazbek's support for the Syrian revolution forced her into exile in London. Similarly, being a political dissident was the reason for Salwa al-Neimi's preference to reside in Paris. The departures of the Lebanese Hanan al-Shaykh and Hoda Barakat were prompted by worsening political conditions during the sixteen-year Lebanese Civil War (1975–91), when the first took up temporary residence in London and the second settled permanently in Paris with only short visits to Lebanon.

Though the circumstances of each author's initial departure from her birth country are varied, they are motivated by a desire to escape similar personal and political constraints. For example, Hamida Na'na''s attempt to flee from the oppressive Syrian regime mirrors the wish of her compatriots Salwa al-Neimi and Samar Yazbek to escape the same authoritarian government. Likewise, Hanan al-Shaykh's and Hoda Barakat's need to flee civil war-torn Beirut defines the impetus for their continued diasporic existence. The authors discussed in this study all hail from the *mashriq* part of the Arab world, although the impact of their literature is evident in the *maghrib* as well. They are chosen because they come from various backgrounds representing a rich mosaic of religions and nationalities; however, they share unique diasporic experience that continues to define their literary output. The political implications of their Syrian and Lebanese origin, coupled with their French and English adoptive nationalities, makes their literature especially apt to the activation of the wa'd trope, and to amplifying the political in Shahrazad's trope. As diasporic subjects, they all live in the liminal "third space" that, in Homi Bhabha's estimation, embodies the diasporic body's hybridized subjectivity (Bhabha 1990b). In the words of Edward Said, they live "in a median state, neither completely at one with the new setting nor fully disencumbered of the old, beset with half-involvements and half-detachments, nostalgic and sentimental on one level, an adept mimic or a secret outcast on another. Being skilled at *survival* becomes the main imperative, with the danger of getting too comfortable and secure constituting a threat that is constantly to be guarded against" (Said 1994, 49, italics mine). To ensure both detachments and attachments, they learn to embrace what Gloria Anzaldúa calls the "mestiza" consciousness as they continue to straddle different languages and cultures, and write tales of loss and survival (Anzaldúa 1987). Furthermore, relishing the positionality of the forever shifting third space means avoiding fixity by adopting a nomadic and rhizomatic lifestyle. I contend that rhizomatic belongings are manifold in diaspora Arab women writers, and they are manifested in the constant shuttling between their diasporic sites and their homelands as well as in the insistence of the majority of them on using the Arabic language as their medium of literary expression.

Salwa al-Neimi, a Syrian who is the daughter of a Muslim Isma'ili father and a Christian mother, grew well aware of the beauty of harmonious coexistence among the various ethnic and religious factors of the Syrian society. She studied Arabic philology at Damascus University and embarked on her journey to Paris in the mid-seventies initially to pursue her graduate study in Islamic philosophy and theater at the Sorbonne. In addition to her current position at the Institute of the Arab World in Paris, she has been a regular contributor to Arab newspapers such as *Barid al-Junub* and the magazine *Arabies*. Although poetry is al-Neimi's favorite literary genre, she has a collection of short stories (*Kitab al-Asrar* [1994] [*The Book of Secrets*, not published in English]), a recent autobiographical novel (*Shibh al-Jazirah al-'Arabiyyah* [2012] ["Arabian Peninsula"]), and is best known in the Arab and Western worlds for her renowned novella *Burhan al-'Asal* (2007) (*The Proof of the Honey*, 2009), which was translated into several world languages and received much acclaim.

Hanan al-Shaykh, a Muslim Lebanese writer with a conservative southern Shi'i background, contributed considerably to contemporary Arab women's literature with works that touch upon the two main events defining her life: The Lebanese Civil War and her diasporic experience in London. Congruent with the other authors' experiences with journalism, she has worked for a woman's magazine, *al-Hasna'*, and the newspaper *al-Nahar* in her early career. With the outbreak of the civil war, she left Beirut in 1976 for Khubar, Saudi Arabia, where she lived with her family until 1982. Since then she has moved to London, where she continues to maintain residency. Al-Shaykh is known for her dialogic prose capable of capturing the specificity and angst of her tortured characters. In addition to the novel, she has dabbled with other genres such as short stories and plays, the latest of which is a theatrical production entitled *One Thousand and One Nights*, directed by the British director Tim Supple, which premiered at the Luminato Festival in Toronto in June 2011 and at the Edinburgh International Festival in August/September of the same year. Her collaboration on this project has earned her the title "the new Shahrazad" in British literary circles (al-Shaykh 2011, 17–23, 21).

Hoda Barakat is a Maronite Christian Lebanese writer who hails from the same mountainous village of Bshareé as Gibran Khalil Gibran (poet and founding member of al-Rabitah al-Qalamiyyah). Her initial journey to Paris (1975–76) was motivated by her desire to pursue her doctorate in French literature. However, she opted to return to Lebanon at the outbreak of the Lebanese Civil War because, as she puts it, "[she] could not stay in magnificent Paris, the city that accumulates a reservoir of grand memories, while Beirut is burning and bombarded in this manner."[5] She worked as a teacher, journalist, and translator, and in 1988 she helped the launching of a women's magazine, *The New Shahrazad*.[6] Nevertheless, the escalating deterioration of security during the war, coupled with her concern for the life of her two children, finally forced her to leave Lebanon for good in 1989 and to reside permanently in Paris. Despite her physical distance, she remained deeply attuned to the pulse of Arab citizens through her editorials in the daily *Al-Hayat* (published in Arabic in London) and recently in the electronic magazine *al-Mudon*. Until 2010 she worked for *Radio Orient*, an Arabic-language radio station, while continuing to write in Arabic. Barakat's literary oeuvre covers several genres: short stories, plays, novels, and epistolary essays. The original, daring topics she raises in her novels have earned her several prestigious Arab and foreign literary

5. Personal interview with Hoda Barakat, Paris, Aug. 20, 2008.

6. Hoda Barakat informs me that the choice of the word "New" in the magazine's title was intended to reflect the erased political and intellectual dimensions of Shahrazad's persona, not just the literary aspect. Personal communication, Charlottesville, VA, Jan. 18, 2014.

awards, such as the al-Naqid (The Critic, 1990) prize, the Naguib Mahfouz Medal for Literature (2000), the Order of the French Ministry of Culture for Arts and Literature (2004), the French Knight of the National Order of Merit (2008), and the Italian Amalfi literary award (2008). These awards were given for *The Stone of Laughter* (1995 [1990]), *The Tiller of Waters* (2001 [1998]), and *Rasa'il al-Ghariba* (2004a) ("Alien Letters") respectively.

Hamida Na'na', a Sunni Muslim Syrian writer and journalist, first left Syria, where she was pursuing a bachelor degree in Arabic literature, for Jordan after the Arabs' defeat in the 1967 Arab-Israeli war. She joined the armed resistance for Palestine's liberation and only returned to finish her degree in Damascus after the death of a beloved comrade. With the military coup that brought Hafiz al-Assad to power in 1971, she and her husband left Syria for Algeria. After her divorce, she moved to Paris, completed a doctorate at the Sorbonne in literature and Islamic studies. She was forced to assume permanent residency in France after the Syrian government's refusal to issue her passport. As the head of the European and North African bureau at *al-Safir* newspaper, the senior correspondent for the French magazine *Le Nouvel Afrique-Asie*, and the editor of the Parisian-based Arabic magazine *al-Wifaq al-'Arabi*, Na'na' credits her work in journalism with making her "a daughter of her time" (Na'na' 1998, 100). In fact, it was under the auspices of her journalistic career and her periodic work at UNESCO that she penned short stories, novels, memoirs, and a collection of interviews with prominent European thinkers and writers (Michel Foucault, Roland Barthes, Jean-Paul Sartre, and others), thereby initiating a dialogue between her Arabic and European audience, diasporic locales, and her country of origin (Na'na' 1990).

With nearly forty books, Ghada Samman is the most prolific of all of the writers in question. A Sunni Muslim Syrian writer who has left an indelible mark on the Arab literary scene since the early sixties, she is one of the pioneers of contemporary Arabic literature. Samman is most known for her short stories and novels; however, her literary corpus encompasses travelogues, poetry, and journalistic and philosophical essays. Diaspora continues to define the very essence of Samman's personal and literary experience from her early residency in Beirut in the late fifties, to London in the mid-sixties, and finally to Paris, where she has assumed permanent residency since the early eighties. Samman hails from a prominent and conservative Muslim Damascene family. Her father (Ahmad al-Samman) was president of the Syrian University (currently Damascus University), and then Syria's secretary of higher education in the mid-fifties. With his unwavering support, Samman finished her Masters in English Literature at the American University in Beirut and started pursuing a doctorate on the literature of the absurd in London in 1965. However, faced with the death of her father in 1967 and the ensuing restrictions of her extended family back in Damascus, she decided to stay in Europe, supporting her nomadic wanderings with journalistic work. The family's punishment for Samman's decision not to return to Syria was to cut her off financially, while the government's penalty was to sue her in absentia for leaving her teaching-assistant academic post and subsequently to deny the renewal of her Syrian passport. After her marriage to the Lebanese critic and publisher Bashir al-Daouk, Samman assumed Lebanese citizenship and took up permanent residency in Paris, with only intermittent visits to Lebanon, owing to the prolonged Lebanese Civil War. In addition to her numerous literary publications, Samman continues to write a column entitled "A Moment of Freedom" at the Lebanese London-based *al-Hawadith* magazine.

Samar Yazbek's diasporic living came as a result of her stance in support of the Syrian revolution against the Assad regime. Yazbek is an 'Alawite writer from the coastal Syrian city of Jableh who in 2010 was recognized as one of the Beirut 39, a group of promising Arab writers under the age of forty. Her oeuvre encompasses novels, short stories, film scripts, television dramas, and revolutionary diaries. Her outspoken criticism of the brutality of the Assad regime against peaceful demonstrators during the revolution earned her the ire of the regime. After several detention visits, she was forced to flee Syria to London out of fear for her life and that of her daughter. Her daring work *Taqatu' Niran* (2011) (*A Woman in the Crossfire: Diaries of the Syrian Revolution*, 2012) won her the prestigious PEN/Pinter Prize "International Writer of Courage" and the Swedish Tucholsky Prize in 2012, in addition to the Holland Oxfam/Pen prize in 2013.

What distinguishes these writers from other Anglophone or Francophone Arab diaspora writers, of both genders, is their insistence on being connected to the pulse of the ordinary Arab street through their ongoing engagement with journalism and the exclusive use of Arabic in their writings. Their fidelity to their native language is rewarded by wide distribution and sale records among their Arab readership in their home countries, and by the adaptations of their works for cinematic and theatrical performances, thereby highlighting the significant public intellectual role they are playing in reshaping public and political opinion in their homeland.[7] The fact that most of the authors still write columns in Arabic newspapers (Na'na' and Samman), have their own radio shows (Hoda Barakat), and work in Arab cultural centers in the diaspora (Salwa al-Neimi) is proof of their effective agency. It is through these venues that they develop and maintain their role as public intellectuals. Engagements with journalism and with multiaxial discourse, and the dialogic project so prominent in their narrative techniques, honed their skill of reporting past traumas and crimes committed on both the personal and the national body. There lies their critical role in redefining Arab gendered diaspora, and in activating poignant cultural myths (Shahrazad and wa'd) that are central to inspiring Arab Spring's revolutions. Employing Arabic in this meaningful way is a safeguard from the danger of passing as non-Arabs. It acts as a constant reminder to carry the homeland's wounds within, and to relate to their Arab readership back home. Arabic functions as a marker of difference that forces the colonial Other to see their angst, their pains, rather than seeing through their assimilated invisibility had they shifted their creative expression to English or to French. In this manner, they are able to tap into certain cultural registers seeking to redefine Arab women's authorship through the political transformation of Shahrazad's literary trope, and through the deployment of the somber and powerful female infanticide trope (wa'd al-banat), the ramification of which I will discuss

7. Ghada Samman's *Al-Riwayah al-Mustahilah: Fusifusa' Dimashqiyyah* (1997a) (*The Impossible Novel: Damascene Mosaic*) has been adapted into a film entitled *The Guards of Silence* directed by Syrian film director Sameer Zekra and debuted in 2010. Also, Hoda Barakat's play *Viva La Diva* (2010), a one-act, one-woman black comedy, directed by Nabil Al Azan and starring Randa Asmar, was performed with great success in Beirut for the first time at Babel Theatre on October 13–24, 2010.

fully in chapter 2. By tracing the wa'd trope from the buried feminine body (Samman), to the buried literary mother (Samman and Al-Shaykh), to the buried nation and city (Na'na', Barakat, and Yazbek), and finally to the buried erotic heritage and Arabic language (al-Neimi), these authors are uniquely positioned to access and transgress debilitating traumas so as to depict the political turmoil of the nation with its demands for democracy and social justice, and to engender healing on the personal and national levels. No doubt the discussion put forth by these Arab diaspora writers is timely in an age in which the newly revitalized Arab states, affected by the Arab revolutionary spring of 2011–15 and the West, have realized that dialogue on both the local and the global levels is paramount. The writings of diaspora women facilitate this dialogue vertically (on the level of their cultural roots), as the literary texts are mostly written in Arabic and consumed voraciously by their Arabic audience, and horizontally (on the rhizomatic level of their current diasporic sites), since by virtue of their immediate translation they contribute to promoting this ongoing and urgent planetary discussion.

Arabic Is My Home

The authors' decision to write in Arabic, to publish in distinctly Arab presses with wide Arab readership, charges their literature with a poignant social and political mission. With the shifting borders of their diasporic experience, Arabic replaces the fixity of place and changes it to a "dynamic concept" that ultimately, to use Doreen Massey's words, "stretch[es] beyond that 'place' itself" (Massey 1994, 115). Arabic, then, becomes the means of connecting past local experiences with global new ones, and of maintaining the authors' dialogue with the homeland's constituency albeit from a distance. Commenting on how writing in Arabic erases geography's borders, Hoda Barakat asserts, "Geography does not denote a tangible entity when we carry places inside ourselves. Upon writing, language itself becomes our place of residence; for it compensates, to a great extent, for our lack of physical presence inside the homeland. For that reason, I always wanted to write and research in Arabic, despite my ability to write in French" (Muhaisin 2009).

During our interview in 2008, she emphasized her love and reverence for the Arabic language, which "hails from a magnificent heritage." She also stated that her desire "to rediscover the language," which she only came to love as an adult, is a response to "the nuns' erasure of Arabic" during the years she attended Catholic schools in Lebanon. Barakat even attributes the two honorary awards that she received from the French government to the French realization that "the kind of writing that comes from the depth of the Arabic experience is what matters, and is distinctly different from the kind of writing that only reports" and caters to the West.[8] The process of "unearthing the Arabic language" from the "coffins" of orientalist francophone views that claim that Arabic cannot express "individuality" or "eroticism," or the Islamist trend that claims that Arabic should be restricted to "sacred discourse," is, in Salwa al-Neimi's opinion, an urgent project. For, in her opinion, Arabic is the language most fitting "to express erotic and philosophical matters" (Nujaim 2009). Similarly, Hanan al-Shaykh insists on writing in Arabic, not English, stating, "I think in Arabic, dream in Arabic, and write in Arabic" (Maha Hasan 2010). For her, Arabic represents "the last wood [she is] attached to" in the midst of the "sea." "My language," she reiterates, "if I lose it, *khalas*, finish, NO Hanan, no writing. So I will never write except in Arabic" (Schlote 2003). The connection between writing in Arabic and the survival or erasure of Arab identity is reiterated in Ghada Samman's insistence on writing in Arabic and on maintaining an Arab citizenship. She insists, "I want to swallow every public pain till the point of intoxication so as to keep writing letters that are not foreign from [the readers'] world. For when the letter is severed from its roots, it dies" (al-Samman 2003a, 138). Maintaining their Arab cultural roots through language is designed both to "inscribe" and to "transcribe, to write from the depths (*'en creux'*), to bring back to the text, to the paper, to the manuscript, to the hand, to bring back at the same time the funeral chants and the buried bodies: yes to bring back the other (once considered the enemy, unable to assimilate) through language" (Djebar 2003, 26).

8. Personal interview with Hoda Barakat, Paris, Aug. 20, 2008.

Indeed, Arab women writers' determination to follow foreign routes, while still insisting on tracing back their Arabic roots through language, is, in Samman's words, an example of being "shaken by the winds of the world without being uprooted" from the pleasures and pains of their homeland (al-Samman 1990, 204). My focus on Arab diaspora women writers who write primarily in Arabic, and who mostly belong to the first- and second-generation immigrants, inevitably obscures the contributions of other Arab diaspora writers who write in French (Evelyne Accad, Andrée Chedid, Assia Djebar, Leïla Sebbar) or English (Ahdaf Soueif, Fadia Faqir, Mohja Kahf, Diana Abu Jaber). Because of the book's primary focus on women writers, regrettably it does not address prominent male diaspora writers such as Halim Barakat, Amin Maalouf, and Antoun Shamas. Dealing with such a huge host of writers and languages would have necessitated a larger scope than this book sets out to encompass. It is my hope that the issues raised here regarding Arab women's authorship, and its relevance to their mobility, locality, orality, the written word, cultural myths, and historic traumas, will open avenues of further discussion by other scholars.

History is full of tales of literary exiles who enjoyed a duality of vision and perception; however, the case of Arab women diaspora writers presents a unique example of doubling the duality because of the internal alienation of females within Arab societies. Unearthing their female predecessors' stories and reclaiming their voice are integral parts of the survival project. Indeed "survival," both personal and collective, is their goal, particularly since coming into writing and the acquisition of their literary voices entail the reinscription of Shahrazad's authority and authorship, and reactivating the voice of the buried female infant (al-maw'udah), thereby transforming the sites of the Arab traumatic past into healing narratives of resurrection. This goal defines and haunts their works as they articulate moments of conflict and resolution, rupture and reclamation.

2

Anxiety of Erasure

Arab Women's Authorship as Trauma

When asked to introduce herself to Italian readers, prominent Syrian writer Ghada Samman stated, "I am a two-thousand-year-old Arab woman. They tried to bury me in the desert, but they failed. They killed me several times, but I always resurrected myself from the ashes to fly, and to write" (De Capua 1992, 103). The trope of female infant burial (wa'd al-banat) is a recurrent cultural myth in the literature penned by Arab diaspora female writers. It presents the reader with a terrifying image of physical erasure. As I argued in my introduction, the wa'd image borders on obsession, an experience denoting rejection and the threat of total annihilation of the physical and symbolic existence of the female self. However, in the literature of diaspora women writers, the wa'd trope is activated to also signify the suffocation of political freedom, the legitimate demands for democracy and social justice, and the curbing of feminine potential. One wonders why an extinct practice that was outlawed by the Prophet Muhammad at the advent of Islam in Arabia around the seventh century AD would still be present so forcefully in the imagination of the daughters of Arabia. The custom of wa'd al-banat itself was first practiced in the pre-Islamic jahiliyyah era when unwanted female infants were buried alive in the sand for a variety of reasons, chief among them fear of dishonor and of economic destitution. The warring, tribal lifestyle with its austere, nomadic conditions meant that tribes could only invest in raising boys who would increase the tribe's army and, unlike girls, could never dishonor it by being captured as war spoils.[1] As war captives, females would be forced to be concubines and to give birth to enemy offspring, thus bringing the foreign "Other" home. Indeed, the perception of daughters as more prone to dishonor and to betray the tribe than sons is rooted in the historical background of the first recorded wa'd incident in pre-Islamic Arabia. One account states that the first Arab father ever reported to practice female infanticide was Qays ibn 'Asim al-Tamimi from Tamim's tribe, whose adult daughter was taken as a war captive when the army of al-Nu'man bin al-Mundher (king of al-Hira)[2] raided their encampment. When truce was declared among the warring parties, al-Nu'man gave the abducted women the right to choose between staying with their abductor or returning to their homes. Qays ibn 'Asim's daughter chose to stay with her abductor rather than to return to her husband. It was at that point, the story goes, that Qays swore to bury in the sand any subsequent daughter born to him upon birth to avoid any such dishonor in the future. The second account as to the origin of the wa'd practice is eerily similar. The tribe this time is reported to be Rabi'ah, with the daughter also preferring to stay with her abductor rather than returning to her father (Fadhelallah 2000). At the root of wa'd practice is the need to quell free will, which threatens and challenges authority. Wa'd's discourse, then, is inextricably linked to the politics of dissent and dishonor. The dishonor factor originates from the women's willingness to abandon their homelands,

1. Male children were considered to be an asset to the tribal society of the time because they had the potential to enhance the tribe's wealth in many ways. First, they could participate in the raids on other tribes—the only means of survival for the tribe— and thus bring spoils and fame to the tribe. Second, they could enhance the tribe's prestige and number by fathering more offspring, preferably more males. Since children in the patriarchal Arab society are considered extensions of their paternal family line, mothers do not have the right to bestow their own family name on their children. Thus children become the sole property of the father, and the daughters of the tribe can only produce offspring to enhance the prestige of tribes other than their own.

2. Al-Hira was an ancient city south of the modern-day Iraqi city of al-Kufa. It was ruled by the Lakhmids (the Mundhereds) in the fifth and sixth centuries CE. The Lakhmids were a group of Christian Arabs who helped the Persian Sasanid Empire to contain the nomadic Arabs to the south.

to embrace mobility, and to initiate a forbidden encounter (spiritual or sexual) with the Other, thereby leading to an adulteration of the pure Arab lineage and to alliances struck with the foreign enemy. The concept of dishonor or shame represented in the Arabic original *'ar* interestingly has its linguistic roots in the words *'awra* (deficient, shameful, genitalia) and *'ara* (to bury a spring well). All three terms are linguistic derivatives of the Arabic trilateral verbal root *'awr*, a verb that encompasses the meanings of deficiency, shame, and burial. The female infant symbolizes the essence of this unholy trinity in the sense that her deficient femininity (*'awra*)[3] will bring about dishonor (*'ar*) and is thus deserving of being buried (*'ara*) in the sands. This tribal fear of the female child's threat and potential danger to the stability of the patriarchal institution is manifested, for example, in the legends that filled the imagination of the Syrian author Hamida Naʻnaʻ in her early childhood. Naʻnaʻ would hear about how Saʻda, daughter of Zanati Khalifa, the governor of the city of Tunis, had fallen in love with a youth from the wandering tribe of Bani Hilal and opened the city's impenetrable gates to the enemy's tribe, thereby betraying her family. At this point in the story, Naʻnaʻ recalls that "those listening heaped curses on Saʻda's head . . . My story [she adds] began in the same way" (Naʻnaʻ 1998, 94–95). It is a risky endeavor all around, then, to raise girls, and the easiest solution, at the time, was literally to bury the potential danger away.

Despite the thirteen centuries that have elapsed since the banning of the waʼd practice in the seventh century AD, Arab women writers still revive it as a cultural myth on the national and the personal levels in their literary corpus, thereby engendering waʼd's presence as a collective trauma that haunts their writings. It is no wonder, then, that most of the diaspora women writers examined in my book share this horrific experience subliminally as a distant, traumatic memory. Like the story of Shahrazad's co-optation, the waʼd trope haunts contemporary Arab women writers

---

3. One hadith attributed to the Prophet Muhammad by two lexicographers, Ibn Manzur (d. 711/1312) and al-Zabidi (d. 1205/1791), states, "Woman is an *'awra*." On what constitutes *'awra* in a woman's body, the legist Ahmad ibn Hanbal (d. 241/855) categorically declares, "Everything in women is an *'awra*." See, for example, Ibn Manzur n.d. 290–99; al-Zabidi n.d. 154–70; and Ibn Hanbal 1986, 29ff.

with an anxiety of erasure both literary (Shahrazad) and physical (the wa'd tradition), with a nightmarish presence that denotes its posttraumatic, intergenerational occurrence. Most of the writers in question, particularly Salwa al-Neimi, Hoda Barakat, Hamida Na'na', Ghada Samman, and Samar Yazbek, found this ritual to be an apt metaphor for their own experience. They materialize this historical nightmare in their narratives, thus bringing it to the surface and using it as a distant memory that propels the writing of their literature and inspires, above all, their survival. These mashriq authors, mostly Syrians and Lebanese, found in the wa'd trauma a confluence to the national traumas of civil war and surviving under the yoke of authoritarian states. They neither subscribe to Harold Bloom's postulations of Western male authorship as dialectic, Oedipal interactions with their predecessors causing their "anxiety of influence" (Bloom 1973), nor do they fit in Sandra M. Gilbert and Susan Gubar's description of Western female authorship as an "anxiety of authorship" caused by a lack of female predecessors (Gilbert and Gubar 1979). Rather, Arab women writers experience their authorship as an anxiety of erasure caused by a double sense of erasure: not only that of Shahrazad's authorship, but also that of the female's physical eradication exemplified in wa'd al-banat's jahiliyyah practice. Both tropes evince different angles on the anxiety of erasure, silencing, and oblivion. In Shahrazad's case, the very intimacy and power of her spoken word betrays its ephemeral dimensions, the need to defy erasure through writing. In al-maw'udah's case, the burial of that body and voice foreshadows society's entombment and the erosion of Arab citizens' civil liberties. It further underscores the urgency of the maw'udah's resurrection through revolutionary change. It is interesting to note that this anxiety crosses religious boundaries and is not restricted to Muslim women writers. For example, Hoda Barakat, a Lebanese Christian, and the Syrian writer Salwa al-Neimi, who hails from an interreligious marriage between a Muslim father and a Christian mother, employ the wa'd trope in a powerful way in their writings. The reference to real or symbolic feminine wa'd is vividly alive in Arab women's diasporic poetics, proving that such traumatic postmemory, to use Marianne Hirsch's words, is indeed intergenerational and collective as it crosses temporal and geographical borders. Hirsch contends that "postmemory is a powerful and very particular form of memory precisely because its connection to its object or source is mediated not through recollection but through an imaginative investment and creation" (Hirsch 1997, 22). Diasporic locales provide the needed distance to recall the wa'd trauma while simultaneously purging it from its immediate threat. In this manner, diaspora women writers are able to reactivate the nightmarish wa'd postmemory without having to suffer the traumatic consequences of its reality.

The Wa'd Trauma

Pre-Islamic Arabia was not the only society to practice female infanticide. For example, in ancient Greece and Rome infanticide was legitimate until the fourth century AD (Giladi 1990, 185). Likewise India and China are also reported to have engaged in such a practice and continue to do so today with the aid of contemporary medical technologies such as fetal ultrasound, sex-selective abortions, and selective chromosomal conception.[4] Obviously the wa'd was not practiced by all Arabian tribes; otherwise, the whole Arab line would have been obliterated.[5] Rather, only three tribes of northern Arabia were reported to practice it on a regular basis: bani Tamim, bani Kinda, and bani Rabi'ah. Among the Arabian tribes who practiced wa'd, the female infant was buried either immediately

4. For Chinese infanticide cases, see Mungello 2008. For Indian incidents related to poverty, fear of having to pay for the girl's expensive dowry, and sex-selective abortions, see Agnivesh 2005. Surprisingly, there is even a report regarding a recent female infanticide case among an Iraqi immigrant family in the Germana district of Damascus, Syria, where a father buried his infant daughter at twenty-three days old. He later admitted to police investigators that the motive was his suspicion that the child was not biologically his own (Dawarah 2008).

5. The grandfather of the famous Umayyad poet al-Farazdaq (641–730 AD), Sa'sa'ah bin Najiyyah bin 'Iqal, used to save female infants destined for burial by offering their fathers one male and two female camels for their lives instead. He is reported to have saved 280 female infants in this manner. After his conversion to Islam, Sa'sa'ah asked the Prophet whether God would ever reward him in the hereafter for the kind deeds he did in jahiliyyah times on behalf of these infants. The Prophet's response was affirmative. See Giladi 1990, 189–200.

upon birth, at six years of age, or in one account even in late adolescence. Burial upon birth accounted for the majority of the cases, whereby a shallow grave was dug next to the laboring mother. If the infant was male, he was allowed to live. A female child, however, was immediately buried in the prepared grave. Fathers often instigated and perpetuated the practice, although reluctant mothers were also reported to do so for fear of abandonment by their husbands. Initiating wa'd at the later age of six or adolescence seems to have been more rare, although occurring occasionally as a form of human sacrifice of both male and female children to pagan gods, or to appease the ire of fathers unwilling to marry their daughters off to foreign husbands as a result of the pagan *hamiyya* (zeal). The second caliph 'Umar ibn al-Khattab (634–44 AD), for example, tearfully recalled burying a daughter, before his conversion to Islam, old enough to attempt to dust off the rising sands of his beard while he covered her little body with it. Two other incidents of burying adolescent daughters are attributed to the previously mentioned Qays ibn 'Asim al-Tamimi and an unnamed man from al-Ansar (the Prophet's Madina allies). The men sullenly inform the Prophet that the daughters were spared an early wa'd owing to the intervention of their mothers. Qays was away on a trip when his wife delivered a girl whom she sent away to be raised with her family, meanwhile informing Qays that the baby was stillborn. Similarly, the second man's wife implored him not to bury the infant girl and, in a moment of weakness, he conceded. When the girls reach the marriageable age of adolescence, Qays is suddenly introduced to the girl that he thought was stillborn, and the second father is struck by hamiyya and is reluctant to marry his daughter off to prospective suitors. The two fathers trick both mothers and daughters when they promise to take the daughters on a trip to visit their relatives, but end up pushing them down a well in the desert, despite the heartbreaking entreaties from the daughters pleading for their life. Qays's daughter asks, "Father, how could you bury me in the sands!" The second daughter's statement is equally touching: she holds her father, asking for mercy, and he is torn between keeping her alive or throwing her in the well. When he finally performs the latter, she cries out, "Father, you killed me?" Both men stay next to the well until the pleading voices of the dying daughters fade away. It is reported that upon hearing these stories, the Prophet burst into tears, and told Qays that "he who does not have mercy, does not deserve mercy," and said to the second father, "If I had to punish somebody for crimes committed in the time of *jahiliyyah*, I would have punished you" (al-Qurtubi n.d., 96–97, commentary 6:141).

A close examination of the wa'd stories—those transmitted to us by the pre-Islamic misogynistic tradition, or those recorded by the Muslim gender-justice-conscious tradition—reveals only the patriarchal side of the wa'd story. We have two patriarchies at play here: the jahiliyyah patriarchy that committed the wa'd, and the Muslim one that strongly condemned and outlawed it. In both of these narratives, however, the voice of the buried daughter (al-maw'udah) remains unheard. Similarly, the voices of the mothers who lost their daughters and the other women who were forced to cope with this atrocity are erased as well. The writings of the diaspora female authors are but one attempt to resurrect the maw'udah, and to rewrite the wa'd and national narratives with her occulted voice.

Furthermore, the men's accounts of their daughters' burial highlight two important issues: the incriminating voice of the buried daughter (al-maw'udah) as she reaches out from the grave demanding to be heard, and the trauma that this act has inflicted not just on the girls but also on the grieving fathers, who, after their conversion to Islam, are suddenly aware of their wrongdoings. They relive the traumatic event years after the act of the wa'd took place, experience posttraumatic symptoms of crying, harbor the fear that God will still punish them for their crimes, and continue to be haunted by the voices of the buried daughters. Indeed, it is precisely the voice of the maw'udah, the one the fathers wanted to suffocate, that takes center stage in one of the primary Qur'anic verses that condemn the wa'd practice as one of Islam's grave sins punishable in the hereafter. Although the wa'd practice is referred to in four other suras (6, 16, 17, 60), verses eight and nine of *Surat al-Takwir* represent the only place in the Qur'an where the root *w'd* is used and the voice of the maw'udah is revived.[6] They highlight the crucial moment of the maw'udah's resurrection and the

6. See, for example, *Surat al-Ana'm* 6:151; *Surat al-Nahl* 16:58–59; *Surat al-Isra'* 17:31; *Surat al-Mumtahinah* 60:12.

return of her voice at Judgment Day: "When the female (infant), buried alive, is questioned / For what crime she was killed (*wa-idha al-maw'udatu su'ilat bi-ayyi dhanbin qutilat*)" (The Holy Qur'an, *Surat al-Takwir* 81:8, 1905–6). The maw'udah's body stands as a trace, as evidence of the crime committed against her in secret collusion. At Judgment Day, she will finally receive justice by presenting her buried body as proof of the insidious wa'd crime. Hence "the proofs will be drawn from the very means used for concealment" (commentary on *Surat al-Takwir* 81:8, 1906); both body and voice join together in pointing the accusatory finger at the guilty fathers, thus giving a punitive meaning to the daughter's cries: "Father, you killed me (*laqad qataltani ya-abati*)."[7] It is no wonder, then, that after realizing the error of their jahiliyyah ways, the fathers are haunted by this traumatic past. This history may explain why the motifs of body and voice are forever intertwined in Arab women's literature.

In her summation of Freud's writings on trauma, Cathy Caruth points out that trauma "is always the story of a wound that cries out, that addresses us in the attempt to tell us of a reality or truth that is not otherwise available. This truth, in its delayed appearance and its belated address, cannot be linked only to what is known, but also to what remains unknown in our very actions and our language" (Caruth 1996, 4). If the voice of the maw'udah can remind the newly converted Muslim fathers of the traumatic reality that they initiated during jahiliyyah times, how could this voice be heard and the traumatic wound felt by the rest of the contemporary Arab women who did not experience the wa'd trauma directly? The

---

7. There is an eerie similarity between the girl's statement—"Father, you killed me"— and Freud's analysis of a deceased boy's statement made to a grieving father in a dream: "Father, don't you see I'm burning?" In *The Interpretation of Dreams* (1915), Freud links his theory of dreams and wish-fulfillment with the external reality of loss and trauma. The son, who had died earlier that night, returns to alert his sleeping father to the fact that his own corpse is burning from a fallen candle. Freud maintains that this dream fulfills the father's wish that the child be still alive. In his analysis of the same dream, however, Jacques Lacan claims that awakening the father to the reality of the son's death and the responsibility of passing on this traumatic information to others is the true meaning of this dream. For more on the intersections of dreams and trauma, see Caruth 1996, 91–112.

answer lies in what Freud refers to as the "latency" of the traumatic experi-ence—the period during which the effects of the traumatic experience are not apparent—the period from the event, to its repression, to its return.[8] The answer is also evident in the cultural, secretive nature of the wa'd act that, in turn, forces contemporary women to experience a secondhand, intergenerational trauma, one that feminist therapists Maria Root and Laura Brown call "insidious trauma" (Brown 1995, 107). According to Root, insidious trauma is characterized as "the traumatogenic effects of oppression that are not necessarily overtly violent or threatening to bodily well-being at the given moment but do violence to the soul and spirit" (Brown 1995, 107). Recent mainstream trauma theory, Brown contends, has begun "to recognize that post-traumatic symptoms can be intergener-ational, as in the case of children of survivors of the Nazi Holocaust." Still, it has yet to admit that these symptoms could "spread laterally throughout an oppressed social group" whose membership could mean "a constant lifetime risk of exposure to certain trauma" (Brown 1995, 108). The act of remembering, of putting the painful, absent pieces together, is crucial, then, and evident in the process of postmemory. For, as Hirsch contends, "postmemory characterizes the experience of those who grow up domi-nated by narratives that preceded their birth, whose own belated stories are evacuated by the stories of the previous generation shaped by trau-matic events that can be neither understood nor recreated" (Hirsch 1997, 22). This is certainly the case for contemporary Muslim and Christian Arab women, descendants of both Shahrazad and the maw'udah legacy. For these women, the wa'd trauma is experienced on both the intergenera-tional and the lateral levels as heirs of an archaic, albeit extinct, practice intended to eradicate traces of the female buried body and silence their recently resurrected voices.

It is the desire to understand, to retrieve the "inaccessible" wa'd trauma that propels our writers to engage the wa'd archetype person-ally and politically in their writings. However, it is this "inaccessibility,"

---

8. On Freud's use of the terms "incubation period" and "latency" in reference to Jewish religion and history, see Freud 1939, 84.

argues Cathy Caruth, drawing on Freud, which makes it impossible to tap into the historical truth of traumatic events. Trauma, she claims, renders the event itself elusive and absent from the moment of its initial occurrence and, as such, "irretrievable."

If these postulations hold true, how can one believe in contemporary women writers' ability to represent the "incomprehensible?" (Caruth 1996, 18). They accomplish this task by avoiding fixity, assuming multiple positionalities while simultaneously insisting on listening to the archives. In fact, unlocking the traumatic historical truth starts by rejecting rigid frameworks of understanding, as Claude Lanzmann contends, "a refusal that is also a creative act of listening."[9] Only in this manner can untapped spaces in women's narrative open themselves up to our contemporary comprehension so as to reverse the "obliquely suggestive and esoteric narrative inferences" of trauma theory, to make it accessible to Shahrazad's and the maw'udah's granddaughters who will, in turn, embody this traumatic past in their contemporary narratives.[10] It is only through activating these dual icons and reclaiming this history of literary and bodily trauma that Arab women writers can unlock traumatic experiences, undo the tradition of its "inaccessibility," and rewrite death into survival stories. James Clifford asserts that "[r]ecalling older histories of discrepant cosmopolitan contacts can empower new ways to be 'traditional' on a more than local scale" (Clifford 1997, 276–77). The goal for current diasporic writing, then, is to simultaneously maintain the discourse of loss and survival from both the local and the global sites. Realizing that "entanglement is not necessarily cooptation," and engaging in "recovering non-Western, or not-only-Western, models for cosmopolitan life," ultimately leads to the

---

9. See, for example, Claude Lanzmann's commentary on the making of the film *Shoah* in Caruth 1995, 154.

10. I am indebted to Lisa Woolfork's literary revisions of trauma theory, and its application to the body of the African American literary and cultural experience. Woolfork argues convincingly that contrary to current postulations of trauma theory, recent African American artistic and cultural reenactments of slavery's past do, indeed, make the traumatic experience "retrievable" and embody it in the contemporary African American imaginary, thus making it more accessible to contemporary survivors (Woolfork 2008).

creation of "nonaligned transnationalities struggling within and against nation-states, global technologies, and markets" (276–77). In fact, diasporic authors' recovery of cultural memories and the past archival corpus is meant to defy global and local hegemonies of essentialist nation-states and patriarchy. The act of listening to Shahrazad's oral (hi)story and the muffled voice of the maw'udah constitutes the nucleus upon which the story of reconstructing Arab female authorship begins—a story of resurrection from the wa'd trauma, of rewriting the history of female selfhood in print and reframing it from multiple, forever shifting diasporic centers.

Trauma in Theory and in Practice

Trauma experts define trauma as a sudden and violent event that threatens the life of a person who has experienced or witnessed it, or those in his/her surroundings (Herman 1992, 33; Vees-Gulani 2003, 26–27). Such a traumatic event causes unusual stressors to the conscious mind, to the point that the brain has to resort to several defense mechanisms to protect the affected subject from a total psychological breakdown. These mechanisms involve psychological numbness and dissociation, in which a subject splits off part of herself from the experience, thereby leading to a dissociative identity disorder (DID). Still, the repressed traumatic events have an insidious way of creeping up into the subject's mind through the intrusion of distressing images, dreams, and/or fantasies. This intrusion leads the affected person to further engage in avoidance mechanisms that, in turn, force the return of these traumatic memories with a vengeance, thereby leading to the subject's hyperarousal (Vees-Gulani 2003, 27).

At its inception in the early 1880s, trauma studies focused on the physiological manifestations of the traumatic event as evident in the pioneering work of the French neurologist Jean-Martin Charcot and his Sorbonne colleagues on hysteria and war neurosis patients. However, the term shifted to a more psychological application as a result of Sigmund Freud's and Joseph Breuer's studies in 1890. At that time Freud advanced his famous "seduction theory," which proposed a certain sexual childhood trauma as the cause for a patient's hysteria. However, at a later date Freud came to abandon the seduction theory's premise, which suggested that a real sexual event might have triggered the patient's hysteria, and conceded that the traumatic causation might be attributed to innate desires and fantasies of the patient's imagination. During the period of 1906–13 the field of trauma studies was invigorated by Carl Jung, who, like Freud, believed that dreams hold the key for unlocking the origin of neuroses. Unlike Freud, however, he disagreed vehemently with the notion of restricting the dream's interpretation to the individual's private world. Jung argued that a more apt interpretation of these dream symbols might be located in the individual's cultural mythology and in the "collective unconscious" (Jung 1966). The shift from Freud's limiting individual definition of neurosis to Jung's collective understanding of it moves the trauma subject from paralysis to creativity. I contend that writing and connecting the individual's trauma with cultural myths, such as that of the wa'd and Shahrazad, enriches the cultural narrative collective and transforms traumatic outcomes from negative to positive ones. My understanding of the wa'd trauma in this regard moves beyond the direct individual's experience of this traumatic event, addressing its collective effects on the authors in question and their readership. A case in point is the poignant way in which the wa'd icon has been collectively adopted by the rebelling Arab masses in the Arab Spring, specifically in the Syrian revolution, to symbolize political oppression. Through invoking the maw'udah's story, diaspora women writers are able to overcome the paralyzing and limiting individual wa'd trauma, and to activate the creative and forgiving realm of the collective trauma. My application of this new trauma definition benefits a great deal from the concept of post-traumatic stress disorder (PTSD), advanced in 1980 to denote the traumatic experience of Holocaust, Vietnam, Hiroshima, and rape survivors, and the mechanism of trauma's intergenerational transference among members of the same affected group. In light of this new understanding of the traumatic occurrence, one does not need to be a direct victim of the traumatic event to experience its consequences; rather, being a member of the same oppressed group or a transmitter of the traumatic knowledge suffices to inflict the same traumatic triggers on the narrator and also on the reader. Despite the spatial and temporal distance that separates the early wa'd victims from these contemporary women writers, the various personal and political persecutions they endured or witnessed in the homeland, in times of both peace and war, have led to the survivability of the wa'd motif in their literary output, thereby attesting to the ability of intergenerational trauma to cross spatial and temporal boundaries. In this context, Shoshana Felman speaks of a "post-traumatic century" that we all live in (Felman and Laub 1992, 1), while Cathy Caruth pinpoints a traumatic history that "is never simply one's own," since we are all "implicated in each other's traumas" (Caruth 1996, 24). Consequently, it is possible then to speak about a collective historical trauma experienced not only *inside* the targeted traumatized individual, but also *outside* in the cultural undercurrents of one's community. This traumatic sense is compounded by successive political traumas such as the *nakba* (1948), the *naksa* (1967), the Lebanese Civil War (1975 until 1991), the Gulf War (1990–91), and the current tumultuous scene created by the Arab Spring's project (2010–15).

The influence of this collective historical trauma is clearly evident, as I will demonstrate in the following chapters, in the invocation of the wa'd intergenerational trauma in the works of Samman, al-Shaykh, Barakat, Na'na', and Yazbek, and in al-Neimi's poetry, specifically in *Ajdadi al-Qatalah* (2001) ("My Murderous Ancestors"). In their corpus, the wa'd image takes on several symbolic vestiges focusing on the feminine body that bears the brunt of burial, suffocation, sexual violation, and imprisonment. It is also evident in thematic pursuits of the authors in which the wa'd trope is at once fabricated, iconized, and deployed to interrogate discourses on women's body, identity, subjectivity, their role as literary women and voice, nation as a woman, and tradition as a woman. Indeed, the literature of Arab diaspora women writers articulates a moral and a political obligation to act as a witness to the wa'd and erasure traumas of Arab women, and to their various manifestations in the burial of memories, history, cities, and nation. This systematic process of "narrative witnessing" (quoted in Vees-Gulani 2003, 21) is a way to document the forgotten voice of the maw'udah who has reached our ears through the two competing patriarchal stories of the pre-Islamic and the Muslim accounts, but never through her own voice. Her story is still buried in the sands waiting to be unearthed through the narrative of contemporary diaspora women writers who inherited this traumatic bequest, and who insist on resurrecting and rewriting her untold story.

Wa'd Nightmares

Such "narrative witnessing" and intergenerational trauma are outlined in Ghada Samman's poignant recounting of the wa'd trauma in the following nightmare:

> Someone is burying me alive in the sands. I do not see his face, nor do I want to. The sands are pouring inside my throat, I gasp for air, but I breathe only sands, sands that fill my lungs, and I suffocate. My fear increases when I relive the same nightmare once more while reading it in my mother's memoirs. It appears that she used to have the same nightmare! I wonder whether my grandmother and her great-great grandmother also experienced the same nightmare, for eternity onward. (al-Samman 1997a, 381)

Samman's heroine, Zayn, whom we will encounter in the following chapter in *Al-Riwayah al-Mustahilah* (1997) (*The Impossible Novel*, not published in English), relives the horror of the wa'd nightmare on a daily basis. Her nightmares replay this feeling of asphyxiation associated with the sensation of being buried alive. She shares with the reader this constant, intense fear that she suspects had haunted her mother's and her grandmother's nightmares before her as well. In this context, the wa'd motif manifests itself both literally and symbolically in images of imprisonment, enclosure, and fear of bodily persecution in a majority of the texts in question. The postmemory of wa'd haunts Zayn, who tries to trace its intergenerational trauma so as to heal its damaging effects through retelling the wa'd story. Additionally, wa'd can be understood to inform the experiences of burial and suffocation in works like Samman's *Al-Qamar al-Murabba'* (1994) (*The Square Moon*, 1998, 148–49), to represent the buried national map and city in Hamida Na'na''s *Al-Watan fi al-'Aynayn* (*The Homeland* 1995, 84, 139), Barakat's *Harith al-Miyah* (*The Tiller of Waters* 2001, 46–47), as well as Samar Yazbek's *Taqatu' Niran* (*A Woman in the*

Crossfire: Diaries of the Syrian Revolution 2011 and 2012, 12, 30), and to denote the forgotten Arabic language and heritage in Hanan al-Shaykh's *Innaha London ya ʻAzizi* (*Only in London* 2001, 125, 227), and in most of al-Neimi's poetry collections. For example, several protagonists are buried alive in coffins (Samman) and urns (Barakat), or left as dead corpses under beds (al-Neimi). The repetitiveness of the waʼd image functions as a promise to affirm subjectivity, and as a signifier representing the dispossession of Arab lands and citizens suffering from the oppression of authoritarian regimes. Repetition, Jacques Lacan asserts, "demands the new." The recall of the traditional waʼd, in the authors' narratives, forces readers to confront its new political manifestations in the Arab world's contemporary cultural scene. It further serves as an awakening of sorts, alerting the female subject not only to the unknown reality of the original traumatic past, but also to the responsibility of being the "ethical witness," and of "passing on this awakening to others," through retelling the story so as "to engage less the past than the unknown future of the bond" between others—the remaining survivors. The focus, then, is on the responsibility to survive, and to create within the folds of one's narrative a space for others to survive as well (quoted in Caruth 1996, 110–12), to resurrect al-mawʼudah as a cultural myth denoting buried human rights and curbed freedoms. Only in this manner can individual traumatic experiences of burial (Samman, Barakat, and Yazbek), honor killing (al-Neimi), sexual abuse (al-Shaykh), and bodily disfigurement (Naʻnaʻ) be transformed into collective projects of resurrection and survival not just for the characters involved, but rather for their readers and the whole Arab nation.

Only My Blood Will Quench the Tribe's Fire: Bodily Persecution Complex

The urgency of the survival message highlights real fears of physical and discursive dismemberment. For example, Zayn resurrects her mother's buried literary legacy by desiring to be a writer herself, and she is convinced that her cousins' bullet, the one they claimed was the result of a hunting accident, was directed at her personally. She is certain that her cousins meant to blind her so as to limit her ability to see and to write (al-Samman 1997a, 489). In her recollection of some of the biographical facts that informed the creation of Zayn's character, Samman recalls how her brother, Salman, "was maddened by the voice of the ancestors seeping through his blood" when he saw her picture published next to her article in Damascus newspapers (al-Samman 1986a, 265). She later divulges that it was her brother who accidently shot her back in this unfortunate hunting accident as if symbolically reenacting the execution of an honor crime (al-Samman 1986a, 264). Fear of persecution is justified. Samman's heroine Zayn explains an old wound as an imaginary excision done by the family's old women to clip her wings (al-Samman 1997a, 365; Samman 1990, 96).[11] Her wound is a reminder of trauma's crying wound, referenced earlier in Cathy Caruth's trauma definition, and of the wa'd's wound as well. Additionally, Zayn's girlfriends are pushed from roofs and forced to swallow smoldering embers to prevent articulation of their romantic desires (al-Samman 1997a, 114, 193). Voice and body are inextricably linked, and the writers' insistence on claiming a literary voice necessitates resurrecting the buried body of the maw'udah. Another form of feminine violation is rape and ultimately murder as in Hanan al-Shaykh's, Hoda Barakat's, Salwa al-Neimi's, and Samar Yazbek's works. Additionally, Hamida Na'na''s Nadia is forced to undergo plastic surgery by the political party so as to alter her identity and hide her revolutionary past. Indeed, diaspora women writers draw a picture of a female body that is often mutilated, violated, restricted, reconstructed, symbolically consumed, suffocated, and buried. It is a terrifying portrait—one that is meant to trigger individual memories and, in Jacques Lacan's words, to *pass them on* in order to enact collective awakenings. It is an awakening that must be passed on to future generations so as to protest the history of women's erasure. It is particularly by engaging in a literary application of trauma theory in Arab women's literary corpus, and by opening up this linguistic female space, that public and national spaces expand as well.

---

11. In an interview with Majid al-Samra'i in July 1980, Samman refers to a similar unexplained childhood wound in her back, and credits it for reminding her of patriarchy's assaults against her creativity (al-Samman 1990, 96).

The focus on examining the confined, dissected, and dismembered female body proves to be crucial to the emergence of a new female selfhood that gains its strength from revisiting the site of atrocities committed on its body, and on the national body as well. By exposing this legacy of fear and violation, these authors engage in a project of reconstruction, rebuilding the body of the woman and the nation rather than reiterating orientalist narratives of oppression that demonize Arab men and culture. The body image is central, and the ways in which these writers and public intellectuals use the wa'd as an icon signifying oppression to remember the fragmented body (mainly female, but in Hoda Barakat's narrative male as well) and the literary canon in order to defy erasure are of utmost importance. Unlike the earlier adab al-mahjar (diaspora literature) male writers, especially proponents of the North American literary circle al-Rabitah al-Qalamiyyah (the Pen Circle), such as Gibran Khalil Gibran and Mikha'il Nu'aymah, who thought that overcoming the limitations of the soul/body binaries could only be accomplished through erasing the body motif in their writings so as to communicate their mystic message of reincarnation, women writers of the diaspora insist that unearthing the body trope is the starting point to challenging the patriarchal discourse that engenders such a duality, with the hope of eliminating it all together ('Abbas and Najm 1967, 41–70; al-Ashtar 1965, 121). They realize that unsettling rather than transcending the patriarchal binaries, through articulating the problematic of the violated feminine body, is what is needed to change its debilitating effects on women and the country. Thus the only practical option is to revisit the traumatic body site so as to exorcize the patriarchal wa'd nightmares from women's and the nation's memory, to trace the wounds enacted on its corporal canvas in the past, so as to transform the present and to illuminate the future. Just as the diasporic women authors transform Shahrazad's corpus from orality to the written word, so in their work the surviving female body enables the physical, sexual, and symbolic resurrection of the maw'udah as she enacts psychological and physical journeys, redefining cultural and political cartographies, thereby proving that acknowledging the presence of the female body, voice, and narrative can and must lead to the transformation of the political and the national as well.

3

Mosaic Autobiography

Ghada Samman's *Al-Riwayah al-Mustahilah* (*The Impossible Novel*)
and Hanan al-Shaykh's *The Locust and the Bird*

In "I Write against My Hand," Hoda Barakat expresses the urgent need
to "raise the spoken word to the level of written language," so as "to preserve its imprint in collective memory and history" (Barakat 1998a, 44).
Her plea articulates a sacred mission undertaken by writers who set out to
resurrect forgotten literary modes and memories in order to claim them
as part of the collective national inheritance, and to protect them from
the violence of erasure. She asserts, "we write to recover the things which
are ours and which the world denies us. We write to retrieve and to take
revenge" (Barakat 1998a, 45). Embedded in her statement is the innate
relationship between writing, particularly that of an autobiography, and
the assertion of an identity often threatened with erasure owing to forgetfulness or death. An autobiographer writes to affirm his/her own voice
amid a multitude of other voices and to assert an existence that would otherwise be forgotten. Richard van Leeuwen contends that "the practice of
autobiography is essentially an effort to conceive, confirm or stress a sense
of identity. Anyone who feels the need to write down his memoirs is at least
partly urged by the wish to assert his position among others, usually his
contemporaries, his cultural background or his social or political environment" (van Leeuwen 1998, 27). Thus most autobiographies emphasize the
individual self/autobiographer, whose mythical "I" dominates the scene
in a Renaissance-like fashion. Recalled memories and narrated events are
presented primarily from the autobiographer's point of view. Locating
the authorial individual "I," however, for female autobiographers is not

an easy task given that it involves working through years of systematic, sociopolitical assault designed to erase that identity. Moreover, an autobiography is by nature an account of the private self's trials and tribulations as it struggles to leave an imprint on the public sphere. Once more, this proves to be problematic for female autobiographers whose mere societal existence has long been relegated strictly to the private sphere. A simple attempt to leave an im(print) in the public sphere would require a certain level of comfort in breaking out of the private sphere and into print—a double jeopardy for most women.

For Arab women autobiographers, this jeopardy is not just a figurative, but a real one, as the "I" of the female self is faced not just with a symbolic threat of erasure, as is the case with Western female autobiographers, but rather with the fear of physical annihilation! The two autobiographical novels examined in this chapter, Ghada Samman's *Al-Riwayah al-Musta-hilah: Fusifusa' Dimashqiyyah* (1997a) (*The Impossible Novel: Damascene Mosaic*, not published in English) and Hanan al-Shaykh's *Hikayati Shar-hun Yatul* (2005, translated as *The Locust and the Bird*, 2009), are haunted by the nightmare of the traditional wa'd al-banat (female infant burial) that threatens not just the construction of the individual autobiographical "I" in the literary sense, but rather literally its very own existence. Naturally, Arab female writers are keenly aware of the limitations of a female self-hood with contested access to history and language. Furthermore, owing to this physical threat of persecution, they are cognizant, even more than their Western female counterparts, of the repercussions of breaking away from the prison of their private worlds in light of an Arabic cultural convention that values concealment and clear demarcation between private and public spheres. Building on Farzaneh Milani's observation of the Iranian culture and how it lacks a "tradition of confession, in either its catholic or secular sense" (quoted in Faqir 1998, 14), Fadia Faqir draws similar conclusions for the Arabo-Islamic tradition, thus leading, in her opinion, to the scarcity of female autobiographies in the Arabic literary canon. She states, "The public and private spaces are neatly divided in many Arab countries, especially now with Islamic revivalism. To expose the inner self publicly, is to risk losing the respect of the family, immediate community and society at large. When writers commit their lives to paper they go against a culture which is based on concealment" (Faqir 1998, 14). In fact, it was this desire to break away from the isolation of the private sphere and the legacy of concealment that motivated Samman and al-Shaykh to author autobiographical novels of themselves and of their silenced mothers. Their diasporic sites at the time of penning these autobiographies—Paris for Samman and London for al-Shaykh—offered a much-needed sense of security, a crucial factor for reducing the anxiety of erasure and of self-expression, thereby providing the necessary detachment for an overall view of the narrated events. Furthermore, the diasporic sites allowed them to reflect on their positionality and placement in their family's and country's cultural frames. Through their resurrection of their mothers' forgotten life stories, both writers activate the Shahrazad archetype in such a way as to transcend the limitations of her orality and the exclusions of a solitary autobiography for the sake of a collective one. Furthermore, both transform diasporic *routes* into *rhizomes* that ultimately connect them to their personal and cultural *roots*. Additionally, both works access the lost temporal, familial, and cultural connection to the past through piecing together a collage of faded pictures, ready to be resurrected and incorporated in the national frame. Consequently, the two autobiographical novels bespeak an outcry for an identity location that refuses erasure and insists on its inscription onto history and language through mastering the laws of script. By articulating their call for authorship as a final fulfillment of the erased mother's literary trace, both authors inscribe a mosaic autobiography that articulates its identity politics *with* rather than *against* the collective familial and national persona in a final reconciliatory tone.

The Collage of Collective Autobiography

Ghada Samman's *Al-Riwayah al-Mustahilah* (*The Impossible Novel*) veers from Philippe Lejeune's traditional definition of an autobiography per se, in the sense that it does not follow his "autobiographical pact" in which the author/narrator/character is the same individual who, from the onset of the work, declares to the reader that s/he is about to delve into an autobiographical account (Lejeune 1988, 3–30). Rather, Samman employs certain narrative techniques that enable her to create an offshoot of the autobiography genre—one that promises to transcend the limitations of both gender and genre as well as the immediate individual self of the author/narrator/main character to a collective universal self that includes community and country: namely, the autobiographical novel. In this fascinating "impossible novel," the author defies the traditional rules of both autobiography and fiction proper. Although the autobiographical novel carries certain autobiographical elements that can be traced back to Samman herself, the text moves away from the traditional definition of autobiography proper in its refusal to commit itself to an autobiographical pact and to a chronology of events narrated exclusively from the main heroine's point of view. In addition, the text further resists its allegiance to the traditional fictive genre, despite classifying itself as such on its front cover. By refusing to follow the classical five chapter divisions when characterizing all five of them as chapter 1, and by confronting the reader with a void last page that forms the yet unwritten fifth chapter, this autobiographical novel is breaking grounds on both the fictive and the genre levels. In fact, the text declares the ambiguity of its genre despite its novelistic masquerade as *riwayah* (fiction) by stating that it is, indeed, an "impossible novel!" But what are the reasons for this impossibility, the intangible, autobiographic existence of this text?

In the following analysis of this autobiographical novel, I will argue that the departure from the chronology of the individual unitary self, which is customary with male autobiographies, and from the linear, stylistic chronology of the traditional novel presents a unique opportunity to experience a new genre: that of mosaic autobiography. This genre's uniqueness lies in the transformation of the autobiographer's unitary self into a universal self through the distancing of the diasporic narrator and the introduction of multiple voices in the fictive dialogue. The result is an autobiographical mosaic narrative that subverts illusory unity; parades tension and narrative gaps; acknowledges the tiny mosaic pieces that eventually form the whole story, not just of the female narrator but of her male characters; and exposes the temporal and the spatial properties of her native city—Damascus. This marriage of the autobiography and the novel empowers the new genre of the autobiographical novel with a wide array of techniques or, to use Lejeune's words, "games" through which the autobiographer/narrator can escape from the limitations of the traditional "I." Lejeune asserts,

> Autobiography such as it is practiced today owes much to the biographical model, and undoubtedly also to the novel, both in its most traditional aspects and in its newest refinements. The majority of the games in which contemporary autobiographers indulge are the timid echo of the investigations of modern novelists into narrative voice and focalization. Justified timidity: in fiction, one risks nothing, one can break identity and put it back together, allow oneself all points of view, give oneself any means. (Lejeune 1988, 37)

Samman's means of constructing this unique mosaic autobiography was to present the narrative from the multiplicity of "We"—a collectivity that starts and ends with the point of view of Zayn's "I." *The Impossible Novel* chronicles the childhood memories of the heroine Zayn, the death of her mother, Hind, in childbirth, and the subsequent challenges of single parenthood for her father, Amjad, and ultimately provides a glimpse of Zayn's upbringing in a traditional, Damascene old house surrounded by the warmth of her paternal grandmother's presence and a multitude of aunts, uncles, and mixed-gender cousins. The storyline documents the thorny process of forming a unique female identity, one that is torn between the assertion of individuality and blind allegiance to the collective identity. By following the developmental stages of Zayn's childhood, adolescence, and early adulthood, one discerns an identity that neither conforms to the traditional definition of female selfhood in her patriarchal culture, nor totally rejects her ethnic and cultural alliance with the overall picture of this Damascene mosaic. At the end of her personal and cultural self-actualization process, Zayn embraces her femininity, her cultural identity, and her authorial voice. The discovery of writing as a cure to the ailment of her femininity enables Zayn to transcend the limitations of the individual "I" autobiography as she simultaneously maintains the familial and cultural narratives, and engages in a collective autobiography of "We" that links her back both to her mother's literary tradition and to her cultural roots. As an artist, Zayn pieces together parts of varied individual selves in order to create a stunning masterpiece of mosaic autobiography in which the "we" represents the collective voices of humans, nonhumans, and even the life (his)story of inanimate objects such as the city—Damascus itself.

The technique of presenting the novel's four chapters all entitled chapter 1 and leaving a blank fifth chapter at the end reflects Samman's emphasis on the importance of revisiting beginnings, and her desire to start the narrative anew with each character to reflect various points of view. Furthermore, as customary with most autobiographies, flashback narration facilitates going back in time to recapture crucial memories of birth in the life of the main protagonist, Zayn, and of Syria itself. The setting is Damascus, at the time when Syria was still under the colonization of the French troops during the French Mandate from 1918 to 1946. The actual time frame of the book begins a year or so prior to Syria's Independence Day on April 17, 1946, and ends with Zayn's impending seventeenth birthday approximately 1959 or 1960. It is a period of thirteen years or so during which Samman chronicles the physical and temporal life of Damascus (the city) and its inhabitants (the characters of her book).[1] Four of the chapters reconstruct Zayn's memoirs while the fifth one remains yet unwritten. The first chapter, "Illusory Memoirs," presents a sketchy yet intensely vivid picture of Zayn's early childhood and her recollections of her mother prior, during, and after her unfortunate death during childbirth. Hind (Zayn's mother) is an educated heiress from a wealthy feudal family in Lattakia who inherited, along with her only sister, a vast estate after her father's death. In Damascus, where she worked as a French teacher for a while, Hind met Amjad al-Khayal, a self-made man who acquired his PhD in law from France. Their first meeting took place in a literary club where, as an aspiring writer, she used to recite her poetry. The two fell in love and married in Damascus despite the strong opposition of Hind's male cousin,

---

1. The narrator of *Al-Riwayah al-Mustahilah* mentions that Zayn was almost four years old when Damascus was bombed by French troops in May 29, 1945 (al-Samman 1997a, 80). This places Zayn's birth date sometime in 1941 or 1942. Ghada Samman was born in 1942 in al-Shamiyya, Syria. The biographical similarities between the main character, Zayn, and the author, Samman, are numerous. Also see note 7 below.

who tried to usurp Hind's inheritance by claiming her insane in order to prevent the family's wealth from passing on to a stranger, Amjad (Zayn's father). Hind prevailed in court, was able to keep her inheritance, married the man she loved, and lived with his huge extended family at the "big house" in Harat al-Yasmin (Jasmine Alley) in Damascus. Yet all was not well in paradise! Hind's first pregnancy disappointed her husband, who, as a traditional Arab man, preferred a boy. Instead, a daughter, Zayn, was born, whom Amjad always viewed as only "half" of Zayn al-'Abidin—the son he often dreamed of fathering. As a result of Amjad's disappointment at having a daughter, and in order to please the husband whom she adored, Hind overlooked her doctor's warnings against a second pregnancy and risked her life in order to fulfill Amjad's desire for a son. Amjad's dreams came true with the birth of twin sons but at the expense of Hind's life. In an ironic fateful twist, Hind died after her difficult delivery; the twin boys passed away only hours after.

Catastrophic Beginnings

The first chapter is narrated mostly from Amjad's point of view. He relies on the flashback technique to recall the previous events that led to this catastrophe. Attempting to purge his sins, he ultimately implicates himself as Hind's killer. His sense of guilt emanates from his realization that his selfish desire for a male child has superseded his love for his wife. Furthermore, the fact that he was on a business trip when Hind went into labor has meant that key health decisions were left in the hands of his conservative brother, 'Abd al-Fattah. During her delivery, Hind needed immediate medical attention. However, owing to 'Abd al-Fattah's ignorance and conservative religious beliefs, he refused to transfer Hind to a hospital so as not to allow male doctors to see her exposed body. As a result, Hind almost bled to death in a difficult home childbirth and was only transferred to a hospital when it was too late for the doctors to save her life. Thus the first chapter of this autobiographical novel surprises the reader with its adherence to a standard autobiographical technique in modern Arabic literature, namely, the invocation of a catastrophic death scene. On this topic, Stefan Wild remarks that "the start of many an autobiography is the start of catastrophe, often an early death witnessed by the child." He continues that this phenomenon holds particularly true in classical auto-biographies written by women since "society considers the birth of girls a catastrophe in itself."[2] Indeed, this sentiment is also echoed in Nawal El Saadawi's invocation of death in the initial birth scene in her own exilic autobiography. In *Awraqi, Hayati* (1995), El Saadawi articulates her femi-nine gender as one of the decisive factors in shaping her early childhood, adolescence, and adult life. In this context, it is not surprising that one of the earliest recollections of her autobiography's narrator (Nawal) focuses on the monumental event of her birth as a female, and the subsequent symbolic death experienced by her whole family. After listening to her grandmother's tales, Nawal reconstructs a birth scene similar to that of a deathbed, or a wa'd scene. She recounts the circumstances during which in an early, cold, October morning "a single scream of a woman experiencing labor pains is heard, followed by a long heavy silence as if both mother and child are dead" (El Saadawi 1995, 5). The imagery of death, suffocation, and silence dominates the birth scene as the adult narrator relives the suf-focation sensation experienced by the infant stuck at the vaginal opening. The same smothering sensation is reenacted through the actual attempt by the midwife to drown the infant in the bathwater upon discovering that it is, indeed, an unwanted girl. In this context, the trauma of the traditional wa'd trope is reactivated, albeit differently, through drown-ing so as to highlight the intergenerational trauma that connects moth-ers and daughters, past and present. This physical and symbolic death sentence imposed on the female body and further justified by conjuring up the myth of the castrating vagina, which threatens to suffocate the child, reminds the reader of the inherent disdain and fear associated with the feminine in the collective unconscious. Not unlike the Western nine-teenth-century artists who, as a result of Freud's influential analysis of the

2. Wild recounts numerous contemporary Arabic autobiographies written by both males and females that follow this traditional death opening technique, including Fadwa Tuqan (1985 [1990]); Latifa Zayyat (1992 [1996]); Hanna Mina (2002 [1993]); and Muham-mad Shukri (1982 [1973]). For a comparative study of the beginnings in Arabic autobiog-raphies, see Wild 1998, 82–99.

castrating elements of Medusa's head, used the term "*vagina dentata*"[3] to express the threatening, engulfing qualities attributed to the female genitalia, pre-Islamic Arabia also shared a collective disdain for the feminine genitalia coupled with the fear of its ability to bring the enemy within. As I argued in the previous chapter, jahiliyyah women were perceived as a liability because of their potential to be taken as war spoils, thereby bringing shame and disgrace to the whole tribe. Thus eliminating this potential danger as early as possible was one of the reasons behind the common practice of wa'd al-banat in which female infants were buried alive in the sand before they had a chance to dishonor their tribe. The character Nawal is quick to point out that although this practice had been outlawed by the advent of Islam in the seventh century AD, the silence that befell her paternal and maternal family members after her birth was reminiscent of their secret desire to revert to this custom, to bury her alive and to commit her to wa'd. Hence the formation of an Arab female identity depends on battling a symbolic death and overcoming a debilitating silence that would otherwise lead to her literal and literary suffocation.

Similarly, in Samman's autobiographical novel the reader is transported back in time to witness the "catastrophe" that befell Amjad and his family upon receiving the news of the birth of a daughter—Zayn. Amjad's association of the impending French troops bombarding Damascus and the undesired birth of a girl harkens back to the then catastrophic implication of a feminine birth in traditional households. Amjad proclaims, "I have fathered a girl then! Girl and war at the same time! . . . I do not want to see her. Keep her away from my face. My child is not a boy but a girl! It is only Zayn and not Zayn al-'Abidin. She is only half a son" (al-Samman 1997a, 16, 54).[4] Not unlike war, the birth of a daughter brings about chaos, possible destruction, and fear of the unknown. For the rest of her adolescent years, Zayn would try to make up for her

3. For a thorough treatment of the development and artistic use of the term *vagina dentata* in nineteenth-century Western artistic and literary pieces as well as its relation to the concepts of feminine veiling and male castration, see Showalter 1990, 144–68.

4. All translations of *Al-Riwayah al-Mustahilah* are mine.

perceived gender "deficiency" by pretending that she is the son that her father always wanted. After Hind's death, their close relationship resulting from Amjad's guilt and Zayn's desire to please her sole surviving parent estranges her further from the feminine realm—with the exception of her grandmother whom she adores. However, the grandmother is cast in an asexual role that renders her incapable of helping Zayn return to the realm of femininity that the latter rejects. This chapter is haunted by the presence of Hind's ghost, often manifested through Amjad's own recollections of her, and through Zayn's repeated references to her mother's nightly visits to her bedside as well as their consequent joint flight to the seaside away from the restrictions of the "big house." Amjad's narrative voice, however, recounts past and current events surprisingly no longer from a masculine domineering point of view, but rather from a feminine point of view that he acquired only after Hind's death. "My feminine side is awakened," he asserts (al-Samman 1997a, 18). By succumbing to patriarchy's rules, Hind was successful in subverting its dominance in a manner that shook the stability of all the males in the family. After her death, not only is Amjad able to see her point of view on all points of differences between them in the past, but also even the prototype chauvinist in the family, her brother-in-law 'Abd al-Fattah, seems to have undergone a mysterious change that leads to his deterioration and later to his temporary insanity.

'Abd al-Fattah's earlier pronouncements against women, especially in regard to their association with cats only suitable for procreation, all come back to haunt him after Hind's death. In the hospital during Hind's childbirth, he advises his brother Amjad not to worry about his wife because, as he puts it, like cats "women have seven lives" (al-Samman 1997a, 10). In the past, he has been known to destroy cats that bring forth only female litters by throwing them in the river (85). The same sentiment is expressed through a fellow male neighbor's criminal actions toward the house's pet cat, which had the misfortune of bringing a litter with a high proportion of female to male kittens. In a threatening gesture toward his own pregnant wife, the neighbor, Munir, destroys the female kittens by throwing them over Damascus's old fence while cursing the female gender's disturbing ability to procreate indiscriminately (115). This cultural aversion to the female's ability to procreate goes beyond the superficial preference for male offspring. According to Simone de Beauvoir, women and nature are constant reminders of man's futile attempts to transcend mortality—man's ultimate goal in patriarchal societies. Building on de Beauvoir's claims, Ynestra King further elaborates on the ensuing "love-hate fetishization of women's bodies." She points out that

> [w]omen's powers of procreation are distinguished from the powers of creation—the accomplishments through the vehicles of culture by which men achieve immortality. And yet this transcendence over women and nature can never be total: thus the ambivalence, the lack of self without other, the dependence of the self on the other both materially and emotionally. Thus develops a love-hate fetishization of women's bodies, which finds its ultimate manifestation in the sado-masochistic, pornographic displays of women as objects to be subdued, humiliated, and raped—the visual enactment of these fears and desires. (King 1989, 21)

It is clear that 'Abd al-Fattah, for example, has a "love-hate" relationship with the procreative aspect of his wife's body. He particularly despises its inability to produce more male heirs who would continue fostering the family line. Similarly, Amjad's relationship with Hind's body revolves around that procreative element as well. However, his insistence on defining Hind only in terms of her bodily procreation rather than her literary creation highlights his anxiety about the possibility of her achieving transcendence through both activities. His obsession with the refrain "*kam marra amthaluna 'ala hadhihi al-'ayn, thumma dhahabu fi ghamdat 'ayn*" (alas, how many like us have passed by this spring and then departed in a twinkling) (al-Samman 1997a, 89, 250), for example, proves his constant fear of mortality and of the return of Hind's spirit in the physical and textual body of her daughter, Zayn, thereby proving her success and his subsequent failure in attaining immortality.

By highlighting the kinship between the victimized women and the victimized cats, Samman introduces the voice of the nonhuman animal to the narrative to act as a foil to the oppressed feminine. Its radical otherness adds another dimension to the recognition of the degree to which women are victimized by androcentric, patriarchal culture. Furthermore, by gradually allowing the reader to witness 'Abd al-Fattah's slow physical and mental deterioration, the author demonstrates the mastery of her narrative style. The role reversal technique in which 'Abd al-Fattah slowly assumes feminine characteristics, beginning with his newly acquired preference for smoking feminine cigarettes, to his sudden, uncontrolled sobbing episodes, and ending with his imagined pregnancy, are meant to exorcize his guilt over indirectly causing Hind's death by forcing him to see things from a feminine point of view (63). Shortly after Hind's death, 'Abd al-Fattah becomes withdrawn and painfully aware of a strong decay-like odor emanating from his body. In order to hide the smell, which no one else except him seems to notice, he starts to drench himself with a strong perfume similar to that worn by pious men. To his dismay, all his attempts to hide the odor are to no avail. To make matters worse, he develops some feminine psychosomatic attributes that hasten his nervous breakdown. For example, his belly starts to swell with what he perceives as a sure sign of pregnancy, which, one day, eventually culminates in delivery pains! The pain resulting from his contractions becomes so intense that he is immediately transferred to the hospital, where doctors declare that he needs to recuperate in a mental hospital. At the culmination of his delusion, 'Abd al-Fattah is certain that he will give birth to twin girls and will consequently die in a manner similar to Hind's and the house's cat whom he killed in the past. Samman uses a variety of tropes to highlight 'Abd al-Fattah's feminine haunting and the process of his effeminization. For example, the loss of his voice is but one signifier indicating his inability, akin to most female characters in the novel, to communicate his wishes to the outside world (287–91). However, despite the similarities, 'Abd al-Fattah's pregnancy is drastically different from Hind's. It is portrayed as a repulsive decay, a cancerous growth, and an overall deterioration as opposed to the feminine life-generating pregnancy. Indeed, 'Abd al-Fattah's deterioration signals the beginning of the end of the old patriarchal establishment, for it is accompanied by an unexplained mold that invades the whole house and metaphorically heralds the necessity for changing the worn-out aspects of past traditions. Amjad realizes this need, remarking, "there is a decaying world around us, and we are all accomplices in its deterioration" (291).

Embracing the Maternal Muse

The novel's second and third chapters, entitled "From the Secret Diary of an Emerging Teenager" and "The Mosaic of the Moving Shadows," respectively capture Zayn's development through her adolescent years among this discordant collage of old and modern characters and ideologies. It also chronicles Zayn's coming to terms with both her femininity and her mother's writing muse. Earlier in her childhood, fully aware of her father's innate desire for a son, Zayn detested her femininity and any association with culturally assigned domestic female tasks such as cooking, cleaning, marriage, and childbearing. However, her desire to assimilate into the masculine world masked a hidden anger at the latter's dismissiveness of her gender. This desire takes on a dangerous turn when young Zayn attempts to chop off the penis of an unfortunate male playmate with her scissors during a play date. Fortunately the crisis was averted through the intervention of the child's father, who prevented Zayn from performing her emasculating deed just in time (107). At a later time in her life, Zayn substitutes symbolic scissors for her physical ones when, disguised as a boy, she tries to use her role as the leader of a neighborhood boyish gang to subvert some of the gang's initiation rites concerning animal torture. Remarkably Zayn's gender identity development fluctuates from a desire to totally annihilate symbols of masculinity, to emulating them through resorting to cross-dressing (223), or even to entertaining the aesthetics of an androgynous existence "similar to that of a leech," which in Zayn's opinion because of its asexual nature has equal access to both worlds (232). However, the androgynous sexuality alternative is not a practical or even a viable solution, because it threatens to push her even deeper into the ambiguous existence of a cultural and sexual neverland. Furthermore, after taking a glimpse at the violent manifestations of a culturally constructed masculine identity, such as witnessing her cousin's circumcision session as well as the neighborhood boys' systematic torture of animals,[5]

---

5. Particularly see Zayn's comments after witnessing the rituals of what she views as a "masculine cult." She points out that after the circumcision of her cousin, Durayd,

Zayn sheds her desire to become a boy and gladly embraces the initiation of her femininity (178). In fact, the way in which Zayn takes charge of her ear-piercing episode—an act that was meant to announce her deficient gender to the outside world and "brand" her with the stigma of a "contaminated femininity"—shows her final acceptance of the feminine within her (233). This act is meant to juxtapose her cousin Durayd's circumcision act, which marks his initiation to the world of patriarchy, with Zayn's own entry to the feminine world. In "Is Female to Male as Nature Is to Culture?" Sherry B. Ortner points out how almost every patriarchal culture has developed symbols and rituals to clearly demarcate between "nature/woman" and "culture/man." One reason for keeping these dichotomies separate is to keep the pollutant elements of nature/women away from cultural and social constructs. Ortner maintains that "a well-known aspect of purity/pollution beliefs cross-culturally is that of natural 'contagion' of pollution; left to its own devices, pollution (for these purposes grossly equated with the unregulated operation of natural energies) spreads and overpowers all that it comes in contact with." Consequently, the "ritual context" develops "as a purposive activity that pits self-conscious (symbolic) action against natural energies" (Ortner 1974, 72). Seen in this light, Zayn's cousin's circumcision is a way to decontaminate him by removing any feminine characteristics reminiscent of his childhood's association with his mother,[6] thereby clearly marking his entry to the world of the Father; the ultimate Signifier. Undeniably, Zayn's mirroring act of piercing her own ears challenges the value of the Father as the sole signifier and restores the feminine realm of the Mother as a counterpoint of reference. Indeed, it is Zayn's way of embracing her femininity by reclaiming the so-called cultural contaminants associated with her gender, thereby exorcizing patriarchy's negative interpretation of them (al-Samman 1997a, 234).

---

his face was overwhelmed with expressions of cruelty and pride as if the men had injected him with a dose of hostility, as if the circumcision session was an initiation into an evil magic cult instead.

6. For an interesting exposé of the different stages of a boy/girl individuation process as it pertains to object-relations theories, see Chodorow 1978.

Similarly, the same pride in her feminine identity is reflected at other moments in the joy she feels by being present at such gender-exclusive functions as female social engagements and *hammam* (public bath) events. For despite the restrictive private nature of these gatherings, Zayn recognizes their value as empowering, regenerative sites that transform the internal spaces into liberating ones, thereby allowing women to reflect upon their common experiences. In these predominantly female spaces, women finally have the time and the needed space to share their narratives and to shed their figurative and real veils. They are free to put aside their societal obligations for nurturing others, and finally allow their bodies to materialize and, for once, to dominate the whole picture. For example, while visiting her aunt's social gathering, Zayn is astonished to see how varied women's shapes are inside the household as opposed to outside of it. She comments, "Outside the household, all women seem just like her aunt, perhaps a little taller, shorter, or broader. Inside the household, however, they shed off their black long coats and, suddenly, *they grow eyes, hair, luscious arms, beautiful thighs, and loud voices.* Then again, upon exiting they are transformed into mere black-inked spots on the pavement, in the street, followed by a huge *eraser*" (188, italics mine). The flowering of the female body is experienced as a literal and a symbolic transformation of the female self. These private enclosures provide the proper testing grounds for the development of female identity and highlight the empowering value of female bonding. Nowhere is the female body's freedom more expressed than in the hammam scene. No place is more private, yet no other place is more suited to give the multitude of naked female bodies of different ages and sizes a much-needed dose of affirmation and spatial grounding gained through channeling the female Imaginary. Samman's hammam is posited as a site where "women shed off their clothes, but also their caution, and declare an announced truce with tension and anxiety" (279). The anxiety of erasure that troubled their existence is temporarily suspended. It is as if they are reborn, transformed back to a prelapserian stage where they are free from any signs of culturally imposed feminine contamination and Original Sin residues. The abundance of water is significant, especially in the way in which it intermingles with women's fluid heart-to-heart dialogue—reminiscent of a symbiotic language that precedes and stands outside the culturally enforced patriarchal discourse. The freedom gained from this regenerative spa is not just figurative, but also spatial as the widowed Buran, Zayn's aunt, enjoys allowing her obese body to stretch freely after indulging her gluttonous desire fully without having to endure the teasing of her husband concerning her weight. In this context, the hammam becomes a site of subversion where women can laugh at their men and the oppressive traditional system altogether. It is a place where the private space is redefined, and reconfigured as a site of emancipation as each individual self draws her own strength from the collective female selves. Commenting on a similar hammam scene in Assia Djebar's *Women of Algiers in Their Apartment* (1992), Brenda Mehta "describes the *hammam* as a feminine kingdom of mythical proportions, an atemporal female space vitalized by the dynamics of solidarity, fluidity of expression, and the physical uncensoring of the body" (Mehta 2007, 125). It is precisely "by creating a countercurrent of feminine representation," she asserts, that "women can give birth to fluid spaces of self-affirmation within the boundaries of structural hegemony" (123). In this sense, the individual "I" is redefined as part and parcel of the collective "We," gaining strength and energy from the collective without losing her sense of unique identity in the process. Zayn's reaction to the hammam scene is to absorb like a "sponge" all the love and the aesthetics of women's collective lives and to insist on identifying herself as an integral part of this discordant but enchanting mosaic (al-Samman 1997a, 279). In this manner, Samman anchors the framework of an autobiographical narrative of an "I" that gains synergy, that values and insists on its connection to the multiplicity of the "We."

Resurrecting the Maw'udah's and Shahrazad's Voice

Once Zayn's reconciliation with her femaleness is fulfilled, she still has to reestablish her severed ties with the memory of her deceased mother in order to achieve full transformation. Unearthing her mother's hidden literary past, or in Assia Djebar's coinage "underground voice" (Zimra 1992, 208) plays a crucial part in acquiring her own literary voice as well as in asserting her independent identity. This is exactly what she accomplishes in "The Silence Guards/Peeping through Time's Gaps"—a chapter that represents the author's fourth attempt at childhood recollection. In a typical Sammanian interactive fashion, the author calls upon the reader to choose either one of these aforementioned subtitles only after reading the chapter. As these titles indicate, this last chapter represents a triumph over the silence enforced on Zayn, on her mother, Hind, and on all of her female co-characters. It also represents a temporal journey back in time to uncover the cultural conspiracy against women's verbal expression as well as her successful attempts to reclaim the authorial voice of her mother. Not surprisingly, then, the chapter opens with Zayn's symbolic search for the legendary ancient treasure in the "big house" at Harat al-Yasmin. She wonders, "where might the treasure be? I do not know and no one else knows for sure. Does it lie in my grandmother's flower garden? Or underneath the fountain's marble, or somewhere else?" (al-Samman 1997a, 391). By the end of this chapter, Zayn and the reader alike will discover the real hidden treasure, which surprisingly did not lie underneath the big house foundation, but rather within her mother's locked and hidden chest instead. Zayn's discovery of her mother's writings and memoirs, coincidentally written in the form of a novel entitled "The New Woman," awakens Zayn's own desire for writing and puts an end to her enforced silence. Early on she had discovered the redemptive aspect of writing when, as a child, instead of succumbing to the torture of her nightmares and relying on a traditional protective charm *hirz* (amulet) to protect her, Zayn committed her own nightmares to paper and placed her own writing inside it instead of the ineligible scribbles of the hirz. Afterward, she was happily surprised when her nightmares vanished and she enjoyed perfectly happy dreams of her mother and herself flying near the seaside. Her own writings dissipate the traditional function of the hirz by exorcizing the evil restrictive aspects of patriarchy. Nevertheless, her insistence on preserving the hirz's outside cover after replacing it with the confessions of her own nightmares demonstrates her emphasis on cleansing tradition from its destructive forces without abandoning it completely (184–85). Zayn's discovery of the healing power of writing prompts her to adopt the practice of maintaining a daily diary—a form of memoir that, like her mother, she guards with absolute secrecy. It appears that her mother's genie (*'ifrit*)—the one that the rest of the family claims possessed her through the repeated use of the refrain "your mother's *'ifrit* departed her body to possess you"—was nothing but her mother's literary muse after all (56, 394, 405, 434, 440, 444). Upon hearing this haunting refrain—"'the *'ifrit* departed your mother's body to possess you'"—Zayn wonders, "Who is this so-called 'ifrit? Ever since her childhood, she often overheard mysterious references regarding her mother's suggesting either utmost admiration to the point of adoration, as is the case with Faiha' for example, or displeasure bordering on hatred as in the rare moments of the broken silence of her aunt Buran. Silence replaces the word . . . Zayn does not know who enforces the law of silence; almost all the women around her are guardians of silence and of hymens" (434).

As Deniz Kandiyoti points out, maternal figures strike "patriarchal bargains" to attain some control and, as a result, they often conspire with patriarchy to ensure the continuation of the enforced rules concerning women's obedience and silence (Kandiyoti 1988, 274). For example, women such as Zayn's aunt Buran and most of her peers support young girls' initiation into the domesticated roles of motherhood and marriage, because they are incapable of imagining any other suitable roles for their daughters under the structural hegemony of the current system. With the help of the elder maternal figures, patriarchy is, indeed, an indestructible institution in which previous victims are perpetually transformed into voluntary wardens—to put it in Zayn's words, "guardians of silence and hymens." The adolescent Zayn is often outraged at the extent to which paternal figures will suppress any signs of female verbal or sexual mutiny. For example, Zayn is often haunted by distinct images of physical persecution inflicted on two female neighbors as a result of their perceived disregard of the sacred rules of verbal and sexual female passivity. First, there is Durriyyah's mother's act of forcing a flaming coal into her daughter's mouth as a punishment for daring to profess love for her male lover. Second, there is Mu'azzaz, an unfortunate girl whose period delay causes her angry father to chase her in an attempt to destroy the feminine body whose nonconformity will surely dishonor the family's name. In her haste to escape her father's wrath, Mu'azzaz's fear causes her to fall off the balcony and die. Undoubtedly, these two incidents are constant reminders of the verbal castration and the physical abuse that will befall any woman who, whether accidentally or deliberately, dares to defy prescribed traditions verbally, symbolically, or even physically.

These examples further highlight the controversial double-edged relationship of women to sacrificial blood. Blood is traditionally associated with painful moments in women's history; it is often the outcome of women's physical abuse, circumcision, virginal hymen penetration, and childbirth. In the absence of a sanctioned outlet for women's verbal expression, feminine blood in these examples serves as the mutilated body's sole means of expression. In asserting the centrality of blood as a symbol, as a product of the female body, and as a prerequisite for their creativity, Susan Gubar insists that "cultural forms of creativity are often experienced as a painful wounding," and the woman writer often "experience[s] herself as bleeding into print" (Gubar 1982, 78).

The sacrificial nature of female creativity and body is further reinforced through Zayn's portrayal of a culture that survives on the consumption of female bodies both symbolically and literally. For example, in the events that followed Mu'azzaz's fall, to which Zayn was the only witness, Zayn is often haunted by the image of Mu'azzaz's outstretched body and its resemblance to a stuffed lamb similar to the ones usually served in funeral banquets (al-Samman 1997a, 193). In fact, even after her death, Mu'azzaz's family and neighbors could not allow her body to rest in peace without physical prodding and inspection. Ironically, it is the intactness of Mu'azzaz's hymen, not her body, that her family was concerned with after her fall. To her horror, Zayn observes them as they rush to summon the neighborhood's midwife instead of the ambulance in order to check on the intactness of her hymen, but not her body. This incident provides physical proof of the symbolic consumption of women's bodies under patriarchal hegemony, and further serves as a crucial milestone in Zayn's struggle for self-expression. In essence, Mu'azzaz's body has been served up and consumed—a fact that strengthens Zayn's resolve to struggle and achieve the salvation of her own feminine self, but not before her own body faces a similar threat of disintegration. Indeed, the trauma of witnessing Mu'azzaz's death forces Zayn to fall prey to a nervous breakdown during which she battles feverish nightmares about the former's guilty father for days. It is only after she decides to write down her nightmares on paper as well as on the door of Mu'azzas's father, pointing the accusatory finger toward him, that her fever goes down and she starts to recover. Zayn's only defense against a culture that thrives on female bodily consumption—as in the case of her deceased mother, Mu'azzaz, and other female victims—is to fight off the conspiracy of silence with real words that serve as corporal reminders of the female corpses that have been sacrificed on patriarchy's altar. In this context, resurrecting the "underground voice" of the maw'udah and Shahrazad, of the corporal feminine through unearthing and inscribing women's buried stories, chief among them her own mother's, is the only way through which Zayn combats the collective "erasure" of women's bodies and literary corpus.

During her adolescence silence, nightmares, and fear of expressing herself have often plagued Zayn since her mother's death. However, she learns how to temporarily overcome them by transforming them into hidden, secretive memoirs. Nevertheless, it is only after she unearths her mother's literary treasure that Zayn is finally able to claim both her lost authorial voice and her mother's, and to permanently rid herself of her daily nightmares. Let us accompany Zayn on her adventure of discovery! When Zayn turns sixteen, she finds herself writing something other than her nightmares in her secret diary. For the first time ever, she writes a resolution instead. She is determined to try her best to acquaint herself with her deceased, forgotten mother. She writes, "knowing my mother . . . my curiosity will not be cured if I do not know who she was exactly, but how? By spying on the past through time's gaps . . . by cross-examining the witnesses before they die . . . and . . . and by piercing through the fortress of the past that is locked in my father's closet" (436). The occasion of unlocking the secrets of the "fortress of the past" presents itself to her one day when her father leaves his keychain behind, and Zayn is left alone in the house after her grandmother departs to visit their relatives in the big house. Finally she is alone in front of the "chest of secrets," but to her horror, she is unable to unlock it! Even worse is the ominous feeling of having experienced the same repetitive frustration before in her dreams: "is this the same dream, or is this reality? And when will [she] learn how to distinguish between the two?" (444) The rusty key presents her with the challenge and the threat of breaking the lock if she suddenly turns it in the wrong direction. However, with plenty of courage and some luck, the chest finally unlocks and opens with a squeak similar to those of historic tombs. The dust and the smell of forgetfulness, death, and mummification attack Zayn as the "shrill of Pandora" resounds clearly in her head upon opening the "chest of sins" (445). Inside the chest, Zayn encounters another locked silver box and a collection of her mother's papers, old correspondences, her mother's locked memoirs, and the unpublished manuscript of "The New Woman." For the moment, she focuses her attention on the novel manuscript kept within a leather-bound notebook. The look and the feel of the cover of the old notebook resemble the "touch of a faint body." The forgotten, unpublished writings of her mother acquire a corporal quality to serve as a reminder of the absence of her mother's physical body. It is a resurrection of sorts through which the woman, whose literary production was denied earlier for the sake of her biological reproduction, comes back to life to reclaim both her textual and physical body. Zayn continues to excavate her mother's old papers and letters as a "nameless sad smell" attacks her nostrils. Sadly, she writes, "it is the smell of hidden things that remain untouched, unseen, and unloved by either wind or light. A smell that resembles the unwept tears, the silent crying of the throat that I excel at" (446). The Shahrazad trope is activated in the mother's return, and in reclaiming the literary corpus she was forced to surrender to oblivion and to the control of her husband.

In the process of reading through her mother's old letters, Zayn is reacquainted with the lost, mysterious mother that she never knew before. The letters present Zayn with the historical background of her mother's struggle for personal and literary independence against the debilitating forces of tradition and familial dominance. For example, she reads with keen interest the letters between her mother and her male cousin Munir. Munir's letters threaten Zayn's mother with locking her up in a mental institution on account of her unveiling and her intention to publish her literary work even under a pen name. Furthermore, Zayn happens to find a picture of what seems to be her mother's face—"a face of a twenty-year-old girl with the look of a woman a thousand years old. Her features indicate the faintness of a girl who has just escaped the sands she had been buried under away from daylight. So that is my mother!" Zayn exclaims. In a marvelous narrative technique that unites mother/daughter and victim/witness, Samman allows Zayn to travel back in time to enter the surroundings of an old picture in which her mother is portrayed with the rest of her family members. Picture, Roland Barthes argues, is the "umbilical cord" that connects past and contemporary generations despite temporal distances (Barthes 1993, 76–77, 80–81). The technique through which Samman allows Zayn to break away the temporal and generational barriers by entering her mother's picture highlights the reassertion of the umbilical bond, brings to light the shared intergenerational trauma, and ushers in the ensuing dialogue that will lead to the resurrection of the mother through her daughter's text. Once inside the picture, Zayn overhears her mother's cousin (Munir) protesting the involvement of Hind's lawyer and future husband (Amjad) in their inheritance dispute. Suddenly Hind is aware of Zayn's presence in the picture, and the latter is aware of her mother's dilemma and of the potential danger that awaits her should she choose the easy way out: marriage. Zayn tries to warn her mother:

> I tell her, "Do not marry him . . . do not escape one trap to fall into another . . . This might be a snare!" She replies, "I cannot help it . . . I have to marry him in order to bring you to life; it is destiny. If I do not . . . you will not be able to enter the picture . . . Do you want to erase your existence?" . . . Suddenly, Munir lights a match and threatens me with it: "If you do not leave this picture at once, I will burn it with all of us . . . We do not wish Hind to have a daughter, a husband, and children who will share the inheritance with us . . . We do not want you, and we will not allow Hind to procreate!" I warn her again, "Please do not marry . . . Continue to defy them on your own." She says, "I cannot anymore . . . I am fading." (454)

Unfortunately, Hind was unable to escape the control of her male cousin without falling into the gilded trap of another patriarchy representative, her future husband, Amjad. She is forced to tame her rebellion, her literary aspirations, and her anger behind the guise of marriage and propriety until it finally, literally, kills her. Zayn is saddened to see how her mother hid and erased her true, private feelings behind the deleted lines in the drafts of her letters, keeping only the words that were culturally acceptable in public. She is also disappointed by the fact that most of her mother's unpublished articles were written in erasable pencil—a fact that had symbolically contributed to her literary exclusion from fame and recognition. She wonders,

> Were these articles ever published? And if they were published, how come I am unable to find any article clippings! Was she [my mother] forced to always remain an oral author! . . . I search carefully amongst her papers, but I cannot find a single published word. Is it possible that Dad tore them up? But why would he target the published works specifically? Why would he keep the "solitary" originals and only tear up what is owned by everyone! Was he jealous? Contemptuous? Or was he afraid that I will repeat my mother's saga? . . . Did he oppose her writing aspirations? . . . What is the truth? It seems that it is a fleeting, mysterious truth—one I cannot grasp hold of. No, it is clear. Perhaps he tolerated her writing as long as it did not spread to swallow her other duties: a baby-making machine, and a "defective" one indeed—one that exploded with the second delivery. (457)

Samman addresses a plethora of issues in regard to the literariness of Arab women—issues universally shared, I might add, with other women writers, especially when it comes to autobiographical writing. How can a female author avoid Shahrazad's trap of orality? Zayn's previous inquiries suggest her awareness of the detriments of orality, of keeping one's work locked in the vaults of privacy, such as the privacy of memoirs, without acquiring the stamp of full authorship and authority through public validation and publication. Hence one can understand Zayn's hatred of pencils, of orality, and of hidden memoirs in general. It is important to point out that Hind's memoirs, though present in a separate diary notebook, are still locked and inaccessible to her daughter since the key to those memoirs, not unlike the key of the original chest, remains under the patriarchal control of Zayn's father. Certainly this situation conjures up the similar image of Shahrazad's written version of the *Nights* all locked up in the royal vaults of her husband (King Shahrayar) as well. Hence defying orality and escaping the sequestration of the private through asserting the right of female authors and their feminine texts to public(ation) are the answers for resurrecting female authority from oblivion as well as from patriarchal literary erasure.

Frustration over her inability to unlock her mother's memoirs drives Zayn to search frantically for some clues to the former's life. She finally finds them within her mother's novel "The New Woman," which, to Zayn's satisfaction, contains a mixture of novel writing and memoirs—a sort of autobiographical novel. It seems that Zayn's mother has found a way to escape the isolation of her private memoirs by incorporating them into the collective narrative fabric, thereby allowing them to enter the public arena in a disguised narrative format. However, because her autobiographical novel has lacked true access to the public arena through publication, it also remained hostage to the private, patriarchal sphere of the father, and consequently to forgetfulness. Upon her discovery, Zayn vows to finally bring her mother's novel to light by submitting the manuscript to a novel contest, thereby completing her mother's unfinished task. Consequently, she enlists the help of her cousin Faiha' in the typing and the submission process, and the two are delighted to see their efforts culminate in the novel's publication upon its winning the literary award's first prize. This success presents a monumental victory not just for the departed Hind, but also for her daughter, who decides to gather the courage to launch her own literary career by publishing her first short story in the school newspaper.[7] Zayn's statement affirms this decision: "I will rewrite [her] tombstone in my own way, since we seem to be one woman born in two separate periods!" (459) Indeed, intergenerational bonding and trauma are alive and well as mother-daughter identification is later affirmed by Zayn's decision to publish her mother's novel. The union is complete when Zayn chooses

---

7. It is important to note that Samman published her first short story, entitled "Inspired by the Math Muse," in 1961 in her school's newspaper. See, for example, al-Samman 1992, 13. Furthermore, on several occasions she addresses confronting her father with her decision to study English literature instead of the medicine specialty he originally wanted her to pursue instead. These biographical similarities, coupled with the fact that Samman's mother, Salma Rwaiha, was a budding writer at the time of her death at the early stages of Samman's childhood, affirm the autobiographical aspects of *The Impossible Novel*.

a pen name that reflects compound elements derived of cherished parts of their identity, namely, Zanoubia al-Tabiyyat, a name that represents a mixture between her first name (given by her mother), and her mother's favorite neighborhood in her birth city of Lattakia.

However, such a bold act of defying patriarchy's cherished rules of private/public demarcation by seeking public presence and recognition through the flagrant act of publishing on the part of both Zayn and her mother will not go unpunished. Upon the discovery of the publication of Zayn's first short story and picture in the newspaper, she faces the same threat that her mother had previously faced from her male cousins. When she refuses to succumb to her male cousin's verbal threats, Zayn receives a more serious message attached to the neck of a slain owl (her favorite bird) and hidden under her pillow.[8] The attached card reads, "this will be your destiny if you repeat your mother's path" (480). Symbolically, Zayn has always identified herself with the owl because they are both wrongfully rejected by society. Therefore, she clearly understands that her male cousins will literally break her own neck next if she insists on following her literary dreams. The threat, however, is double-edged. As much as Zayn's cousins form a physical threat to her, she, on the other hand, constitutes a symbolic threat to them. By committing the act of writing, she brings to the public certain elements that are supposed to remain hidden in the private sphere, such as woman's voice and body. Certainly Zayn's provocations do not only constitute a flagrant violation of patriarchy's rules, but also indicate the failure of her male cousins in performing their roles as patriarchy's guardians, thereby highlighting their inadequacy. Despite the culture's repeated denial of their existence, the bodies of women demand more spatial presence, and constantly present physical reminders that challenge the hegemony of the tribal cult. Their voices eternally threaten to report patriarchy's crimes committed against them. In this context, a woman's voice and a woman's body become inextricably linked

---

8. Samman's preference for the owl is no secret to her readers. She strongly opposes societal perceptions of the owl as bearer of bad omens. The owl is also the emblem of her publishing house, "Manshurat Ghada al-Samman."

in the Arabic collective imagination. Historically, this linkage locks both body and discourse in the static position of the *'awra*—the most private of privates, the site of secrets and shame.[9] For that reason, the publication of Zayn's picture alongside her text conjures up, in her cousin's imagination, the shameful image of the belly dancers on a billboard advertisement. With disgust, he insists, "your picture next to your name in the newspaper resembles the advertisement of the 'Siriana Cabaret' dancers. Respectable women do not publish their names, intimate thoughts, and pictures in newspapers" (al-Samman 1997a, 485). However, contrary to her cousin's expectations, the slain owl reminds Zayn of her slain mother, thereby strengthening her resolve to never again succumb to patriarchy's threats. As a result, she decides to become a writer and finds the courage to inform her father of her decision to study literature instead of medicine. Consequently, Zayn's insistence on actualizing the body of her text in a published form brings about a dire punishment on her own physical body. On a hunting trip during which she antagonizes her male cousins by boasting of her superior hunting skills, she then becomes the hunted. Her defiant body has to be taken out so as to curb the spread of her words. Zayn receives a stray shot in her back, presumably from one of her cousins, as she walks to retrieve a fallen bird that she has just taken down. As she loses consciousness, she cannot help but thank God that the shot had hit her in her back instead of her eyes—its original destination. Afterward, she writes in her memoirs, "what a catastrophe! To be unable to write and read and to become blind as they wanted me to be. . . . They have to prune the senses of the girl who aspires to capture the birds of astonishment, the impossible, and the unknown . . . They have to inflict a certain handicap on a woman's body to prevent her from rebelling" (489). Intentionally depriving Zayn of the ability to see further demonstrates her "defective" social status in her cousins' eyes—a status that she opposes vehemently. So Zayn is rather happy when the doctor is unable to extract all parts of the bullet, thus enabling her to keep the remaining parts as a souvenir, a trace

9. On the interconnectedness of "woman's speech and woman's sexuality," see Malti-Douglas 1991, 29–53; on *'awra* see pages 121–27 of the same reference.

of the everlasting attempts to suffocate her authorial voice. In this context, remnants of the bullet become witnesses to Zayn's cousins' violence against her body. Indeed, they offer a testimony and a counter feminine narrative to the hegemonic masculine one. Similarly, the body of her textual writing bears evidence of their cruelty, and its publication threatens to indict them in front of the whole world. Interestingly, the heroines of several Arab women's autobiographies share a mutual belief that patriarchy's insidious plan to inflict bodily harm on them ensures their exclusion from the realms of authorship and authority. For example, similar to Zayn's fear of being deprived of her sight, of being the subject rather than the object of the gaze, the young heroine of Nawal El Saadawi's *My Papers . . . My Life*, Nawal, is certain that the school principal wants to handicap the very same hand that she employs to write (El Saadawi 1995, 173). Once more the enigmatic interplay between women's body and women's discourse is defined in traumatic enunciations, revisited and delineated with bloody ink.

Nevertheless, it seems that, contrary to the initial intent of her male cousins, Zayn's unfortunate accident has the opposite outcome. Her close encounter with death has revived the strength of her mother within and the power to fight back. Not only does she reclaim her authorial voice, but it returns stronger and clearer than ever before. To her surprise after the shooting accident, her memoir entries assume the subjectivity of the first person pronoun, the "I," instead of the distancing and othering of the third person pronoun that she was previously accustomed to employing in her diction. In a touching interior monologue Zayn remarks,

> For the first time in my life, I am writing my memoirs in the first person pronoun and I speak about myself fully knowing that it is me that I am speaking of. For the first time I do not write something that is half truth and half fantasy; I am not afraid if anyone recognizes my person in my writing; not afraid of committing the act of speech. The bullet that was supposed to kill, hurt, or perhaps scare me has revived me instead. Even my nightmares and my dreams were before written as if they happened to some *other* person. As if I was two shadows walking side by side, often intermingling but never coinciding . . . Today, I felt that I stepped into my shadow and *we* became one. (al-Samman 1997a, 487, italics mine)

Suddenly the female autobiographer is free to shed her self-doubts and fears, reconciles reality with fantasy, and steps out of the private into the public sphere. The reuniting of the shadows, however, although it is an erasure of the domination of the male shadow cast upon her ever since her childhood, does not necessarily include an erasure of all shadows, certainly not that of her mother's literary shadow. On the contrary, Zayn's authorial voice will echo the legacy of her buried mother's voice and of all the other collective female voices in her life. In it the motifs of the maw'udah and of Shahrazad converge and resurface to usher in a new dawn for Arab women's authorship. Hence Zayn will pen her autobiography with the multiplicity of the first person plural "we" instead of the isolation of the essentialist "I" of traditional solitary autobiography. It is significant that the only night that Zayn was able to sleep without her usual nightmares was the night that she was informed of her mother's literary success and the subsequent publication of the latter's novel. That night introduced Zayn to two concepts that she vows to adopt for the rest of her life: the "magic of the word" because it immortalizes its writer, and the "magic of action" because her resolve to submit the novel in the literary contest had led to its publication and her subsequent agency.

Dreams of Flight

Zayn's reconciliation with her authorial anxiety of erasure leads to the fulfillment of another childhood dream: flying, her literal and symbolic final soaring over patriarchy and tradition. Zayn had long sought to convince her father to allow her to train to fly a single-engine plane with her German trainer, Captain Schiller. A couple of months before her seventeenth birthday, she takes off with her trainer in one of their routine training sessions. However, as soon as they take off Captain Schiller suffers a heart attack, and Zayn finds herself alone trying to land a spiraling airplane. Suddenly, aspects of a debilitating past, her ancient fears, the monstrous genie that lurked under her childhood bed, the memories of her abused female neighbors Badriyyah and Mu'azzaz, as well as numerous mysterious voices and hands come back to haunt and undermine her self-confidence (497). Along with the self-doubt caused by these traditional voices comes the reassurance of her mother's voice from deep within urging her to "not be afraid," followed by the voice of her father: "you can get up, rely on yourself" (498). In a final liberating act, Zayn takes control over the plane just minutes before it crashes, managing to land it perfectly while symbolically shedding the internal patronage of tradition as well as the external patronage of her foreign trainer, Captain Schiller. In fact, the rejection of local and global guardianship is a recurrent motif of most Arab diaspora women writers in this study. I should note, however, that the transcendence of the heroine over tradition in Samman's narrative does not lead her to a total rejection of it. On the contrary, in the process of summoning her strength to land the plane on her own, she calls upon all the benign elements of her city and culture to lend her a helping hand: the old neighborhood, her grandmother's traditional house, the Omayyad Mosque, her childhood playgrounds, and even nonhuman life forms such as the blessed snake of the big house.[10] Zayn's salvation is actualized through making peace with and accepting all the discordant pieces of her life. Indeed, Zayn's final victory and realization of her female selfhood are not accomplished through a total rejection of her heritage, but rather through transcending the debilitating, traditional values and keeping the positive ones close to heart. Her wings will enable her to soar high to explore new horizons; nevertheless they will always remind her of Damascus and the homeland. The process of narrating Zayn's autobiography could not have happened without incorporating the collective voices of her mother, father, city, and society at large. The "we" is part and parcel of the "I"—a positive extension of its layering rather than a negative one. Contrary to the common practice of autobiographies past, the "we" does not replace or erase the autobiography of the "I," but rather expands its

---

10. The household old snake, fondly nicknamed by Zayn's grandmother as al-Alfiyyah (the thousand-year-old one), is a benign figure that coexists peacefully with the numerous residents of the "big house." It is a presence of bliss and tranquility, and an eco-critical reminder of the beauty and necessity of humans' coexistence with other nonhuman elements of nature. This ecological voice adds yet another dimension to the multiplicity of Samman's narrative discourses.

focus to include the polyphonic voices of animate and inanimate objects alike. Even the house-residing snake, the owl, the old tree, and Damascus's ancient walls and buildings partake in narrating this mosaic autobiography. The collective voices of the "we" enrich rather than limit the autobiography of the "I." Indeed as Julia Kristeva points out, an autobiography of the "first person plural" is

> a "we" of complicity, friendship and love. . . . What the "I" loses in delegating itself to the group is partially regained in the metamorphoses of the "we." It is by transforming itself, by changing itself totally that the collective image, the group portrait, proves it is a momentarily fixed passion. To speak of "us" is not an analysis, it is a history that analyzes itself. But isn't any autobiography, even if it does not involve "us," a desire to make a collective public image exist, for "you," for "us"? (Kristeva 1987, 219–20)

Despite the fact that the text displays an initial premise of focusing on Zayn's own childhood journey, on the singular third person feminine *"hiya"* (al-Samman 1997a, 9), still it eventually evolves to represent the voice of the father, mother, indeed of all the other inhabitants of the novel, including even the most traditional characters, such as Zayn's aunt Buran and uncle 'Abd al-Fattah. By following this technique, Samman enables her text to come alive with the dialogism and alterity of all the multiple voices in her narrative, thereby allowing the polyphony of voices to create the irregular parts of her mosaic autobiography. Undoubtedly Zayn's effort to overcome a crippling silence, to locate her individual identity and authorial voice, is not an individual quest. On the contrary, in the process of her quest for self-assertion, she discovers that her identity, for better or for worse, is intrinsically tied to the rest of her community, to her family heritage, and especially to her matrilineal tradition. Zayn's final redemption is not complete unless she is willing to make peace with the destructive demons of her past. Even the villain 'Abd al-Fattah finds redemption through the agency of the feminine manifested in the love and care of his daughters, who took it upon themselves to rescue his textile business from total oblivion through the incorporation of their feminine designs in his traditional damask craft (360). The survival of the homeland is dependent on the collective participation of its inhabitants, men and women alike. There is no place for "singular" myopic views and solutions, and dialogue is a must among the multiple selves so as to weave cohesion in this discordant, but nevertheless complementary mosaic (360–61). The exilic site from which Samman writes her autobiographical novel is essential in unifying the various multiple pieces of this mosaic of memoirs. The diaspora provides the writer with the proper spatial and temporal distance needed to appreciate the beauty of the irregular mosaic pieces, thereby enabling her to reconcile the disparate, tender, and traumatic moments that shaped life in her motherland. One cannot help but feel the exhilaration of her heroine, Zayn, as she embarks on a journey of selfhood with her feet firmly planted in the unsettled yet harmonious soil of the homeland.

Samman is fully aware that the expected salvation of a woman's autobiography lies in her control of "graphé" or writing in Cixous's *écriture féminine* sense of the word. To escape from the traditional role of being artifacts or mere objects of the male text, female writers realize that their heroines have to be the authors and commentators of their own published feminine texts. Whether it is Gubar's "bleeding artist," Hélène Cixous's "white ink" (Cixous 1986, 312), or my own anxiety of erasure, the experiences of feminine writing are closely related to the feminine body as text. The desire to caress, and to resurrect this historically buried physical (al-maw'udah) and textual (Shahrazad) body is the driving force behind female writers' autobiography. Their insistence on transcribing their own annotation to their confessional stories, to alter Freud's "talking cure" therapy with their version of the "writing cure" (Friedman 1988),[11] highlights the therapeutic aspect of their autobiographies. Unlike Freud's "talking cure" model, in which the therapist appropriates the patient's narrative in his final written evaluation, thereby rendering the cure temporary and ineffective, these autobiographies provide the actual cure for the patriarchal

---

11. For a history of Freud's implementation of the "talking cure" in treating Dora's case of hysteria, see Freud 1963. Also, for a feminist criticism of the "talking cure" as a methodology for therapy, see Katz 1987.

"dis-ease" (Gilbert and Gubar 1979, 45–92). Furthermore, they provide Arab women writers with a viable alternative for Shahrazad's orality and with agency because their authors have full control of the production and the final transformation of the stories from their oral form to their written version. Having abandoned the mediation of a male therapist or publisher, as is the case with Samman, who owns her own publishing house, thus achieving full control over not just the production but also the dissemination of her literary productions, our female author is fully empowered. In this manner, Samman's version of a mosaic collective autobiography possesses the ability to manipulate diasporic voices and transform them to a site of empowerment rather than weakness. Consequently, it promises to go beyond the feminine wounded body so as to achieve its ultimate reconciliatory mission. Ultimately, the outcome is not just a healing literature, but a transformative and an immortal one; for it speaks in the polyphony of all of its characters. As Samman herself asserts, immortality in literature is achieved only when "the author's own life is fused with that of others, and vice versa . . . it is the 'we' in the mold of the 'I' that ultimately creates an immortal literature" (al-Samman 1992, 17).

Reframing Postmemory in Hanan al-Shaykh's *The Locust and the Bird*

The tradition of encapsulating personal and collective national experiences in mosaic autobiographies penned by the literary daughters of occulted mothers continues with Hanan al-Shaykh's latest novel *Hikayati Sharhun Yatul* (2005), translated as *The Locust and the Bird* (2009). Al-Shaykh deploys the Shahrazad trope effectively by positing the discourse of the oral mother vis-à-vis the written inscription of the daughter. The novel portrays an autobiography of Kamila, Hanan's mother, written by the daughter but from the point of view of the illiterate mother. The reader traces back Kamila's journey from Nabatiyeh in south Lebanon in 1931 to preindependence Beirut in 1934; from abject poverty after her father's desertion of the family, to the harsh life of having to work to support the family's modest means at the age of eleven; and being forced to be a child bride to her brother-in-law, three decades her senior, at the age of fourteen. After having two daughters from this loveless marriage (Fatima and Hanan), the mother decides to divorce her husband in order to marry her lover (Muhammad), but at the expense of losing custody of her daughters to her former husband. A period of blissful life ensues, during which Kamila brings forth five more children from her second husband, only to be violently disrupted by Muhammad's sudden death in a car accident.

Throughout her life, Kamila compensates for her severed connection from the written word with an exceptional ability to memorize poetry and proverbs, and to draw pictures. At an early age, she learns to escape to the magical world of motion pictures to forget, albeit temporarily, the dreariness of her real life. After Kamila's death of an incurable thyroid cancer, the author (Hanan) pieces together the details of Kamila's life story from the various leaflets, family pictures, and drawings of her illiterate mother. Combined with Muhammad's love letters and personal papers, and Kamila's own oral rendition of her life communicated verbally to her daughter Hanan, the author reframes through these various modes of remembrance her mother's life story and the story of Lebanon's transition from the French mandate, to national independence in 1943, to the upheavals of the 1975 civil war and beyond.

The novel tactfully addresses the tenuous relationship between the mother "Kamila" and the deserted daughter "Hanan," a relationship that can only be mended when the latter finally agrees to pen her mother's story posthumously. This relationship is somewhat similar to Arab women's relationship with Shahrazad, their literary predecessor, simultaneously grateful and adversarial. Hanan wants to erase the painful past of the mother's abandonment of her two daughters for the sake of her lover, and the marks of her mother's bites from her hand (Al-Shaykh 2009, 16–18). However, at the insistent requests of her mother, she ends up writing her mother's story as the only means to unlock and heal the traumas of the past. Because she was illiterate, Kamila always needed a medium to help commit her thoughts to paper. This medium was often dictating her thoughts to others (Al-Shaykh 2009, 299, 301, 302), or resorting to her favorite modes of self-expression: narrating stories and drawing. Having no access to the written word, Kamila resorts to drawing childish images of flowers, hearts, and birds instead. In addition, her literary talent is often displayed in the oral enunciation of metaphors and storytelling, and in her ability to recite poems and memorize proverbs. Nevertheless, Kamila remains painfully aware of the limitations of this oral medium and its inability to convey her stories to the outside world, or to preserve them for posterity. In desperation, she confesses to her daughter, "I was never so desperate to read and write as I am now, if for no other reason but to write my story. Let me tell you how it hurts when a piece of wood and a piece of lead [pencil] defeat me" (18). Therefore Hanan commits the maternal story to paper, thereby preserving it from erasure.

As in Samman's *The Impossible Novel,* old family pictures play a pivotal role in reconnecting the characters to the site of trauma, thus highlighting the temporal and the spatial loss of the mother. For example, when the adult Zayn or Hanan look at their mothers' pictures, they attempt to place their missing self in relation to the maternal line. Articulating their place in the intergenerational trauma is an attempt to mend the broken link between mothers and daughters, past and present. Al-Shaykh's *The Locust and the Bird* documents the difficulty with which the author approaches her mother's story. Her initial resistance to seeing the value of her mother's life narrative stems from more than the temporal and spatial barriers rendered visible in the distance that separates the pictures of mother and daughter in the English version of the book (Al-Shaykh 2009, 1); rather, it stems from the emotional trauma of her mother's desertion in early childhood. The coping mechanisms adopted by little Hanan in order to deal with her mother's absence do not exactly fill the resultant void. She states, "I could show how little I cared about our mother's desertion. But her absence was a kind of presence, like a photograph that fell down and shattered into a million pieces, leaving its dusty contours etched forever on the wall where it had hung" (7). The mother's absence turns into a haunting presence, a vestige not so dissimilar from Shahrazad's own trace, demanding to be heard. Indeed, the mother's repeated complaints to her adult literary daughter—"what about my life story? When are you going to write that?" (10)—remind the author that her own literary history is incomplete if it does not include the missing piece of her illiterate mother's life story. Al-Shaykh realizes that her dismissal of her mother's story does not muffle just her mother's voice, but ultimately hers as well. She states,

> I need to write. Yet, to my horror and bewilderment, each time I sat down to write I saw myself as a five-year-old, hiding in the dark behind a door with my mother's hand covering my mouth as a face spied on us. The image kept recurring. I was scratching old scars. Why, in London of all places, had the war inside me erupted? I had been confident that I had released my mother from that box inside my mind; and that marrying and having my own children had mended the rupture between us. And now I was being taken by my fountain pen from the cold of London to the haze of that room in Beirut where we had hidden behind the door. (14–15)

The author's recollection of the hazy room in Beirut, where hiding with her mother behind the door of her lover Muhammad renders both mother and daughter "as close as the orange and its navel," is both tender and traumatic as the daughter realizes later that her mother had used her daughter as a pretext to concoct fictitious doctor's visits to cover up her secret meetings with her lover (15).[12] Hanan's rhetorical question "Why, in London of all places?" articulates the importance of diaspora in creating the distancing needed for evacuating traumatic memoirs from their destructive potential. Indeed, Hanan's act of "scratching old scars" in the diaspora reaffirms Gloria Anzaldúa's notion of the émigré's old scabs that repeatedly hemorrhage as they grate against the site of border crossing (Anzaldúa 1987, 3). If left unaddressed, the trauma of these wounds will haunt the daughter, thereby leading to a paralysis of hand and a muffling of her literary voice. The emphasis, of course, is on the importance of the diasporic locale in creating the needed spatial and emotional distance to allow the protagonist to revisit the traumatic past. Certainly, as Kamila asserts, to "reconcile [oneself] to the past" is of utmost importance (Al-Shaykh 2009, 274).

---

12. The same haunting image of the hiding of the mother and daughter as well as the imagery of "the orange and its navel" are repeated in the first page of Hanan Al-Shaykh seminal novel, *The Story of Zahra* (1995b, 3).

Equally crucial is the awareness of the impossibility of embarking on a woman's future narrative that does not acknowledge and unearth the past unofficial narratives of forgotten mothers. In fact, the mother's insistence on the centrality of the hidden informal aspect of women's lives to the advancement of the contemporary, official versions becomes the motivation for correcting the author's myopic vision. Toward this goal al-Shaykh narrates the following incident: "when I became a journalist, Mother would have family or friends read aloud what I had written. Illiterate, she couldn't read for herself anything that I wrote. However, it was a series of articles about prominent women that got to her" (Al-Shaykh 2009, 10). For example, Kamila's objections about al-Shaykh's coverage of privileged, educated women resonate deeply in the latter's narrative. Al-Shaykh's mother strongly criticizes her daughter's choice of grandes dames and socialites in her feature article about Lebanese women. She states, "those women were privileged. Maybe nobody encouraged them to do what they did, but at least they were not oppressed. But what about women who are treated as less than human because they are born female? You don't need to go out looking for such women. Here I am, right in front of you! Why don't you interview me?" (11). The daughter needed to be convinced of the value of illiterate women's unofficial narratives, of the need to acknowledge the local and the oral maternal tradition in the written texts of their global, published successors. This shift to the local is reaffirmed once more when al-Shaykh invites her mother to a launch of her Arabic version of *Only in London* in Beirut, 2001. Interested in finding out the plot of the novel, Kamila asks her daughter what the book is all about. Upon explaining that the book deals with "Arab women negotiating contemporary London and things not being as they seemed" (11), al-Shaykh's mother cuts her short, chastising her in this manner: "Why are you still nibbling from other people's dishes?" (11). In her defense, the daughter claims that her mother's proverbs always "inspired" her, an answer that the mother emphatically disputes: "I don't want you to be inspired. It only means that you see things from your perspective, not mine" (11). To use Assia Djebar's words, the mother's "underground voice" demands to be resurrected and heard. When Hanan finally relents and sits down to write her mother's story, it is Kamila's voice that forces al-Shaykh to pen her mother's autobiography as the first-person narration of the mother, rather than in the daughter's third-person narrative voice. After starting her autobiography in the latter mode, al-Shaykh is interrupted by her mother's voice: "was it my mother who stopped me? I heard her voice insisting that she wanted the beat of her own heart, her anxieties and laughter, her dreams and nightmares. She wanted her voice. She wanted to go back to the beginning. She was ecstatic that at long last she could tell her story. My mother wrote this book. She is the one who spread her wings. I just blew the wind that took her on her long journey back in time" (Al-Shaykh 2009, 302).

It is significant that the adult Hanan could not write in London until she mended her relationship with her "absent mother" and regained her trace and history. In the process of this reclamation, not unlike Samman's technique in *The Impossible Novel*, pictures act as time-travel vehicles transporting both mother and daughter to each other, thereby mending the rupture between past and present. Moreover, pictures play an important role in postmemory recall in *The Locust and the Bird*, particularly since, because of the mother's illiteracy, the daughter is left to piece together the remnants of her mother's story through examination of family pictures and her mother's childlike drawings created in lieu of the written word. When combined with the verbal rendering of Kamila's life story, the pictorial and oral texts create an overlay, an "imagetext," in W. J. T. Mitchell's sense of the word, that combines the visual and the verbal dimension of memory in "a double-coded system of mental storage and retrieval" (Mitchell 1994, 192). Hanan and Kamila communicate via drawings and pictures both in life and after the latter's death. To compensate for her inability to write, Kamila had long "devised a way of writing things with pictures" (Al-Shaykh 2009, 274). For example, she would draw a picture denoting the person's profession next to his/her telephone number in her phone book. Seizing on this mode of communication, Hanan reciprocates in kind. While skimming through her mother's phone book, Hanan sees a dove that the latter drew next to her name since she was the daughter who "was always flying off somewhere," a gesture that Hanan reciprocates by drawing a rose next to her mother's phone number (275). On another occasion, Hanan puts her face close to her mother's and asks her own daughter, who was taking pictures of the two, whether they looked alike or not (267). Through pictures, Roland Barthes contends, the "umbilical" connection to maternity and life-giving, to "first- and second-generation remembrance, memory and postmemory" is affirmed (Hirsch 1997, 23). The daughter acts as a medium to bridge the oral and the pictorial into the written. However, for her to effectively engage in playing that role, Hanan has to locate her own placement in her mother's picture album first. While examining an old photo of Muhammad lifting her mother up on a family outing that originally included Hanan and her sister Fatima, Hanan is unable to find their image in the picture. As a child, Hanan had always wondered why "a blank spot" existed where she and her sister "had once stood" (Al-Shaykh 2009, 16). Subconsciously, Hanan had always "wanted to be included in that moment, but [she] didn't know how," thereby blaming her mother for the erasure of her children from her life and family picture frames (298). However, it is only after she reads her mother's will, written by Muhammad's hand only one year after Kamila's marriage to him, that Hanan realizes how often her mother thought of her daughters to the extent of planning to bequeath family heirlooms to each daughter after her death. It is at that moment that Hanan realizes that she had always occupied a special place in her mother's life. Consequently, she overcomes her feelings of abandonment and the traces of her mother's painful childhood bites in order to jump-start the healing narrative anew (17–18). Furthermore, it is through reading Muhammad's own letters to her mother, often transcribed on pictures and official clippings of national significance, such as the message of the French high commissioner (Jean Helio) to the Lebanese people in 1934 urging them to vote for the first national assembly for an independent Lebanon, that Hanan is able to piece together a collage of personal and national history (299). As a writer, Hanan becomes connected to Muhammad's poetry, thereby creating a bond that erases her earlier jealousy of him. After reading his letters, she asserts, "Muhammad touched me deeply as I read and understood how much his existence was tied to the written word. And yet he fell passionately in love with my illiterate mother, embracing with such ease that vividness of hers, which unnerved so many others. . . . And how powerful a thing to have these words left to me, particularly since my mother didn't write" (300). This sentiment seems to be shared by Hanan's daughter, who reminds her mother that "it is as if Muhammad wrote everything for you to read in order to write their story" (Al-Shaykh 2005, 376). Undoubtedly Hanan's own mother seems to agree with this interpretation when, after divulging her life story, she tells her daughter, "I have never felt so light, so content, because I have dumped my life and strife on your shoulders and we have finally bonded. Oh! Telling you my life story was better than a hundred Prozac pills" (Al-Shaykh 2009, 279).

Kamila's reference to the healing aspects of the talking cure can only find its permanence, its survivability, through the daughter's transfiguration of it into a writing cure. The daughter's duty is in preserving "the condition of plentitude" of the mother's poetry and songs, which, according to Jacques Derrida, belongs to a "sound-image" phase that predates writing in her own rendition of the mother's story.[13] While searching through her mother's old papers after the latter's death, Hanan discovers an undelivered letter addressed to her and dictated to her younger brother by her mother. The letter emphasizes the generational responsibility imparted to the daughter by virtue of being entrusted with her mother's life story, and by embracing her newly anointed witness role through reporting the mother's untold narrative. In her letter, Kamila highlights the importance of challenging the status quo, overcoming the traumas of the past, and never severing the connection with one's roots. She states,

> Don't measure things by a past that is gone. It was sweet indeed, because I challenged the executioner and the chains that bound my wrists. I regained my freedom from all those virgin maidens who were sold without a price. But fate was stronger than I was, and it crushed me. It took everything I had, absolutely everything. I turned into a tree that had been stripped of all of its leaves, leaves that jumped from pavement to pavement in the company of their friends, the breeze and the howling wind. I became a ship with no shore in sight. When I saw your lovely picture and heard the sound of your sweet, melodious voice, I received back my own beauty from yours and my intelligence from yours as well.

13. For further discussion of Jacques Derrida's distinction between "arche-writing" and writing as it relates to the "sound-image" phase, see cooke 2001, 30–35.

That stripped tree once again started to sprout gleaming leaves, and they will stay that way just as long as life and capacity stay with me. (Al-Shaykh 2009, 301)

It is significant that the local Shahrazad, Kamila, delineates the importance of returning to the maternal tree that, though seemingly dead, has the power to spring back to life, to embrace mobility, through a rejuvenation process initiated by its rhizomes: the successes of her daughter. The daughter's accomplishment as a writer bestows authority and authorship on the oral maternal pronouncements as it embodies their orality in text. The fact that the mother signs her letter, in the Arabic version, with the inscription *"Kalam Kamila"* (Kamila's words) is indicative of her desire to inscribe her words in script (Al-Shaykh 2005, 377). With her daughter's help in making this transition a reality, Kamila's narrative acquires a distinct feminine imprint when it couples her feminine name (Kamila) with the masculine narration denominator (*kalam*), thereby simultaneously reinscribing the value of the "illiterate" oral (*kalam*) into the written and highlighting the feminine linguistic and national contribution to Arabic cultural remembrance.

As she retraces the landscapes of her mother's letter, Hanan becomes increasingly engaged in a process of rereading, a "landscape" reading in Matei Calinescu's estimation, which has "the potential to become a subversive and procreative act" (Diaconoff 2009, 42), thereby simultaneously unearthing the mother's/Shahrazad's literary oral trace and inscribing it in print. The fact that this landscape rereading is facilitated by Hanan's diasporic positioning allows for the proper distancing needed to piece together disparate family frames and fables in one elegant mosaic. With the guidance of her mother's voice, pictures, and Muhammad's own notes delineating the circumstances of their own courtship, Hanan is able to negotiate between the graphic and vocal plentitude of the mother, between the "imagetext" and the "sound-image," so as to create a liminal space between "loss and a new beginning" (cooke 2001, 33–35). The ongoing engagement in this collaborative mosaic autobiography simultaneously bestows agency and materiality to the mother's voice, and heals the traumatic rift between mother and daughter as it charges the latter with listening to the whispers of the former. The daughter finally accepts her role as a witness to document her mother's multiple traumas: abject childhood poverty, child bride rape experience, the death of Muhammad in a car accident, and finally Kamila's own death. In this process the author is capable of regaining what miriam cooke calls the "mother tongue"—the lost maternal "archaic alphabet" consisting of "embroidery, of music, of light . . . [and] of poetry" (cooke 2001, 31–33)—and of further inscribing it permanently into print.

It is the insistence on incorporating the mother's forgotten stories that inspire the awakening that must be passed on to future generations so as to nullify the history of women's erasure. In the final scene of *The Impossible Novel*, Zayn's authorial voice unites with her mother's and the multiplicity of their "We" propels the assurance and agency of her authorial "I." Similarly, Hanan al-Shaykh's rewriting of her mother's autobiography in *The Locust and the Bird* demonstrates a desire to overcome temporal, spatial, emotional, and generational barriers to repair a broken link in their past that engendered a traumatic event of separation and loss. Narrating both autobiographies from the diaspora allows for the mosaic merging to occur, for the oral and the written to unite, for Shahrazad's voice and the maw'udah's body to merge, for maternal spirits to be embodied in future generations' narratives, and finally for the traumas to gain physical and temporal distance so as to heal old wounds. Indeed, both of the women writers in question are forever indebted to their literary mothers, who gave their daughters the power to claim and to rewrite the past, and to reinforce their right to shape their future. It is particularly by reclaiming this lost linguistic female space that the ghosts of the past are conjured up to be interrogated and ultimately rehabilitated into public and national spaces.

4

Diasporic Haunting

Ghada Samman's *The Square Moon*
and *A Masquerade for the Dead*

Upon reflecting on her enigmatic relationship with the past, Hanan al-Shaykh stated, "the past resided within me; it haunted and tired me out. I feel that I have returned there (the homeland) to mend what was destroyed" (quoted in al-Abtah 2004). In the same vein, Salwa al-Neimi's engagement with the past is even more contested, as it is manifested in nightmares of corpses buried under her bed. Her verse "under my bed, there is a cemetery" (al-Neimi 2001, 78) beautifully captures the chilling haunting of this past. Both writers articulate the attraction and the ambivalence of diasporic haunting, of unearthing memory's "cemetery," and of recalling ghosts from a distant fantasyland. But why would a female Arab writer in the diaspora choose the fantasy fiction genre as her medium of expression? How could this genre chart innovative possibilities for trauma recall and transformation beyond traditional Arabic models? These are but a few of the questions that confront the critic when studying diaspora writers' treatment of the fantasy genre, specifically Ghada Samman's short story collection *Al-Qamar al-Murabba': Qisas Ghara'ibiyyah* (1994) (*The Square Moon*, 1998). Written in Paris and dealing with the problems of the multitude of Lebanese immigrants who were uprooted from their homeland because of the atrocities of the civil war, *The Square Moon* could be viewed as yet another nostalgic text expressing the diasporic experience of its characters, lost souls who were able to create their own marginal existence amid their diaspora—spheres that reduce, albeit temporarily, the agony of exile and connect them on a fantasy level with the homeland.

Yet the employment of the fantasy genre here presents alternative modes of engagement with the maw'udah and Shahrazad motifs. Furthermore, the diasporic locales enable the writer to create strange bedfellows from the Middle Eastern world of Beirut and the Western world of France. The supernatural, the paranormal, and the metaphysical in these stories emerge as the illegitimate offspring of the unusual liaisons between these two opposed worlds. Moreover, Samman's portrayal of the dilemma of the diaspora and its subsequent conflict delineates Arab values and calls them into question.

By exploring these uncharted territories of the supernatural, Samman becomes the first female writer who molded her Arabic narrative into the Western genre of fantasy fiction and its preoccupation with imaginative worlds beyond immediate reality. Certainly the introduction of fantasy literature into the Arabic canon is not new. There is a rich tradition of classical, medieval, and even modern examples of fantasy and science fiction narratives among Samman's male counterparts. Early examples of this genre date back to the premodern Islamic age of the twelfth and the thirteenth centuries, where a certain tradition of reporting marvels was called the literature of *al-'aja'ib*. The primary example of this literature was the early manuscript of Arabic geographical texts entitled the *'Aja'ib al-Hind* (The Wonders of India), which was written by Buzurg b. Shahriyar and was thought to be the predecessor to, as well as the main source of, the famous tales of *A Thousand and One Nights* in the ninth century (*The Encyclopedia of Islam* 1986). Further examples of fantasy literature in the Arabic canon were the two books of Muhammad b. Mahmud al-Qazwini (d.600/1203–682/1283), who wrote *Athar al-Bilad* (Prodigies of the Countries) and *'Aja'ib al-Makhlukat wa-Ghara'ib al-Mawjudat* (Prodigies of Things Created and Miraculous Aspects of Things Existing) in the thirteenth century. One could classify both works under the field of cosmography, for they contain information about astronomy, geography, botany, zoology, and ethnography. *'Aja'ib al-Makhlukat*, in particular, contains, in addition to the above-mentioned fields, sections that address superterrestial beings, mainly inhabitants of heaven (angels) and inhabitants of the lower strata (*Jinns* and *ghuls*) (*The Encyclopedia of Islam* 1986). Despite the fact that al-Qazwini's second book addressed elements of the marvelous, nevertheless his employment of the fantasy element did not go beyond mere descriptions of things reported to him, or quoted by some of his predecessor cosmographers. At the beginning of the twentieth century, however, Arabic literature witnessed another attempt at incorporating the fantasy genre, in the works of male writers of the South American exile (al-'Usbah al-Andalusiyyah) and writers of the North American exile (Al-Rabitah al-Qalamiyyah). For example, writers such as Fawzi Ma'luf and Shafiq Ma'luf (who wrote the epical poem *'Abqar*) from the first camp, and others such as Gibran Khalil Gibran and Mikha'il Nu'aymah from the second camp, authored fantasy literature that dealt with issues of incarnation and subsequent flights to utopias created only in their imagination (Khafaji n.d.; Saidah 1956, 237–49). However, unlike those male-authored fantasy narratives of premodern and early modern times whose main interest was to celebrate the uncanny and unattainable utopian states, Samman's treatment of the genre is laced with the political and social realities of the world left behind in the homeland. Consequently, it is haunted by the diasporic experience that both informs and transforms its appeal.

I submit that, unlike its Western counterparts and even most of its male-authored contemporary Arab fantasy and science fiction narratives, Samman's version of the fantasy genre is not simply a pursuit of yet another undiscovered frontier, but an avenue to recreate and travel back in time to the virtual dimensions of the homeland, back to the hybrid and painful realities of the Arab world. Samman's version of the genre does not conjure up cyborg and alien characters from the future, but rather mythic characters from the past who embody the heart of Arabic myths and culture. These characters do not represent dreams of an alternative liberal world, as is the case in female-authored Western science fiction, for example,[1] but rather traumatic nightmares of a troubled world that

---

1. See, for example, Charlotte Spivack's discussion of Western contemporary women writers of fantasy/science fiction, such as Ursula Le Guin, Evangeline Walton, Mary Stewart, Vera Chapman, and Octavia Butler (Spivack 1987).

needs to be questioned, subverted, and transformed through the medium of fantasy narrative. With no exception, warlocks, sorcerers, ghosts of the maw'udah and Shahrazad, and of ancient and forgotten forefathers, and political and religious apparitions are all beamed up to the Paris of the 1990s to parade in the tormented souls and minds of their Parisian-like, lost, and dispossessed countrymen. The result is a unique Arabic fantasy fiction situated in the diasporic present of its characters, with an eye on the future as well as on the past.

The diasporic site acts as a disorienting factor for the dislocated characters, thereby adding to the poignancy of the fantasy genre. Samman creates a sense of estrangement equally powerful for characters and readers alike. By transporting us to different settings in time (the past) and space (the diasporic site), Samman's narrative forces the reader to open up the past for inspection, to exorcize the sins of the fathers, revise their ideologies, heal traumatic memories, and finally restore the ethics of peace. She endorses a deconstructive project through which demolishing prevalent personal and cultural beliefs is the only answer to solving the homeland's social and political afflictions. With this personally and politically reconstructive goal in mind, Samman's new twist on fantasy fiction distinguishes her from Arab male writers of this genre, such as Nuhad Sharif (1932–2011), Tawfiq Hakim (1898–1987), and Talib 'Umran (b. 1948), whose imaginary utopian worlds are a mere escape from the social and political realities of their time and from their particular locale.[2] By contrast, her version of the fantasy genre is a more committed one, in which her characters and readers revisit their past dystopia in order to confront their demonic memories, thereby building a bridge of healing for their personal and cultural traumatic sites. In this chapter, I will address the following stories from Samman's collection *The Square Moon*: "Beheading the Cat," "The Metallic Crocodile," "Thirty Years of Bees," "An Air-Conditioned Egg," and "The Swan Genie." In these stories, the interplay of wa'd, Shahrazad, and the diaspora motifs uniquely come to life.

2. For a discussion of male science fiction writers, see 'Azzam 1994.

(Re)Writing Arab Identity in the Diaspora

In keeping with Ursula K. Le Guin's definition of fantasy as a "journey to self-knowledge speaking to the unconscious, from the unconscious, in the language of the unconscious, symbol and archetype" (quoted in Spivack 1987, 4), Samman's first story in the collection, "Beheading the Cat," introduces the reader to the unconscious world of "Abdul," a Lebanese man living in Paris with his parents after they were forced out of Beirut by the civil war (1975–91). The story reveals a glimpse of Abdul's disturbed inner world—one that is caught between two contradictory ideologies, Parisian and Arab, vying for equal representation. The story narrates Abdul's encounter with a supernatural character, the matchmaker, whose presence he alone can detect. The matchmaker figure appears in Abdul's life immediately after he decides to ask for the hand of Nadine, a French-Lebanese girl who has been raised in Paris since early childhood. Action is suspended in this story, and the events focus on Abdul's imagined conversations with the matchmaker as well as his own internal monologues. Nadine, Abdul's love interest, is the epitome of a liberated, strong woman. Having been a child when her family immigrated to Paris, she grew up unencumbered with the trappings of Arab femininity, believing in the sexual and intellectual freedom of women. Her MBA education and strong athletic body place her in stark contrast to the women Abdul is accustomed to encountering in his birth country. After a period of courtship, during which Abdul becomes equally fascinated and awed by Nadine's peculiar liberal qualities, he decides to propose. Before his departure that day, he hears a knock at the door and upon opening it, he encounters a mysterious middle-aged lady who barges, uninvited, into his apartment.

Needless to say, Abdul is in shock and thinks that she could be an old friend of his mother, an assumption that is confirmed when the lady calls him by his Arabic name—"'Abd al-Razzaq"—instead of his westernized name, Abdul.[3] Everything about the matchmaker, starting from her black

---

3. Abdul's psychic schism is highlighted by juxtaposing his Arabic name ('Abd al-Razzaq) with his Western hybridized one (Abdul). The very fact that the matchmaker

veil and ancient jewelry, and ending with her extreme familiarity with him, makes her seem to have just stepped out of the pages of a forgotten fantasy book, perchance the *Nights*. Her outward appearance reminds Abdul of conventional matchmakers, and his suspicions are confirmed when she informs him,

> 'Abdul Razzaq, my son, this bride worships God in heaven and you on earth. You can marry a second, a third, a fourth wife, in addition to her, and she will live happily with her co-wives. She will even go out herself to ask the hand of a second bride for you if she can bear you no children. But it is important that on your wedding night you behead a cat on the threshold of your home, in front of her, so she will see and understand that her fate will be that of the cat's, should she disobey you. (al-Samman 1998, 1)

The matchmaker continues to enumerate the extraordinary qualities of Abdul's prospective bride; meanwhile he is trying to discern whether she is an apparition, a product of his exhausted nerves, or a real person. He recalls that his decision to finally propose to Nadine was not an easy one, given that he has been known among friends for his inability to make quick decisions. He recalls Nadine's teasing remarks about his indecisiveness, his unadventurous nature, as well as her favorite epithet for him: the "Lebanese Hamlet" (5, 8). Still, Abdul tries to gather the rational and "Cartesian" side of his nature in order to prove to himself that the matchmaker is merely a ghost (13). Nevertheless, the significance of the decapitated cat story, its relation to Abdul's inaction and sense of emasculation, does not escape the Arabic insider. Decapitating a little kitten is an old wives' tale detailing the steps that the new bridegroom should follow in order to ensure his wife's unquestionable obedience to him for the rest of their marital life. The purpose for such a threatening ritual is to reinforce the male's physical and symbolic supremacy. In this context, I should note that

---

addresses him with the Arabic version of his name reflects his inability to cope with Western cultural ideology and the split persona embodied in his hybrid name.

there is no real historic evidence of actual enactments of the cat's decapitation ritual; however, its persistent circulation in folkloric maxims denotes its status as a cultural symbol, or an archetype in Jungian terms (Jung 1966). The archetype references a set of prescribed rules for the wife's obedience and the husband's supreme leadership within the marriage. In this so-called marital ritual, the wife's voice is muffled like the matchmaker's cat—and like the transformation of Shahrazad from the queen of narrative to an ordinary wife, at least in the longer version of *A Thousand and One Nights*.[4] The threat of violence and death, enacted at the prospect of a couple's first initial sexual intercourse, is a painful reminder of the nexus of sex and death that underlines and eternally haunts Shahrazad's authorial voice with threats of physical and literary erasure.

In the traditional context, however, one should read Abdul's indecision, his inability to wed the perfect "obedient" Arab wife, and his failure to, at least symbolically, "behead the cat" in his relationship with Nadine as an emasculating choice that renders him, in essence, a freak—a "Lebanese Hamlet." In his bewilderment Abdul recalls some troubling signs indicating that the matchmaker is indeed a figment of his imagination. For example, the doorbell rang even though it was out of order, and he did not see the matchmaker's reflection in the mirror when she crossed the corridor, nor did he see her footprints on the dusty floor. In addition, her body did not make an impression on the soft couch pillows where she sat. Still, he finds himself totally captivated and attracted to what she is saying, and he wonders why:

> Is it because she reminds me of old glories gone by, of distinctions I used to possess because of the mere fact that I was a male? Or is it because she awakens deep within me another person inhabiting my body who, I used to think, died and was buried in Paris? Am I happy about my strange meeting with this mysterious matchmaker because she reminds me of my value as a male in my country and in other countries where having certain male organs grants me non-negotiable distinctions and benefits? (al-Samman 1998, 6–7)

4. For more on Shahrazad's transformation, see Malti-Douglas 1991, 3–53.

Abdul's fascination with the matchmaker results from his longings to be, once more, a "true Arab man." She revives in his unconscious the desire to be the "master" in the relationship—a privilege that he no longer has in Paris. It is rather significant that the appearance of the matchmaker coincides with Abdul's decision to propose to Nadine. The apparition also causes time to stop, thus indicating Abdul's difficulty in making this temporal and cultural leap between his modern-day Parisian ideologies and his past Arab ones. Abdul finds himself frozen in time, and his temporal paralysis initiates a journey into the past to replay in his memory scenes from a bygone era. Furthermore, the matchmaker's description of Abdul's imaginary bride enforces a virgin/vamp dichotomy in his mind. Though not exclusive to Arab culture, this dichotomy acquires a new significance to the Arab insider who is aware of the Arabo-Islamic strict demarcations between these two figures. Women can either belong to the virginal chastity camp in their capacity as mothers, wives, and daughters (women who embrace dutifully the gender segregation laws of the status quo); or they can belong to the camp of the "fallen" (*saqitat*) women who refuse to be pinned down by the aforementioned restrictive system. The legendary obedience and chastity of Arab brides, as claimed by the matchmaker, sharply contrast with Nadine's outgoing, liberal, and strong character. The conflict between the two female archetypes frightens Abdul, who admires the Western liberal side of Nadine's character, but, as a traditional Arab man, is simultaneously threatened by its manifestations.

While occupied by one of his inner monologues in the presence of the matchmaker, Abdul recalls that "[Nadine] appeared to me to be a woman of another kind. I love her because she is so, and I am also apprehensive of her because she is so. What attracts me to her is the same thing that makes me afraid of her. And all that impels me to love her impels me also to fear marrying her" (5). When Nadine challenges him to bungee-jump from a bridge overlooking the Seine, Abdul refuses adamantly. He later explains the reasons behind his refusal: "I was afraid of the day when Nadine would be transformed into a huge rook, to whose feathers I would cling in vain— to fly with her in fear" (6). Nadine's association with the mythical *rakh* (rook) bird, long believed to be extinct, conjures images of the *Nights'* mythological traveler Sindbad and his immense fright as he holds onto the leg feathers of the bird that transported him from a snake-infested pit to safety.[5] Abdul's fear is similar to Sindbad's except that, unlike Sindbad's adventurous trips that culminated in safety, he is certain that his western-bound journey with Nadine will surely lead to his demise. The reason for his apprehension could very well be that in the West, he feels threatened by the prospect of relinquishing his myriad privileges as an Arab man. This supposition is confirmed by Nadine's numerous complaints when she accuses Abdul of wanting "to be an image of [his] father in order to preserve [his] gains." Accusingly, she declares, "you want to live your life as though the war did not happen and time did not go by" (al-Samman 1998, 8). In Evelyne Accad's estimation, "the anarchy that reigns" during the war creates a shift in gender roles (Accad 1990, 60). Nadine's complaint stems from this increase in women's mobility and social freedom during wartime. On yet another narrative level, the matchmaker's presence in Abdul's apartment was possibly evoked by Nadine's suggestion when she teasingly told him "to find a matchmaker who will find [him] a bride whose mouth no one but her mother has ever kissed, who is quiet and obedient, as my mother says in her proverbial maxims" (al-Samman 1998, 11). The Arabic proverb Nadine alludes to highlights both the presence and the absence of women's oral agency: "a bride who has a mouth for eating, but not for speaking" (al-Samman 1994, 18).[6] The proverb limits the functionality of the woman's mouth to its denigrating sexual and digestive aspects. Samman uses this proverb,[7] however, in order to deconstruct accepted societal norms, subverting their stifling effects. Nadine's vocalization of the maxim, however, transforms the dehumanized female mouth by empowering it with speech, in a manner reminiscent of Shahrazad's empowering oral narrative, thereby restoring its expressive function as an instrument of combat against repressive cultural practices. By using the vocal capabilities of her own "mouth," Nadine finds an avenue to

---

5. See the account of Sindbad's second voyage in *Alf Layla wa-Layla* (1252 AH).

6. The full proverb is found in the Arabic original, but not in the English translation.

7. The famous Arabic proverbial maxim—"a bride who's never been kissed but by her mother, and who has a mouth for eating, but not for speaking"—is said to portray an exemplary state of female chastity, often preferred in young brides.

reconstruct the female body, to change its sexually dehumanized politics, and to restore its authority.

Samman's abandonment of the classical, diachronic narrative style for a dialogue that fluctuates between the matchmaker's speech, the narrator's description of Abdul's reaction, and the constant interruptions of Abdul's own inner monologues shows Abdul's inner self to be on the verge of a total breakdown. Furthermore, the narrative structure encourages readers to identify, not with a single subject, but rather with a multiplicity of subjects—calling to mind the Bakhtinian "polyphonic" narrative format (Bakhtin 1981). Samman's narrative structure rejects linearity of time, which assumes the superiority of diachrony and reason, and replaces it with refracted vision. This technique is more indicative of disconnected yet fluid multiple experiences. Upon his encounter with the matchmaker, Abdul's watch stops, refusing to follow the monotonous order of time. Its paralysis mirrors the futility of traditional narrative, and ushers in a new kind of narrative, one in which Samman rewrites received notions of both narrative and gender relations. Although rewriting techniques are certainly not restricted to female writers, since the 1980s, however, they have increasingly been employed by Arab female writers who want to break away from the one-dimensional, diachronic frame of narrative. They seem to help the female author to blend the real with the unreal, the factual with the fictitious, in order to create alternative realities in which different feminine ideologies, related to fluidity and connectedness, are presented as viable alternatives to the hegemony of masculine politics and narrative.

Toward the end of the matchmaker's visit, Abdul is left with her amber rosary on the coffee table and the discovery that she resembles the image of his deceased spinster aunt Badriyyah. Later, he envisions that the matchmaker is run over by a car, but when he asks the bellboy and the neighbor for corroboration, they both assure him that they did not see any woman fitting her description. Following the matchmaker's departure, Abdul leaves his home to meet Nadine at her gym; not surprisingly, however, once again he finds himself unable to ask her hand in marriage. Nevertheless, he continues to be haunted by the ghost of the matchmaker (his aunt Badriyyah) walking aimlessly in the dark and cold Parisian streets. The fantastic here is a metaphor of the search for meaning and for identity amid a period of loss and disillusionment for the dislocated, diasporic Arab male. Abdul tries to capture the meaning and the essence of an Arab identity torn between Lebanese and Parisian realities. Just like the preserved fossils in his aunt's amber rosary, he would like his privileged male status to remain intact, unscathed by the passing of time. To his dismay, however, Abdul finds that such an identity is lost in the folds of history along with many other archaic ideologies. Within the confines of their Parisian diasporic site, Arab males have been forced to redefine their relationship with their female compatriots. The new reality of the diaspora necessitates the transformation of despotic identities and collaboration among the sexes. Structurally speaking, the supernatural and the fantastic broaden the schism between Western and Eastern worlds, thereby forcing characters to face the past and question established practices. Both in its presentation of Abdul's inability to resolve his dilemma and in its employment of a narrative structure that does not move forward simply and diachronically, Samman's fantasy narrative challenges these inherited ideologies, deconstructs them, and creates a space for the construction of new, alternative narratives.

Forging Alliances

In the next story, "The Metallic Crocodile," Samman presents the reader with a counternarrative to Abdul's. Here the diaspora is viewed in a refreshing, positive light, enabling the self to transcend traditional outlooks and to reconnect with other, similarly fragmented and dispossessed selves. In this story, diaspora provides an unflattering mirror of exile that, by revealing one's own inadequacies, teaches one to be more accepting of others' shortcomings as well.

The action unfolds on a cold Parisian morning in front of the French immigration offices where Sulayman and many other immigrants of different nationalities are awaiting the renewal of their visa papers. Sulayman reflects sadly on the political affairs in Lebanon that forced him into this diasporic existence. He is completely demoralized and is battling a horrible toothache that is aggravated by the chill of Parisian mornings.

Back in Lebanon, Sulayman was a self-proclaimed magician who had the unfortunate luck of aiding the wife of one of the militia leaders. She comes to him, in tears, complaining about the repeated extramarital affairs of her husband, and asks Sulayman to give her a charm (*hirz*) to emasculate him. However, when the husband discovers what both of them have concocted against him, he threatens Sulayman with death and orders him to leave Lebanon immediately. Recalling this incident, Sulayman asks himself, "what am I doing here?" (al-Samman 1998, 18). His companions in misery and humiliation are two Lebanese women standing ahead of him in line and an African man (Dunga) behind him, along with many others. Amid the fits of his toothache and the attacks of the winter chill, Sulayman hears a soothing warm voice in his head that seems to calm him and appease his pains. The voice identifies itself as that of Dunga, and assures him that he will try his "real" magic in order to calm Sulayman's pains. Sulayman is in disbelief, especially when the African man assures him that he is communicating telepathically and without language mediation. Dunga reminds him that he can use telepathy because, unlike Sulayman, he is "a real magician who comes from the jungles of secrecy" and magic, and "is the descendent of a noble family of magicians from a famous African tribe." "I am not a strange charlatan like you!" Dunga asserts (24). The contrast between the "true" magician and the "charlatan" highlights the importance of identity politics in the diaspora, and provides a commentary on those who maintain their ties to their homelands and others who sever them. Furthermore, it foreshadows the story's ending in which a betrayal of one's roots and "real" identity brings about symbolic death.

Samman's employment of the "jungles of secrecy" constitutes a virtual journey to Africa, an introduction to the invisible, ethereal language that is often shared among oppressed people—a language that emerges from the fluidity of the prelapsarian, to use Hélène Cixous's words, "Dark Continent" of one's unconscious (Cixous 1986, 314). This language, Samman seems to suggest, is one that does not need a voice, syntax, or even two willing participants. Julia Kristeva argues that the presymbolic, preverbal, free floating, and less-defined experiences of the Self vis-à-vis the outside world reminds us of belonging to the realm of the semiotic, of the forgotten mother. For example, the two Lebanese women in line ahead of

Sulayman tell him, "Some of our country's males treated us as the dictator treated them. We'll never forgive either of them" (al-Samman 1998, 22).

Recalling cycles of domination and destruction perpetrated by both warlords and hegemonic war ideology is an equally incriminating stylistic tactic reflected, time and again, in the work of other women diaspora writers as well. Indeed, the soothing, warm sensory feelings that Sulayman experiences replace violent, tangible, and concrete definitiveness of the outside, masculine, and reasonable world. Dunga's voice repeatedly warns Sulayman not to rely too much on reason because "logic prevents [Sulayman] from seeing reality" (26). He seems to suggest that truth lies in the fluid experience of the senses, in preverbal language, and in the dark, repressed, forgotten "Continent." Cixous comments on the necessity of exploring this repressed feminine continent that is present in each individual as follows: "*The Dark Continent is neither dark nor unexplorable. It is still unexplored only because we've been made to believe that it was too dark to be explorable. And because they want to make us believe that what interests us is the white continent, with its monuments to Lack. And we believed. They riveted us between two horrifying myths: between the Medusa and the abyss. That would be enough to set half the world laughing, except that it's still going on*" (Cixous 1986, 314, italics in the original). The fact that Dunga belongs to this "continent of darkness," by virtue of his profession's connection to the metaphysical rather than merely his skin color, is significant because he will be the one to bring Sulayman to recognize his true identity and to recognize himself in the experiences of the other dispossessed, wretched souls of both genders and all races. The death punishment that Dunga delivered to the French black policewoman who "remedie[d] her own oppression by oppressing others," through humiliating him and other Africans in the immigration office, taught Sulayman a lesson in never severing his own roots (al-Samman 1998, 27). The process of integrating the self and the Other demands a depolarization of masculine and colonial values. Once the initial essentialist dichotomy of self/Other is eliminated, there is a return to the original state of blessed unity (the semiotic, presymbolic stage) of the individual, and an acceptance of all the various Other(s) around us. The unique understanding and compassion that Sulayman establishes with the African magician is an excellent example of the initiated dialogue, hence understanding, between the self and the Other, experienced after one gazes in diaspora's two-directional mirror. Once again, fantasy is the medium, and diaspora is the perfect site for this wondrous transformation.

Lost in Paris: What Can an Arab Woman Do?

Although not a self-professed feminist, Samman's next story, "Thirty Years of Bees," qualifies her for this title. In this story Samman reconstructs the culturally determined, dehumanizing sexual politics of the female body, transforming that body into a weapon against patriarchy. She challenges the societal limitations that imprison the female body within its constructed biological roles of maternity or uncontainable sexuality, as either a nurturing mother or an oversexed femme fatale. We witness the heroine's transformation from the human form to a huge beehive that inflicts torture and pain on its male suppressors.

Reem is an educated woman who stood by her husband's side for thirty years while they established their renowned publishing company. After the huge success of their publishing company, a business in which success Reem played a great part, she becomes embittered at her husband's desire to restrict her position to the private realm of mundane household duties. Her husband's chauvinistic attitude is also shared with another male companion of letters, Saduq—a writer who owes the launching of his literary career to Reem's support, despite her husband's initial skepticism of his talent. Saduq picks up the couple at the Paris airport, and heads to the site of an honorary celebration where Reem's husband is to reap solely the rewards of their joint work in the publishing house. The couple intends to attend the honorary reception that celebrates their publishing house's contribution to the spread and advancement of Arab literature in the diaspora. When Saduq disrespectfully seats her in the backseat of the car, she recalls vividly his enormous earlier gratitude when she informed him of their publishing house's decision to publish his research, and his flattering words indicating that he will never forget the favor of "a great thinker" such as herself (127). What adds to her sense of betrayal is that the two men (Rida and Saduq) completely ignore Reem's presence and insist on excluding her from their "literary" conversation. At this ultimate form of betrayal, Reem slips back into her private world, experiences numerous epiphanies from times past, and finally turns her forgotten body into a weapon by whose agency she unleashes exacting punishment for the male-dominated publishing industry's betrayal of her. At the reception numerous bees spring out of Reem's mouth and attack everyone who insisted on writing her out of the collective, Arabic literary history.

Relegated to the backseat of the car, Reem's memory slips into a succession of flashback images attempting to position herself vis-à-vis her male car companions. Reem and Rida's first meeting occurred when she visited his office as a young writer hoping to publish her poems. She soon found out that Rida, later to become her husband, was not interested in publishing any poems either for her or for other "cheeky" female writers (128). Rather, Rida opted to give physical dimensions to her poems, to limit and to define them within the context of the body politics. When asked for his literary assessment of her poetry, Rida claimed that he could not assess them critically because he "was preoccupied with reading the book of [her] face, and turning the pages of [her] eyes" (129). Flirtatiously he added, "One cannot read the complete book of your eyes in a whole lifetime! Yet he seemed to finish reading it the night after the wedding, and he threw it out of the window with the screams of our first child" (129). Reem recalls that during their engagement, he said to her playfully, "she who has such beautiful hair [*sha'r*] must certainly write the most beautiful poetry [*shi'r*]" (al-Samman 1998, 128). The verbal homophone (*jinas*) between the words *hair* and *poetry* in Arabic makes the situation all too ironic if not pathetic. Indeed, it is an all too painful reminder of Shahrazad's diminished authorial role at the end of the longer translated version of the *Nights* when the external narrator's focus shifted from her role as narrator to her role as mother and wife.[8] Rida's insistence on shifting the focus

8. Unlike the fourteenth-century Syrian manuscript, the 1835 Bulaq edition has a lengthy epilogue detailing the transformation of Shahrazad from a shrewd, intelligent narrator to a bride parading several wedding attires to the shah. As Fedwa Malti-Douglas points out, "body has been transmuted into word and back into body. Corporeality is

from her literary articulations to her physical attributes symbolizes the dangerous entrapment that body politics poses to Arab women writers. This golden trap is further realized when the couple have their two sons, and Reem feels trapped in the familial expectations of the imposed motherhood role. Reem's dreams of literary grandeur and of symbolic soaring are suddenly thwarted. Instead, they are replaced with the painful reality of her domestication as a housewife as she awakens the next day to realize [her] transformation "from a free bird to a docile sheep. But an invisible bee had started to buzz in [her] chest" (129). Since childbirth, Reem was never able to write a word on paper; however, she continues to write these poems in her head over and over again. The humming of bees starts to grow louder in her head, symbolizing the words trapped in her mind. Reem recalls that Rida's way of domesticating her was never through the use of force, but rather through his subtle use of "honey-coated words" as well as the use of her family and children to mock and discourage her literary aspirations—in short, through her enslavement to institutions of marriage and motherhood. In this story, Samman is voicing a social commentary, asserting that love and paternalistic care can be as big a trap for the budding feminine authorial selfhood as real imprisonment, and verbal and/or physical abuse.

During their lengthy trip from the airport to the institution where her husband is to independently reap the benefits of thirty years of their collaborative work in the publishing house, Reem is painfully aware of their exclusion of her, an instance of how male homosociability functions to isolate women and to prevent them from gaining access to the "boys' club."[9] Disapprovingly, she notices the homosocial couple's (Rida

---

the final word, as Shahrazâd relinquishes her role of narrator for that of perfect woman: mother and lover" (Malti-Douglas 1991, 28).

9. For a comprehensive study on homosociability in the Arabic culture, see Malti-Douglas 1991, 11–28. For a Western twist on the same concept, see Sedgwick 1985, 1–20, 134–60. For an analysis of the threat that women, who embody the concept of *Nushuz* (subversion) in Islamic memory, pose to Arab male homosociability and the political order, see Mernissi 1996, 109–20.

and Saduq) superficial intimacy and the male bonding that often grows between so-called "important" men. Her resentment increases exponentially, especially when she recalls her years of hard toil in the publishing house and her husband's collusion in concealing her contributions. She reflects,

> He is not embarrassed to participate in the coverup of the truth that everyone knows, namely, that I did half of the work at the publishing house and the magazine, in addition to my work at home. There is a collusion to conceal what a woman can do and it is a silent collusion that has continued through history. If my husband boasts that he fought unjust authority here and there in defense of his opinions and was defeated several times, I must say that I shared his fight, and at the same time I also fought my destiny as an Arab female. If he is repressed, I am doubly repressed: once with him and once by him! . . . No, he never said anything. "A male shall have as much as the share of two females," even in work they have both done together, half and half. (al-Samman 1998, 133)

Reem's complaints articulate the systematic conspiracy against women's literary endeavors as well as the urgent need to unearth women's literary history so as to save it from the imposed generational silence. It is important to note, here, that men's control over women does not stop at bodily reproduction, but extends to their literary productions as well. In Reem's case, her silenced literary productions are her unpublished, forgotten works. It should be noted that in most Arab countries, upon divorce mothers have custody of their children only during infancy and early adolescence. Fathers almost always win the full custody of their children after adolescence. By the same token, women's intellectual productions are controlled by the male-dominated publishing industry. Samman portrays a dismal picture of the fate of Arab women's selfhood, given that even those who are highly educated cannot escape male domination and co-optation of the means of their literary production as well as biological reproduction. Her allusion to the Qur'anic verse detailing the rules of inheritance— "Allah (thus) directs you / As regards your children's (inheritance): to the male, / A portion equal to that of two females"[10]—serves as a painful reminder of the negative implications of certain cultural interpretations and application of the Qur'anic exegesis, whose result is an inequitable status for women that, through inheritance laws, is extended beyond the death of their legal male guardians. But her quotation is also an ingenious narrative technique by which Samman calls on women to engage in Qur'anic textual hermeneutics, to reinterpret, and to reclaim Islam's gender-based justice from its misconceptions so as to resurrect the voice of the maw'udah and to regain its egalitarianism.

Reem attempts to join in the conversation of Rida and Saduq, but she is met with their cold silence as if an immature child "has interrupted the discourse of adults" (126). She then lapses into silence while engaging in her own inner monologue. It is then that the bees' humming increases in her head, and it seems that when she opens her mouth a bee comes out of it. From now on, the outside symbolic world and its accompanied language become peripheral to her experience. Instead, she immerses herself further into a unique internal, to use Julia Kristeva's term, "semiotic" world. This linguistic world consists of free-floating, less-defined experiences of the self that seem to belong to the presymbolic world, which connects her to feminine "imaginary language" (Kristeva 1986, 89–136; Cixous 1986, 308–20) as well as to elements of nature that represent the eternal mother figure. Saduq fails to recognize the benevolent nature of the bee, and he pulls over to squash the "annoying bee." He further explains that months ago a testing lab in Paris imported a species of ferocious African bees to conduct experiments on, but that they managed to escape and settle in the neighboring area where repeated efforts to find and destroy them have failed. During the remainder of the trip, they continue to be visited with bees that Reem believes have originated in her mouth.

Upon reaching the center where her husband is to be honored, Reem experiences unusual audible and visual manifestations of the distorted nature around her. The distorted surroundings reflect the carnivalesque reality of women's existence in a male-dominated environment. Hence the

---

10. The Holy Quran, *Surat an-Nisa'* 4:11.

subsequent epiphanies highlight the need to break away from these suffocating restrictions. First, "the sky is well paved with cement, and the clouds
are of baked bricks and fired clay." Second, "the trees run in space with the
scarecrows; the trees' dark leaves are gray saturated with black. Behind
them, a petrified river does not run but fills its bed, almost overflowing
its banks" (al-Samman 1998, 39). Along with these entangled consecu-
tive images, Reem sees an apple tree with strange-looking fruit. The fruit
seems to have acquired carnival masks and, strangely enough, mustaches!
At this point, Reem crosses the boundaries of the real world and is aware
of the presence of "an inner river of obscure suffocations [that] stretches
its dark veins between [her] and the elements of the universe, joining [her]
to the circulatory system of an unknown, mysterious planet" (139). In a
world dominated by masculine ethics, nature loses its fluidity and beauty
and acquires the appearance of a masquerade. Estranged from this world,
Reem is driven to the realm of the fantastic where meaning can be found.
Reem's estrangement is embodied in numerous "flashbacks" or epiphanies, including certain scenes from tradition, her past, and the present.
The importance of these epiphanies lies in their universal applicability not
only to Reem but to multitudes of Arab women. On the subliminal level,
these epiphanies play on Arab women's collective unconscious fear of the
threat of wa'd al-banat,[11] and symbolically reaffirm culturally prescribed
norms of women's confinement. The first epiphany reveals a number of
women being carried in shackles in a metallic trailer that resembles a
steel train. The second vision uncovers a woman willingly lying in a tomb,
while simultaneously giving orders to the worker on how to best secure the
locks of her coffin. The third epiphany introduces us to an exploding well
that spits out all of the translated and literary works that Reem edited and
authored for the publishing house, while the fourth vision reveals a number
of old ladies who gather to circumcise a little girl only to discover that she
grows wings, which they hasten to clip off, all the while cursing Satan. Still
the wings grow again and the old women keep clipping them off over and
over again. Other visions consist of a crying little girl, locked in a closet,

---

11. See, for example, my discussion on the wa'd concept in chapter 2.

whose voice disappears when a mummified hand reaches out to suffocate her. Yet another epiphany represents a shackled dying woman who calls out for help as a balloon loaded with medical instruments and medicine is flying away from her reach. Finally, Reem views her own transformation to a giant bee that is prevented from flying because of a thread tied to her leg. This thread is controlled by a little boy who has a mustache and a face resembling "'Antar," the famous macho epical hero of *Sirat 'Antarah*.[12] The epiphanies function on more than one level: thematic, linguistic, and syntactic. Subsequently, these epiphanies erupt into the outer world in various manifestations. As soon as Rida starts to deliver his acceptance speech, Reem finds herself calling telepathically to swarms of bees, which invade the auditorium and start attacking Rida, Saduq, and the audience. Indeed, she "is in a state of semiconsciousness, like one having a familiar dream over and over again. She sees what is happening with glazed eyes and does not know whether those bees have really come through the windows or have rather come out of her eyes, ears, throat, nails, and hair. She is frozen stiff, and all those present scream like crazy people while the bees sting them during a horrible long nightmare" (al-Samman 1998, 141). Reem's dehumanized and debased body transforms itself into a hive of killer bees, thus turning into a killing machine that avenges itself on her oppressors. Furthermore, Samman's use of the image of the exploding well that spits out all of Reem's unpublished works, as well as the recollection of the traumatic images of confined and mutilated women of past eras, reminds us of Cixous's description of *écriture féminine* as "volcanic," an act of *voler*: both stealing the language and flying with it, thus restoring it to the feminine realm. The exploding well seems to embody the transgressive possibility she has imagined: "If I were to explode, to publish, to dare to fly at night above the roofs of the city in order to contemplate its innards, then write about them, that would be a breach in the law that forbids women to visit the planet of creativity—unless they do so within the conditions

12. This twelfth-century folkloric epic details the heroic accomplishments of 'Antarah, a pre-Islamic poet and warrior whose war victories were motivated by his desire to prove himself worthy of marrying his cousin 'Ablah.

of clownish social conventions" (137). "A feminine text," Cixous affirms, "cannot fail to be more than subversive. It is volcanic; as it is written it brings about the upheaval of the old property crust, carrier of masculine investments; there is no other way" (Cixous 1986, 316). Reem's memory of the tribal ritual of wa'd al-banat as well as several images of women's mutilation connects the traumatic past to the present, and in turn over-comes and transforms the negative impact into a positive, regenerative one. For the first time, Saduq notices that the swarms of bees are com-ing from Reem's mouth, and cries for people to arrest this "witch," all to no avail (142). Rida seeks protection in Reem, and she conceals him with her body bent in a fetal position. When the bees' raid ends, everyone is fatally stung by the bees except for Reem. The doctor insists on provid-ing a "scientific" rationale for this strange phenomenon and designates a female signifier (Reem's perfume) as the reason why she was spared from the painful stings. With this explanation, the doctor assures Reem as well as himself that it is her perfume that acted as a repellent for the bees. She remains silent since she knows that she never wears perfumes, owing to her allergy. Samman's discrediting of the medical scientific rationale is but an example of the transformative intent of her use of the fantasy genre. Science, as a symbolic masculine construct, has its own limitations and is incapable of comprehending the realms of the metaphysical and the fan-tastic. Reem's experience suggests that women, on the other hand, because of their marginal position in the symbolic world, have access to the meta-physical and the supernatural because they still maintain their original ties with the semiotic world.[13]

After the bees attack, Reem feels a great sense of serenity and relief. For the first time in thirty years, the humming in her head seems to van-ish. Her freedom from the humming bees, however, is only momentary, for she is still trapped by Rida's unctuous flattery. When she goes to check

---

13. My use of the symbolic/semiotic dialectic here reflects, as Julia Kristeva points out, their "inseparable" interrelated relationship "within the *signifying process*." Often the symbolic references the Father and the semiotic the distinctive mark, and trace of the Mother and the modalities of poetic language. See Kristeva 1986, 92–93.

on Rida he tells her that during the bees attack, it seemed to him that she was protecting him from the bees, and that "motherhood was [her] talent always." He continues, "You secrete tenderness as bees secrete honey. A woman is like a bee. For her, giving is a secretion she is never thanked for" (al-Samman 1998, 143). Upon hearing yet one more example of her husband's honeyed rhetoric, Reem feels the humming of a single solitary bee in her chest. In a final commentary, Reem states that "this is how it started, a long time ago: a few bees and a low buzz. This is how I started thirty years ago—thirty years of bees!" (143). By now, it is no secret to the reader that the bees symbolize Reem's repressed creativity and co-opted authorship. First, the "ferocious" bees came from Africa, and we learn that Reem and her husband established the publishing house in North Africa to escape censorship and oppressive journalistic practices in their home country. Second, the bees are brought to be exploited and controlled by the purportedly "scientific" male-dominated labs. One assumes that they will be exploited under the pretext of science and the benefit to humanity. Likewise Reem is manipulated on the biological (reproduction) and the intellectual (literary production) levels under the pretext of society and family. Furthermore, the circular narrative ending assures us, with great pessimism, that there will be another outbreak perhaps thirty years later as long as Reem's constant co-optation and disempowerment continues through flattery. For the new generation of Arab educated women, flattery is the new method of disempowerment that replaces the old methods of verbal and physical abuse of their less fortunate female compatriots.

Nevertheless, in this story, the fantastic offers a unique opportunity to unveil the limitations of the real, to criticize it, and to present new ideological constructs to replace its tyranny. The supernatural expresses the traumas and the frustrations of a certain segment of Arab women. It replaces their present inaction with action, albeit a reactionary one in this story, and offers alternative modes of imaginative expression. This fantastical genre creates ruptured spaces in the narrative that women can fill with their own semiotic language, where dreams, telepathy, and sensory experience can replace the cold, repressive, and calculating male expressive modes. The goal is not to replace one model with another, but rather to shatter the whole male/female binary opposition paradigm. By focusing on the tremendous, unutilized potential of the liminal space that separates the two sides of the binary, one can eliminate the divisive nature of this solidus and the violence associated with its diachronic inception. As a result, this space will open up to the myriad possibilities of communications and negotiations. Recalling past traumatic memories of Shahrazad's literary co-optation and reenacting the wa'd symbolically through multiple epiphanies are essential to creating this semiotic rupture, ultimately to identity and cultural reclamation. The images of shackled, confined women as in the first epiphany; the flashbacks of women who confirm to the patriarchal system and even exceed its expectation by literally giving workers directions to nail their own coffins shut as in the second epiphany; coupled with images of female circumcision, child abuse, disregard for women's health, the metamorphosis of Reem into a giant bee with a human head that becomes a child's toy; and finally the eruption of the subterranean well that spews all of Reem's unpublished works in the subsequent epiphanies—all contribute to the disruption of the narrative, to the convergence of the Shahrazad and wa'd archetypes in a manner that articulates a need to dismantle the stagnant past, replacing it with a gender-inclusive future. It is the past that cripples both the present and the future of these diasporic characters, and prevents them from ending their exiled political status. Samman's fantasy genre challenges this past in order to reveal the invisibility of, and the challenge to, female subjecthood in the context of a male-dominated society. The outcome, though not totally optimistic owing to the fatal reenactment suggested in the circular plot, is not apocalyptic either, for revisiting past traumas prevents the reenactment of new ones, and fosters healing and female empowerment.

X in Wonderland

While images from the past drive Reem to rebel in Paris, albeit temporarily, flashbacks from the past increase the confusion and sense of isolation often experienced by the next, unnamed heroine in New York.

In "An Air-Conditioned Egg" the unidentified heroine, whom I will refer to as X, suffers from the consequences of a diasporic, hybrid identity.

By day, she is the epitome of the successful Western business executive who dominates a big financial firm in the World Trade Center. However, at night she reverts back to the sixteen-year-old teenager who yearns to go back to Damascus to relive the warm and tender memories of her engagement to her now deceased fiancé. X's choice of decoration in her New York apartment exhibits the same contradictions that she suffers from internally. For example, her father's Ottoman fez (*tarbush*) rests proudly beside the fax machine. Likewise, her grandmother's amulet (*hirz*) sits beside a champagne bottle in the fridge. Additionally, scattered pictures of her in a revealing bikini lie beside her female cousin's, her aunt's, and her grandmother's pictures in full veiled attire. The collectivity of the cultural artifacts she surrounds herself with highlights the spatial and temporal contradictions so prevalent in her New York life. Reflecting on this cultural divide, she states, "this is the mosaic of my life, stretching between the present and the past, in between two continents, two lifetimes, two modes of wakefulness and sleep" (180). The diasporic experience is accurately described through the doubling of meanings, the juxtaposition of her previous and present life, and the plurality of her images. Luce Irigaray points out that "there is always for women 'at least two' meanings, without one being able to decide which meaning prevails, which is 'on top' or 'underneath,' which 'conscious' or 'repressed'. . . . For a feminine language would undo the unique meaning, the proper meaning of words, of nouns: which still regulates all discourse" (Irigaray 1990, 84). There is a plurality in female language—a plurality that is further manifested through the doubling of X's identity. The schism in X's double Western and Eastern identity widens when her ex-mother-in-law calls her unexpectedly from a hotel in New York and asks to see her immediately.

All these years, X has been visited with the "ghosts of the past," those of her fiancé, her father, and her previous life in Damascus. She reflects that "the past does not really go away. It remains deep inside . . . like an engraving on stone that time cannot efface. No exorcist can expel the faces of yesteryear's loved ones who inhabit [her] like dear ghosts" (al-Samman 1998, 165). The fantasy aspect in this story serves as a metaphor for X's search for a lost identity, for a meaning amid the discordant collage of past memories and present realities of her life. Amid the cold and isolated New

York environment, X's quest for her lost identity materializes in several vivid memories. X's flashbacks reveal that she was engaged to a wonderful, one-of-a-kind, liberal Damascene man who often reminded her that he is not "a descendant of Shahriyar" and that he is "from a new breed" of Arab men (171). He later made good on his promise when he insisted, despite the objection of both of their parents, that she pursue an MBA degree in the United States. After his unexpected death during a routine operation procedure, she decides to stay in New York, unable to go back home without him, or to assimilate totally in the cold and calculating Western environment. X's rebellion against the traditional Arab conventions that refuse to recognize a woman on her own unless she has a male "guardian" is enormous. She often remembers her resentment at being born both a woman and an Arab. "Sometimes I feel that having been born a woman and an Arab at the same time is an unforgivable sin. It means depriving me of my civil rights" (171).

She tries the Western alternative and its solution to women's disempowerment, namely, to assume power and to be the "man" in the relationship with the opposite sex. However, this solution does not offer her any personal satisfaction, specifically since she becomes guilty of dominating and controlling the life of another human being (her Arab-American young secretary/lover) just as her male compatriots would have done with any unfortunate Arab woman back in the homeland. Samman introduces a switch in male/female relationship dynamics in order to reevaluate, subvert, and rewrite them on a more equitable basis. When the secretary asks X whether she will visit him that night or not, X's answer is as cold and collected as any busy male executive answer can be. She responds, "Not this evening. I'm tired, but if I change my mind, I'll call you." Her secretary's answer is typical of that of a love-stricken woman who is tired of waiting on her busy lover: "you treat me as an Eastern man treats his lover. Say, 'Yes, I'll come' or 'No, I won't come' and leave me to dispose of what remains of my time. You know that I love you" (164). Responding to his complaints calmly, X points out that she cannot be bothered with such matters at the moment, since she has an urgent meeting to attend with her ex-mother-in-law. However, her lover's protests escalate and continue to prevail in the following manner:

"I loved you because I thought that you are Shahrazad, and lo and behold, you are Shahriyar."

"Excuse me, but I'll not embark on a discussion of all this now."

"You're not an Eastern woman. You're an Eastern man!"

"Excuse me, but I'll not embark on a discussion of all this now"

"I'm a desert man, but you treat me as the harem used to be treated. Why have you chosen an Arab to torture? Why don't you have a relationship with Richard or Johnny?"

"Excuse me, but I'll not embark on a discussion of all this now." (165)

The invocation of the story of Shahrazad and Shahrayar is anything but innocent here. To the Arab reader, it summons the nexus of sex and death that Shahrayar was in control of, which Shahrazad can only avoid through her never-ending narrative. The gender role reversal between X and her secretary does not just put her in Shahrayar's position, but allows her to be in control without resorting to Shahrazad's oral play. The fact that X does not feel the need to elaborate orally on her reasons behind her inability to meet her lover speaks volumes here. It also relieves her from the necessity of enacting Shahrazad's act of self-defense through her reactive, endless narration. Significantly, X's answers are short and fixed; they do not even attempt to add any details to her decision, or provide her lover with any further explanation. Ironically the Arab-American secretary, in an act similar to that of Abdul in "Beheading the Cat," voices his discontent with this role reversal and demands his right to a Shahrazad of his own, but to no avail. He is transformed into a mere sex object and his emasculation is complete when he admits that, indeed, he is in a relationship not with an "Arab woman, but [with] an Arab man!" instead. Specifically, the deliberate framing of the Arab man in the essentializing fixed role of the oppressor draws attention to the need to revise this taxonomy by both Arabs and Westerners alike.

Still, is X's role reversal the answer to Arab women's dissatisfaction with the status quo? Definitely not, given that only shifting the player's position from the oppressed to the oppressor does not question the binary or change the rules of masculine power and domination. In her discussion of the characteristics of female fantasy heroines, Charlotte Spivack points out that "in the fantasy novels the female protagonists . . . demonstrate physical courage and resourcefulness, but they are not committed to male goals. Whether warriors or wizards, and there are both, their aim is not power or domination, but rather self-fulfillment and protection of the community" (Spivack 1987, 8). Despite X's dissatisfaction with certain chauvinistic aspects of her culture, she still wants to preserve some aspects of its heritage, particularly familial connectedness, love, warmth, and compassion. Her yearnings for all of these memories come true, albeit only in a dream, through the magical agency of her ex-mother-in-law's diamond earrings. Wearing the earrings as she sleeps that night, X travels back in time to her youthful days in Damascus and relives her happiest memories with her fiancé, who hands her in the dream a jasmine necklace as a memento of his love. When X awakes the next day to the same harsh realities of New York City, she is pleasantly surprised to see that she is wearing a jasmine necklace! The fantastic element in this story intensifies the oblique and pessimistic reality of X's situation. It is significant, perhaps, that a liberal man such as her fiancé, 'Arfan, dwells only in fantasyland, as if his real presence on earth was just a dream. The goal, then, becomes replicating his presence among other Arab males in order to foster a less stereotypical representation of Arab masculinity.

Living in Limbo

The next story features yet another nameless heroine who also doubles as the invisible narrator of the "The Swan Genie." In this context, we encounter another facet of the Arab woman's struggle in the diaspora. The story chronicles the life of a well-to-do Lebanese family who is forced to immigrate to Paris because of the atrocities of the civil war. After living for a short while at their accustomed level of financial comfort, the family's financial assets are depleted. Therefore they have to rely on the heroine's work, as a department store's sales clerk, for support. The heroine adjusts well to this newfound sense of purpose; however, conflict arises when her husband decides to take the family back to Lebanon upon the conclusion of the civil war and the return of his wealth. Upon hearing this unsettling news, the heroine is upset, and finds herself unable to make a decision between keeping her newly acquired independence by staying in Paris, or returning home with her husband to the house of patriarchy. Enter the magical element, once more, in the form of a swan genie, which turns the couple into two statues to protect them from having to make this difficult decision. However, our heroine remains unhappy with their inanimate state as well. She then asks the genie to remove the spell, and wanders aimlessly with her husband in the streets of Paris.

During the heroine's employment, she discovers a whole new world of work ethic, financial independence, and self-fulfillment. She starts to enjoy her early morning Metro rides, and the chances that they offer her to read a good book, even preferring them to the comfort of a limousine. Her opening lines surprise both the reader and herself when she admits that she "no longer feel[s] [as] a stranger in Paris." Elaborating further, she admits, "I feel like one who has betrayed an old lover named Beirut" (al-Samman 1998, 96). Her dilemma, contrary to X's dilemma, is not in having two contradictory Eastern and Western identities but in having assimilated all too well in the sociopolitical fabric of a culture that professes and practices gender equality. Needless to say, she does not want to go back to Beirut where she will be reminded, on a daily basis, of the restrictions on her female subjectivity and her husband's treatment of her as a prized possession. Samman makes a startling assertion of the positive effects of the civil war on women.[14] Strangely enough, our heroine admits, her "real life started with the war, which set [her] free" (al-Samman 1998, 97). This revelation bears a striking resemblance to Evelyne Accad's observation that the Lebanese Civil War has liberated women by turning the restrictive patriarchal norms upside down (Accad 1990, 60). Men were just too busy, or simply too weak, to preserve the essentialist, masculine politics

---

14. Several Arab writers (Evelyne Accad and Hanan al-Shyakh) pointed out the relative freedom women acquire during wartime owing to the disruption of the social norms that usually govern their mobility. This topic will be addressed fully in chapter 5 of this book, "Transforming Nationhood from within the Minefield."

of dominance that was upset by the unbalancing war factor. However, one cannot help but notice the separation and the subsequent contradiction between the political and the personal in the lives of Arab women. Hence the solution to their dilemma, as Samman seems to suggest, is to engage the personal with the political, in simultaneously eradicating masculinity's invasive domination over their land and their bodies.

Still, the heroine of "The Swan Genie" is incapable of foreseeing this solution at this moment, and is haunted by the contradictions as well as by her inability to decide whether to stay in Paris or to go back to Lebanon. She acutely feels the pangs of an identity crisis manifested in this bewildered pronouncement: "I am no longer an Arab woman, and I am not yet a Western woman. Who am I?" (al-Samman 1998, 120). This question continues to puzzle her, and the answer, of course, is in the introduction of the fantastic element as part of a *deux ex machina* to solve her dilemma. At the Allée des Cygnes, an island situated in the midst of the Seine near the Eiffel Tower, a swan genie appears and offers the choice of three wishes. Our heroine's first wish is to be shown what her life would be if she opted to stay in Paris. The swan genie points to an old lonely woman sitting on a bench feeding the pigeons, and informs her that she will be this old lady in the future. At the prospect of this lonely existence, the heroine asks the fairy to transform her husband and herself to statues right there on the island. She does, but in spite of her stony outside appearance, the heroine keeps feeling the cold, the rain, and the pain of the etching that the kids in the park try to inflict on them. She still feels miserable, so it is not surprising when she uses her last wish to undo the charm that transformed the couple into stones. The swan genie flies off, disappointed, after stating that "human beings don't know how to deal with miracle[s]"; thus they constantly waste the opportunity (122). When the protagonist meets the swan genie for the first time, the latter's "huge body" reminds her of the "legendary rook," and "her white feathers iridescent with rainbow colors [look] as if she has just come out of the tales of *The* [sic] *One Thousand and One Nights*" (117). As I pointed out in chapter 1, Fatema Mernissi conjures the image of the same figure from the *Nights'* corpus, whom she calls "The Lady with the Feather Dress" in her *Scheherazade Goes West*, and uses her example to stress the importance of women's mobility and creativity.

Mernissi stresses the importance of women living "as nomad[s]" to avoid a prison-like fixity (Mernissi 2001, 4). The magical powers of the swan genie, and perhaps of "The Lady with the Feather Dress," are redefined as their ability to straddle two cultures and to stay unattached, unfixed in their belongings. Specifically, their strength springs from within, rather than from outward fantastical solutions.

According to Tzvetan Todorov, the fantastic presents us with a variety of supernatural powers such as genies and sorcerers: "these beings symbolize dreams of power" (Todorov 1973, 109). The metamorphoses that the heroine requested from the swan genie failed to bestow on her the power that she was seeking. Her imaginary empowerment is ineffectual because it is rooted in inaction; after all, statues are made from stone. Instead, the metamorphosis the couple should seek is not only physical but an ideological one, with its locale firmly placed in their homeland rather than their host country. This sociopolitical transformation should recognize the negative consequences of hegemonic domination over the personal and the sexual (women) as well as the political (civil society) domains in the Arab culture.

Lost on the verge of two contradictory worlds, what is an Arab woman to do? Thus far, Samman offers the reader four alternatives: First, Arab women may accept an inferior position and male co-optation and be sacrificial lambs, with the occasional rebellion every thirty years or so, as we see in Reem's case. Second, Arab women can masquerade as males, thus enacting the same oppressive ideologies of power and domination, as we see in X's story. Obviously, the second solution constitutes treason to women's very own feminine nature. Luce Irigaray points out that "[i]f women allow themselves to be caught in the trap of power-seeking, in the game of authority, if they allow themselves to be contaminated by the 'paranoid' mode of functioning of male politics, they no longer have anything to say or to do *as women*" (Irigaray 1990, 87). A third option presents itself in the denial of one's Arab identity, as Zakiyya-Gloria, the protagonist of another short story in the collection—"Register: I'm Not an Arab Woman"—intends to do. Finally, a woman's fourth choice would be to live in limbo beyond the realms of time and space, frozen in time in the diaspora until the repressive realities of their culture dissipate on their own accord, as seen with the heroine of "The Swan Genie." Obviously, none of these four alternatives presents a viable solution for the dilemmas suffered by some Arab women, for they involve surrendering to patriarchy's power, betraying one's womanhood and/or ethnicity, or waiting pessimistically in an eternal state of limbo and inertia. The answer lies not in individual solutions, but rather in collective ones that view the project of finding a way for dislocated, diasporic Arab selves to forge a new inclusive community back in the homeland. So, is there any hope for a lost Arab Self in the diaspora? The answer is yes, there is hope as long as the sins of the past are exorcized and purged. Conventional ideologies and traditional forefathers have to be summoned to be questioned, criticized, and reincorporated into the fabric of the collective narrative. The future can no longer depend solely on the language of the Father, but should include the discourse of collective national voices, including that of the feminine. Fantasy genre becomes the vehicle for social critique, and the mode that facilitates trauma recovery, reconciliation, and synthesis of conflicting histories and archives.

A Masquerade for the Dead and the Promise of Dystopia

In Samman's novel *Sahra Tanakuriyyah lil-Mawta* (2003) (*A Masquerade for the Dead*, not translated into English), she continues to explore the option of homecoming and the difficult choices the characters make as they negotiate their positioning among diasporic and homebound ghosts. The fantasy genre frames and articulates the increased level of deterioration and contamination of Lebanese society, and the transformation of Beirut from civil war violence to a postwar dystopia. Similar to the previous short-story collection, the novel continues the tradition of having the fantasy genre serve as the liminal "third space" for negotiating the relationship between the two contentious sites of diaspora and home. "Capturing such boundaries between spaces," according to Brenda Cooper, "is to exist in a third space, in the fertile interstices between these extremes of time and space" (Cooper 1998, 1).

The Beirut of today that six expatriate characters (three men and three women) return to in postwar Lebanon is far different from the utopian, idyllic pre–civil war world that they preserved in their mind. In this novel, dystopia serves as an oppositional narrative strategy to expose the exploitive nature of a colonialist legacy and a materialism-based global economy, to create a space to critique an imperfect utopian framework, and ultimately to resist closure. The main cast consists of Maria al-Harani (an accomplished writer); her childhood friend Suleima and her daughter Dana; Fawwaz (a French-Lebanese bank manager returning to Beirut to sell his father's villa after the latter's death while in Paris); and two young expatriates, Naji and Abdulkarim, whose failure to achieve wealth after years in the diaspora drives them to engage in illegal acts of identity theft and con-artistry leading to the schizophrenia and consequent death of the former and the assassination of the latter. On the plane that transports them to Beirut from Paris, they are accompanied by Marie Rose (a middle-aged French obstetrician), who hopes to encounter in reality the romanticized and erotic "Orient" of her dreams, and Walid, a Lebanese self-made businessman whom Suleima perceives as the incarnated young version of her deceased husband.

A Masquerade for the Dead constitutes the last volume of Ghada Samman's four-novel series on different facets of the Lebanese Civil War, which started with her prophetic *Beirut '75* (1975), through which she predicted the onslaught of the civil war four months prior to its actual occurrence. The series continued with *Beirut Nightmares* (1997b) (*Kawabis Bayrut*, 1976), a novel that documented accurately the state of ruthless sniper killings, the accompanying state of fear and recurring personal as well as national nightmares from the vantage point of several characters, some real and some fantastic. The third novel, *The Night of the First Billion* (2005) (*Laylat al-Milyar*, 1986b), chronicles the 1982 Israeli invasion of Beirut and the subsequent trials and tribulations of some Lebanese immigrants in their Swiss exile in Geneva. Set in Beirut at the turn of the millennium in 2000, the fourth novel in the series, *A Masquerade for the Dead*, transports its six Lebanese expatriates back to the site of their initial civil war trauma in Beirut, confirms the author's earlier prophecy of the impending war of *Beirut '75*, and further enlists the readers to be witnesses to the traumatic haunting of the characters by the war's postmemory (Hirsch 1997, 22).

The narrative revolves full circle as the nightmares shift from dreams and predictions, as in *Beirut '75*, to reality in *A Masquerade for the Dead*. These nightmares further materialize in postwar Beirut in the form of the living dead zombies and vampires, and the ghostly presence of ancestors always ready to haunt those offspring who insist on selling their country.

The narrative techniques of *A Masquerade for the Dead* and *Beirut '75* are hauntingly similar, yet different. It is as if one is looking at a reversed mirror image twenty-eight years in the future. The political and social decay of Lebanon is portrayed in the degeneration of the fantastic element from the benign in *Beirut '75* to the morbidly gothic in *A Masquerade for the Dead*. For example, the three ominous ladies, representing the Greek mythological three Fates, at the onset of *Beirut '75* are transformed into three carnival-like figures who instead of wearing black and mourning the impending war, as they did in *Beirut '75* (al-Samman 1975, 7), are laughing feverishly at men's obsession with war, celebrating the death and destruction that engulf the city. They inform the author Maria that their hysterical laughter is the result of the recurrent "stupidity" of men who from time immemorial have engaged in wars that led to their destruction. One of the ladies declares that "[they] have been laughing since the Crusades . . . Men never grow up. They play with military figurines in their childhood, and continue to fool around with catapults, cannons, and nuclear bombs when they grow older" (al-Samman 2003b, 29). Furthermore, the transformation of yet another motif, the dogs' barking, originally representing the symbolic victimization of Farah, the main character, in *Beirut '75* (al-Samman 1975, 106) into actualized wolflike dogs roaming the city in *A Masquerade for the Dead*, is indicative of the hellish societal descent into a cannibalistic postwar jungle. In this jungle green spaces have been uprooted and octopus-like cement buildings have invaded the city. The city has become a site where "cement is the Master of the house; and where concrete hearts, the age of mafia and sharks prevail" (al-Samman 2003b, 33, 120). In *Beirut '75*, a taxi brought five characters from Damascus to Beirut, but in *A Masquerade for the Dead* the six main characters arrive by plane from Paris, their diaspora having taken them further away. The compulsive narrative repetition and recurrent events between the two novels constitute what

Susan Friedman calls a Freudian "return of the repressed" (Friedman 1989). Friedman argues that one can find traces of repetitions, of acts of remembering, that function "as a site (cite) of resistance," in the "intertext" of women's narrative (Friedman 1989, 143–44). In comparing two texts by the same author, for example, Friedman asserts that "the early text may be the most distorted or 'timid,' while the last text might represent the author's success in working through a performative repetition to remembering" (146). The ultimate goal is "to work through the transference," to move beyond the repetition because, as Freud reminds us, "once an adult can 'remember' the past, he or she is no longer doomed to 'repeat' it" (146).

In *A Masquerade for the Dead*, Samman sets out on a project of remembering the personal and national dismemberment caused by the civil war. To this end, she reenacts the trauma of the multitude of Lebanese expatriates who, upon returning to postwar Lebanon, cannot recognize or relate to the degenerated postwar Beirut society. The pre–civil war Lebanon that they and other middle-class citizens knew has been buried under the rubble. Simultaneously, it is replaced by a capitalist, impersonal, global economy that controls people's lives. Through the author's portrayal of Fawwaz's return and his intent to sell his father's ancestral house, his subsequent haunting by the ghost of his deceased father, and his final realization of the importance of belonging to his homeland, Samman underscores the importance as well as the trappings of postmemory. To put it in Marianne Hirsch's words, the "generational distance" that separates Fawwaz's French-Lebanese identity from his Lebanese father's hi(story) presents some challenges to Fawwaz's process of postmemory. Yet despite the son's temporal separation from his father's traumatic past, he remains deeply invested in resurrecting his father's memories, for they offer a clear path to Fawwaz's understanding of his own lost heritage. Hirsch explains that "postmemory characterizes the experience of those who grow up dominated by narratives that preceded their birth, whose own belated stories are evacuated by the stories of the previous generation shaped by traumatic events that can be neither understood nor recreated" (Hirsch 1997, 22).

Fawwaz's reluctance to embrace his contested postmemories articulates Hirsch's claims succinctly. He grew up in Paris listening to his father's recollection of the idyllic world of prewar Beirut, and its traumatic demise after the civil war. As a child he recalls fleeing from the burning city; however, as an adult he adamantly refuses the demonic hold of this memory on his consciousness, stating, "I do not want my memory to be transformed into a Hiroshima or a mass grave" (al-Samman 2003b, 15). However, it is the death of Fawwaz's father in the diaspora and the subsequent denial of his last wish to be buried in Beirut that continues to haunt Fawwaz's memory. Instead of being buried in Beirut, the father was cremated in Paris. Since then, the smell of his burned corpse coupled with the intense feeling of his presence haunts Fawwaz, particularly after the latter's decision to sell the family's house in Beirut. Understandably the father's ghost is protesting the double robbing of his death rights: once when he is cremated against his wish in Paris, and once more when Beirut postwar business opportunists bulldoze his burial site to erect financial establishments in its place. Lamenting, the father states, "the thieves of mottoes and revolutions have robbed us of everything, even of our tombs. They raided our ancestral tombs where your grandfather and his grandfather's tomb existed for generations. They sold the ivory tombstone and bulldozed the rest, scattering part of Beirut's history to the wind" (57). The theft of Beirut's history, of its citizens' legacy, demands a retribution of sorts and engenders a curse that the ghosts cast upon those who betrayed the country's heritage. In fact, the living dead's act of roaming the city, of masquerading as the living, reflects the true corrupt identity of those who sold their souls and ideals to the devil. The situation creates a dystopic atmosphere when zombies and vampires contaminate and consume the city. Ultimately, the employment of the fantasy genre manifests the state of dystopia and utter loss for the Lebanese citizens. It further provides the author, argues Fadia Suyoufie, with "the agency of probing beyond the deceptive veneer of external reality" (Suyoufie 2009, 187).

Unlike Fawwaz, who chooses to be oblivious of his traumatic past, Maria (the author) wants to revisit traumatic war memories and to unearth buried archives and people alike. She achieves this goal through returning to traumatic sites represented by the multiethnic graves populating the graveyard where her assassinated lover (Fadi) is buried. On her way to the graveyard, Maria recalls how they were both stopped at a checkpoint during the civil war, how, when it was realized that the lovers belonged to two different warring religious sects, Fadi was shot, while the militia soldier, who belonged to her own religious denomination, carved the symbol of her religion with a knife on her arm as a reminder of the prohibition against dating outside one's religious sect (128–29). At Fadi's gravesite, Maria is met by several living dead who depart their grave to sunbathe, to dance, and to roam in the city undistinguished from the living residents. She even encounters the ghost of Beirut: the city personified as a widowed woman who changes her clothes from black to screaming red because she has no patience to grieve for her departed husband (the idyllic, patriotic past) any longer. The intermingling of the real and the fantastic displays, through the fictional interstices of the third space, the real trauma of the Lebanese population, particularly women. A weeping spirit of a little girl informs Maria that she was killed by mistake in lieu of her activist father, and that she is crying because "they [the warlords] killed her before she reached her adult potential" (173).

The fact that women's persecution during the civil war was not instigated by their gender, as was the case in the tribal infanticide ritual in jahiliyyah times, but rather by their political or religious affiliations, marks an interesting shift in the modern recasting of the maw'udah literary motif. In this contemporary framing, burial imagery is no longer restricted to females; rather it extends to men and country as well. Toward the end of the novel, the evil twin of Naji (who sold the desperate Lebanese entry visas to an imagined country called Utolia) tries to bury him alive at a gravesite because Naji's awakened conscience threatens to expose their conspiracy to defraud people (230–31). The spread of the traumatic burial motif from women, to men, to cherished ideals, to the buried nation as a whole indicates the enormous postwar national tragedy, and the urgency of reclaiming the country from the grip of internal and external special interest groups. Furthermore, the linguistic transformation of a traditional Utopia into a nonexistent "Utolia" highlights the distortion and increases the urgency of real, rather than escapist, imagined solutions.

Samman's interplay of death and resurrection in *A Masquerade for the Dead* does not cease at the wa'd motif; rather it expands it to revive the

Shahrazad archetype as well. Recalling Shahrazad's image, some critics have argued that the prevalence of death in the fantasy genre is symptomatic of the authors' postmodernist condition. According to Wendy Faris, "[t]hese postmodern storytellers may need magic to battle death, a death more depersonalized even than the one their mother [Shahrazad] faced from King Shariyar [*sic*]; they inherit the literary memory, if not the actual experience, of death camps and totalitarian regimes, as well as the proverbial death of fiction itself" (Faris 1995, 163–64). Indeed, death and subsequent resurrection play an integral part in Samman's project of reclaiming fantasy genre—a project that entails reinscribing the female author's agency and the country's citizens in the national narrative. In the novel, this transformative role is given to the author, Maria.

The prevalence of death threatens to erase Maria's fiction and person when the ghost of one of her former characters, Mustafa in *Beirut '75*, resurfaces under the new name of Munir Najib and threatens to kill her. No longer the honest ideologue of the past, Munir represents a sector of past revolutionaries who become opportunist militia leaders benefiting from the death of their fellow citizens. Maria's decision to resurrect and then kill him in her upcoming novel threatens his very, albeit imaginary, existence. It represents her rejection of partisan politics and global economic frameworks that seek to dismember Lebanon's prewar unitary identity. Hence Munir's fierce resolve to kill his author (Maria) is akin to Shahrazad's literary erasure. Maria's presence and recollection of past memories is a constant reminder of Lebanon's prewar stability, a far outcry from the dystopic reality of today's Lebanon. In a nightmarish episode, Munir kidnaps Maria and throws her in his palace's dungeon, threatening "to gag her mouth so as to muffle her screams" and to literally bury her underground. He takes away her pen and papers to prevent her from finishing the novel that will write his death. Nevertheless, Maria's renewed zest for life and for writing prevents her impending death as she writes Munir's demise in her head, and emerges out of the dungeon to find herself asleep at her desk table (al-Samman 2003b, 311–12). As I argued in previous chapters, the authors' physical death and literary erasure are inextricably linked. Maria's attempt to regain control of her narrative, her insistence on inscribing her experiences in writing, her vehement rejection of corrupt characters and the chaos of discordant economic and divisive religious interests, are all symbols of the country's need to protect its future from the destructive factors of internal and external political interests. Furthermore, her heritage reclamation project, which started by revisiting certain Beirut locations (streets, cafes, buildings) and imagining them in their prewar glamour, thereby inscribes a language of peace instead of war in this postmodern dystopia. The merging of the realm of the metaphysical with the real intensifies fantasy genre's critique of the current status quo and highlights the urgency of unearthing the archives of peaceful coexistence in Lebanon's history. Maria's act of celebrating the deceased's birthdays by decorating Muslim and Christian graves alike harkens back to a nonviolent time of Lebanese fraternal coexistence (249). Repeating Ibn al-Arabi's love poetics motto "love is the religion I follow wherever direction it may take," Maria decorates both Muslim and Christian tombs in an attempt "to resurrect the dead" (249). Regaining the memory of the war victims on both sides of the partisan conflict is a way to combat the zombies and the vampires who plan on cannibalizing the idealists left in the country (320). Samira and her nationalist father, Khalil al-Dari' (*The Night of the First Billion*'s protagonist who rejects his diasporic existence in Paris and returns home at the end of the novel), represent those remaining patriots (492). Those benevolent memories are the reason behind Fawwaz's change of heart regarding selling his father's old home to foreign investors. They may also, in due time, halt the steady exodus of Lebanese emigrants to the West.

Despite the final scene's pessimistic ending, resulting in the death of some or the return of other principal characters to Paris, the merging of reality and nightmares as Fawwaz's plane leaves and then assumes the shape of Lebanon's map, as if Lebanon is leaving its essence behind, is not without its advantages. The fact that the father's old house and Fawwaz's nationalist girlfriend, Samira, will forever keep alive his ties to the home country represents a glimpse of hope and the potential promise within this utter dystopia. The possibility of unmasking the corrupt elements and of returning to a premasquerade Lebanon could still be part of the protagonists' future reality. In this manner, exposing the multiple sites of "intertextual haunting"[15] in Samman's *The Square Moon* and *A Masquerade for the Dead* becomes the vehicle of uncovering the role magical texts play in incriminating totalitarian regimes and authoritarian ideologies, and of envisioning a peaceful future from the multicentric locales of home and of diaspora.

15. For more on intertextual haunting, see Suyoufie 2009, 182–207, 186; Fraser 2000, 782; and Faris 1995, 163–64, 179.

5

Transforming Nationhood
from within the Minefield

Hamida Na'na''s *The Homeland*

Echoing Ghada Samman's interplay of war and diasporic haunting, Hamida Na'na''s protagonist, Nadia, poignantly articulates the experiences of loss and alienation particularly as they intersect with diasporic locals and lethal wartime. Her opening scene in *The Homeland* mournfully captures these conflicting affiliations:

> You know it is wartime.
> Death-time. Time for conflagrations and far off lands. Time for vagrancy on the streets of exile. Time to be spent in strange cities, their faces clothed in mist. All links to your distant homelands are broken. Only alienation remains. You gaze in the mirror and watch the woman in front of you dying slowly day by day, and the child within her blood being awakened.
> (Na'na' 1995, 1)

Arab women's narratives of war bespeak an illustrious history of Muslim and Christian women's participation in revolutionary struggles, of their desire to expose totalitarian "imagined communities" paradigms of nationalist ideology, and of the co-optation of their right to participate in national construction by military, male-dominated dictatorship regimes, domestic or foreign. They also deploy the wa'd al-banat trope to unravel Arab male nationalist discourses, which in their view seem to bury the nation alive. Images of death and resurrection often intersect to weave a story of women's erasure from the history of nation-building and their insistence on revival through political activism. This chapter will follow Arab women's struggle to carve out their own feminine space as they embark on dual nationalist and personal liberation missions from local and diasporic sites. By examining Hamida Na'na's *The Homeland* (1995) (*al-Watan fi al-'Aynayn*, 1979), I will demonstrate Arab women's attempts to break the mold of their representation as mere national symbols devoid of any political agency and to escape the victim/heroine dichotomy (Abdo 2002, 592). The manner in which they reinscribe their feminine agency in the national struggle is vital to charting out new dialogic, peace-oriented models for national reconstruction.

History of the War in the Middle East and Its Effects on Arab Women

For most of the twentieth century, the Arab world has been the unfortunate site of many a war. The reasons are varied, although mostly impacted by Western colonial projects in the region that were unwelcome outcomes of the collapse of the Ottoman Empire at the end of World War I. The colonial conquest by English, French, and Italian troops in the region covered the period between 1918 and 1945, from the end of World War I to the end of World War II (and, in Algeria's case, for example, well beyond that date until 1962), and culminated in the 1948 war resulting in the annexation of Palestine and the subsequent establishment of the state of Israel. For almost every Arab individual in the region, 1948 marks the beginning of a reign of terror and trauma (called *al-nakbah* [catastrophe] in the Arabic literary canon) characterized by geographical and spiritual displacement, as well as symbolizing the launching pad for the Arab-Israeli conflict and its subsequent 1967 and 1973 wars. In addition, the onset of the sixteen-year Lebanese Civil War, which lasted from 1975 until 1991, coupled with the atrocities of the Israeli invasion of South Lebanon in 1982 and the 1990 Gulf War, the Israeli shelling of Southern Lebanon and Beirut in July 2006, and the American colonization of Iraqi soil between 1990 and 2011 fanned the fires of an already charged and complex political atmosphere in the region. To this extent, almost every Arab citizen, man or woman alike, has been charred by wars' legacies and has been either an unwilling participant or an innocent victim of its tyranny. On the literary scene, this extended legacy of pain and displacement explains the explosion of what later came to be known as political literature: *adab al-nakbah* (the 1948 literature of catastrophe), *adab al-naksah* (literature of defeat, marking the literature produced after the Arabs' defeat in the 1967 Arab-Israeli war), and *adab al-harb al-ahliyyah al-lubnaniyyah* (literature of the Lebanese Civil War, covering the period of 1975 to 1991).

Although writers of this contemporary political genre in the Arabic literary cannon have been members of both genders, a study of the literary production of Arab women writers in this field yields more than the political commentary of a standard war narrative. Penning a war narrative from a feminine perspective poses more thematic and textual challenges to the female author. For example, national issues so prominent and well-defined in the works of her male counterparts are not so easily pronounced in female war narratives. This is partially owing to the confluence of personal and national issues both seeking presence in a female's literary war text. In other words, how could a female author seek independence for the nation from the external foreign colonizer if she lacks her own personal freedom because of the pressures of the patriarchal internal colonizer—her male compatriot? With his place securely and superiorly defined within the parameters of a patriarchal culture, the Arab male writer can afford to heed the call to subordinate the personal to the national voice in his text. By contrast, from the confines of her private space, how could an Arab female writer afford to voice the concerns of a nation while occulting her own personal voice when by doing so, she in essence annihilates her very own existence? The answer for most of the female war writers lies in the realization that a nation cannot be liberated when only partial citizenship is granted to its female citizens. In addition to freeing one's country from the external colonizer, part of the national struggle is also realizing the interior ideological constructs that allow the suppression of certain individuals within a country, thus leading to the eruption of violence and war and the enslavement of the nation as a whole. For that reason, Arab women writers have combined the concerns of the national with those of the personal and have demystified the idyllic, romanticized image of the nation as a motherland in their depiction of war narratives. By displaying the resulting destruction that befalls the nation and its inhabitants during war rather than offering a cherished romantic ideal, women war writers shatter the sacred war myth. This is accomplished by demonstrating how these wars dismember rather than protect the body of the motherland. When describing the dismemberment of the city during war, for example, these authors mirror these effects in the disfigurement of the female body of their heroines. By employing this associative technique, they also point an accusatory finger at the social and cultural conditions that permit the political to explode in devastating wars. For women war writers, the homeland is still associated with the feminine; however, it is a correlation that exposes the abuse committed on both the female body and the motherland alike. Na'na' highlights the irrationality of the violence committed on the feminine body of both participants and bystanders, while Hoda Barakat's engagement with the same genre, discussed in the next chapter, relays the war's experience from the point of view of male characters at the verge of crises and collapse. Collectively, the war's literary corpus attempts to chart an exodus of sanity from war's insanity. Na'na''s *The Homeland*, in particular, draws a painful depiction of the 1967 Arab-Israeli war and the controversial reality of female participation in the construction of nationhood in the context of a revolutionary war struggle. In all of these contemporary writings, the writers have a tendency to concentrate on the intersection between the sexual and the political, as well as to engender an antiviolence and love dialectic. They have chosen to focus on the dissection of the female body, a foil to the maw'udah's buried body, as a point of departure in their texts for they believe that it reflects and mirrors the dissection of the nation under the war scalpel. In this context, the dilemmas faced on personal and national levels become mutually corroborative—a fact that highlights the urgency of addressing the former if one is to annihilate the causes of war and national displacement.

Diaspora Arab women war novelists exhibit a heightened awareness of the intersection of personal, national, and political borders. Owing to the circumstances of its origin and the double-exiled position of its subjects, Arab feminist literature in general, and war narratives in particular, remain inextricably linked with the nationalistic discourse, thus displaying an equal commitment to the political as well as personal agendas. Consequently, Arab women writers believe that a solitary change on the female, personal level (the Arab woman) will not suffice to bring about the desired overall liberation from the oppression of patriarchy and tradition. They are fully aware that traditional norms of oppression usually affect both males and females and are the products of the sociopolitical ideologies of essentialist societies. Hence the struggle against these repressive ideologies has to be won on *both* the personal (Arab men and women) *and* the political (the Arab society) levels, not just on *either* the personal *or* the political.[1] This is a truth that the heroine of *The Homeland* learns only too well.

Arab Women's Involvement in Revolutionary Struggle

The history of Arab women's participation in wars is a vast one and dates back to pre-Islamic times. It should also be noted that women's roles in these wars go beyond guarding the home front and tending to the wounded, with the level of their involvement ranging from being war leaders as in the example of Prophet Muhammad's favorite wife's ('Aisha) leadership of the Battle of the Camel in 656 AD, to active revolutionary fighters in contemporary independence wars. A glance at recent Arab history demonstrates women's close involvement in independence struggles, producing a host of national heroines such as Safiyya Zaghlul of Egypt (1876–1946) during the 1919 revolution against the British protectorate, the Algerian Jamila Buhayred who was tortured to death by French colonialist forces, and numerous Palestinian women freedom fighters who champion the cause of Palestinian statehood. The challenge has always been, however, to maintain public involvement in the national arena without being relegated to the private sphere of the "home" once independence has been accomplished. In *Egypt as a Woman*, Beth Baron highlights the fashioning of the modern state to reflect patriarchal, familial dynamics and the

---

1. For more on the dialectic of either/or, both/and in Arab feminism in general, and in the literature of Nawal El Saadawi in particular, see Malti-Douglas 1995.

installation of the concept of national honor as an extension of family honor. This association locked women revolutionaries in maternal roles in which their image as the mothers of the nation was used to replace their actual presence in the political arena. As Baron puts it, Egyptian women nationalists "were favored as symbols rather than as political actors, and seemingly confirming that the more women appeared in visual culture as representations of the nation, the less they appeared in the public arena" (Baron 2005, 215). Similarly Algerian women, for example, were asked to return to their private homes once Algerian independence was realized in 1962.[2] To avoid falling into the trap of oblivion like their Algerian sisters, Palestinian women work simultaneously on personal and national liberation projects. In this manner, they can assert women's agency in national reconstruction long after the desired goal of Palestinian nationhood is accomplished. Rita Giacaman contends that this confluence between national liberation (primary front) and the emergence of women's consciousness (secondary front) is what motivates the women's movement in the West Bank (1996, 130). Dissociating women's nationalist agency from the patriarchal agenda that dominates most of the nationalist discourse, however, is an ongoing daily struggle for women who refuse to be the "victims" of nationalism (Abdo 2002, 592), or to play the poster child role in nationally constructed narratives of heroism.

This double struggle is what motivates Nadia, the heroine of Hamida Na'na''s *The Homeland*. The novel reflects the sense of loss and despair that befell the Arab population after the Arabs' defeat in the 1967 Arab-Israeli war. It further registers the heroine's dissatisfaction with Arab and Western revolutionary rhetoric and searches for alternative answers to solve the Palestinian question without resorting to violence. Previous feminine engagements of the war narrative genre in the Arabic literary canon have been the work of female novelists who have experienced the unsettling war encounter either as indirect victims of the war's atrocities, or as concerned

2. For more on Algerian women's participation in the Front de Libération Nationale (FLN), including its comparison with Palestinian women's revolutionary experience, see cooke 1996, 105–66.

outsiders documenting the trauma of war from firsthand observations and from victims' own reports. However, Hamida Na'na''s major contribution is in her depiction of women's commentary on war from the viewpoint of an active female guerrilla fighter who experiences both the perils of violent war participation and the agonies of its subsequent exile. Originally published in Arabic in 1979 as *al-Watan fi al-'Aynayn*, *The Homeland* documents the general sense of loss of Nadia, a former Palestinian freedom fighter, and her current displacement in the diasporic site of Paris. Through the epistolary format that the novel adopts, the reader is thrust into Nadia's current and past worlds through a series of flashbacks and lyrical, interior monologues that transport us magically between Arum (Damascus), Ayntab (Beirut), and Haran (Amman)—the sites of her homeland and previous revolutionary participation respectively—and Paris, the site of her current exile. Nadia, a Syrian intellectual, not unlike most of her Arab counterparts after the Arab defeat in the Arab-Israeli war of 1967, becomes increasingly dissatisfied with the essentialist, revolutionary rhetoric of dominant political parties for they have proven their inability to regain Palestine. She finds herself torn between continuing to be part of the political rhetoric charade through her ongoing membership in a political party that survives on empty slogans, and dissociating herself from the futile engagements of such a bourgeois intelligentsia by accepting the invitation of Palestinian guerrilla freedom fighters to join in the liberation battle to regain Palestine. But Nadia finds herself unable to break through the binary oppositions that define politics and war paradigms.

A Face Unlike Their Own

One of the challenges facing female revolutionary fighters is the resistance of the male-dominated political establishment to attempts to break out of gender-assigned private domains. As I mentioned earlier, full participation in the public political arena is often sought, yet never attained unless it is defined in combative, masculine terms. It becomes imperative, then, for female fighters to negotiate alternative forms of national participation that at once acknowledge and heed feminine national agency. Nadia battles courageously the patriarchal repercussions suffered by women who decide to engage in politics and war; she shuns marriage, pursues higher education, and defies her family's will by joining the struggle of the Palestinian guerrilla fighters. Yet despite all of these sacrifices, societal and familial acceptance for her involvement in the national struggle remains unattainable. Indeed Na'na' herself, whose early revolutionary struggle mirrors portions of Nadia's own life, reflects on society's and family's disapproval of her own revolutionary role in this manner: "the men and society there [Amman] judged me even more harshly than my family had, for how could a girl leave her family to live among men, even for the sake of country? . . . my family searched for a lost daughter; society and the Party considered me an outlaw, and the political leadership regarded me as a troublemaker whom it was impossible to control" (quoted in Faqir 1998, 99). Na'na''s interjection here goes a bit further than the humble attempts of early-nineteenth-century women writers who "tried to steer the concept of honor away from female purity"; indeed, she goes as far as questioning the concept of honor itself and the fashioning of women "as its repositories" (Baron 2005, 216). Na'na' demonstrates that for a female fighter, the struggle is almost always personal as much as it is national, because the national commitment will not erase her personal transgressions as far as family and society are concerned. In *The Homeland* the Arab defeat in 1967 propels Nadia to unmask the empty, ideological rhetoric of her political party and convinces her to seek refuge in organized activism using her body as an instrument of change. By taking control of her own body both sexually and politically, Nadia believes she has found the answer to combating patriarchal and foreign colonization. Yet at this moment in the text she is still imprisoned by the walls of patriarchy, thereby limiting her action and forcing the "war story" to be manifested only through the female body (cooke 1996). Not unlike her fellow women war novelists, Na'na' recounts the national story of fragmentation, dispossession, and loss through drawing a parallel line between the body of a nation and that of the female heroine—Nadia. She seems to suggest that Palestine will forever be lost as long as female sexuality and consciousness remain excised in the Arab world. Throughout the novel, Nadia reaffirms her association with the national body through the process of touching her own body, thereby using feminine pleasure and presence to reestablish the unshakable linkage between women and nation. It is not surprising, then, that Nadia associates her own face with that of national defeat. Her decision to join in the liberation guerrilla missions stems from a desire to replace the face of defeat and inertia with that of victory. Her personal exhilaration at joining the guerrilla fighters bespeaks a promise for subsequent national liberation. She declares, "I walk out . . . I leave my old face behind, the face disfigured by war. I go out into the streets of Arum feeling like a new woman. I am free of the submission which is built into my humanity, free of my own weakness, free of the myth of mourning which had become ingrained in my blood. Free" (Naʿnaʿ 1995, 28). At first, Nadia's work consists of mobilizing the fragmented forces of Palestinian refugees by concentrating her efforts on making rounds in their separate camps in Amman, and by circulating educational material that calls for their deployment in the guerrilla's organized struggle. Then, after a period of arms training, Nadia is summoned along with other comrades to be informed that the guerrilla leadership has decided to utilize their skills, especially her knowledge of foreign languages, in external missions designed to inform the world's public opinion about the Palestinian people's plight. Nadia is unsure about the soundness of such a mission, especially since she believes that "the idea seemed like madness in view of the fact that the struggle was not even established in the Arab theatre" (38). The leadership, in her opinion, still has a lot of fieldwork to do on the level of mobilizing people within the Occupied Land itself. However, the faint voice of a woman historically excluded from political participation prevents her from stating her opinion clearly. When Abu Mashour disagrees with Issam's justification for moving beyond these educational efforts to a plane-hijacking mission designed to inform the world of their cause, Nadia is unable to voice her opinion. She states, "*I hesitate a moment so that the woman-tree can stretch out her branches and free herself from fear and her mortality*" (38–39, italics mine). The reference to the tree is a peculiar reminder of the tension between fixity and mobility, the restrictive aspect of the tree's rootedness versus the liberating potential of its rhizomes' horizontal and vertical movements. It appears that after shattering the familiar myth of family honor represented in a female's sacred virginity, and the restrictive paradigm of women's political participation,

Nadia, at this point, is still unable to define women's political agency on her terms. She simply cannot overcome women's traditional "weakness" deeply "rooted" in decades of political and cultural exclusion.

Subsequently, she joins her comrades in conducting a mission to hijack an Israeli airliner flying from Geneva. She even takes a role of leadership in the mission because she is the only one who can communicate with the pilot in English. Several other plane-hijacking operations finally result in her arrest, imprisonment, and torture in a West German jail. After her escape from prison, she is considered by the revolution leadership as the poster child for armed struggle. Yet, despite her apparent compliance with the leadership commands, she undergoes extensive soul-searching, eventually admitting to her comrade Abu Mashour her growing disbelief in the concept of armed resistance and violence tactics altogether. She asserts, "It is hard to be the killer, and humiliating to be the one killed. Why do we fight wars? Why do we manufacture weapons? Why do we cause death? . . . I thought about what it means to be Palestinian and to live the Palestinian dilemma which says you either live the harsh life of an exile or learn how to kill" (63). Furthermore, her discussions with Abu Mashour involve evaluating the outcomes of other revolutions around the world such as in Cuba, Africa, and Bolivia, particularly the revolutionary struggle of Regis Debray documented in his book *Revolution in the Revolution*—long considered to be the bible for young Marxist guerrilla fighters in the Arab World—and their applicability to the Palestinian struggle.[3] Not surprisingly, Abu Mashour's fear that these outside hijacking missions will only succeed at creating myths of individual heroism at the expense of the Palestinian masses left behind dead and forgotten is later confirmed to Nadia (74).

After her release from prison and return to Jordan, she finds herself stuck in the patriarchal binaries of victim/heroine that long entrapped women fighters between the roles of receivers of war's aggression as

3. See Fadia Faqir's introduction (Na'na' 1995, vii–viii) in which she asserts the resemblance between the characters of Frank (Nadia's French lover), and the French Marxist Regis Debray (a friend of the author who was imprisoned in Bolivia from 1970 to 1976).

victims, or initiators of said aggression as iconic heroines or martyrs. Nadia is thus exalted to the level of sainthood and mythical heroism. Furthermore, she is asked to be in charge of publicizing the cause given that her now well-recognized face at Western airports makes it impossible for her to continue in her previous line of work. Moreover, she is assigned special guards and relegated to work on the sidelines in the media department in Beirut instead of on the front lines. She finds it ironic that even after her numerous sacrifices in order to be part of the national struggle and her attempts to free herself from the socially perceived bondage of her femininity, she is still viewed by the male-dominated revolutionary leadership as a "burden" and as a property to be looked after. Thus, despite breaking away from her patriarchal family and engaging in the revolutionary struggle just like her male comrades, she is once more relegated to the feminine private sphere—to the woman's room. Outraged at the level of her codification, she screams, "you're going to make me into a consumer product" (91). Nadia's resentment at being used and discarded in such a manner grows even stronger when she is strongly advised to undergo plastic surgery to reconstruct her face to further prevent the enemy from recognizing her. Her earlier attempts at exchanging the "face of defeat" for that of victory ironically lead to the disfigurement of her own face, because the sought-after transformation was enacted under the auspices of the same traditional patriarchal paradigms of violence. Nadia has to learn the hard way that violence begets violence, and that it eventually consumes the person who participates in it. It is her own face that has to be mutilated, thus underlining the political leadership's consumption of both her image and her body, reaffirming in the process the unity of a woman's body with that of a nation.

Consequently, when the surgeon's scalpel reconstructs her face, Nadia undergoes a similar dissection of her own, tearing down the essentialist binary oppositions upon which politics and war are built. Increasingly, she questions war's ideology as well as the effectiveness of the revolutionary missions that seem to demonize the Palestinians' image in the public arena and benefit the advancement of some leaders within the organization who want to prove their ideological superiority at the expense of the corpses of their comrades. At the doctor's office, she is asked to choose a new nose from a catalog containing a variety of nose shapes. Despite her unwillingness to undergo the plastic surgery, she welcomes the idea of having a new nose—one that had never "been blocked up by war and the stench of dead bodies and Arab politicians" (105). Remarkably, Naʿnaʿ's narrative does not celebrate the mythological aspect of war and does not bother to hide the havoc that it wages on the bodies of humans and country alike. On the contrary, it demonstrates the disruption created internally and externally for both individuals and the nation by the hypocrisy and the misguided paradigms of both patriarchy and colonialism.

Eventually Nadia feels the need to break away from the organization's center in Jordan. She accepts the courtship and, subsequently, the marriage proposal of her plastic surgeon and moves to Beirut to pursue an ordinary civilian life. However, because of her commitment to the Palestinian cause, and owing to the persuasion of comrades, Nadia agrees to return to work in the media office of the organization in Beirut. At the time of her return to political life, Nadia is also expecting the birth of her baby. Despite this added responsibility, she performs superbly in the organization, spending more time in the press office than is to her husband's liking. Disillusioned by Arab politics himself, her husband prefers to live his luxurious life in his cocoon detached from the national struggle. Shortly after, her guerrilla comrades in Jordan experience a setback, losing yet another battle to Israeli colonial forces in addition to many of their committed fighters including her friend Abu Mashour. Her comrades' aborted revolutionary project leads to Nadia's own miscarriage. Nadia's sense of national loss becomes insurmountable, especially when compounded with the personal loss of her fetus. The death of Nadia's child signifies her subconscious refusal to bring another citizen into a nation divided by futile, masculine war paradigms. Her initial dream of creating a new breed of Arab men, through giving birth to a male child who would usher in a new age of victory and a national dialectic built on love and mutual dialogue, is now shattered forever. She recalls the national inertia and helplessness of that particular historical moment in this passage:

> For a while I dreamt of that dark-eyed child of the East. I wanted him to be a male child because we do not have enough men any more. I was

insistent on creating a man, on bringing one into the world. I would look at every face I saw with hope, I would study it, and I always came to the conclusion that, after the Fifth of June, all our men had fallen to the bottom of a pit of fire where Medusa had turned them into black stones which could no longer move or love. (117)

Unfortunately, as a result of spending some time transporting fleeing Palestinian comrades from the battlefront of Amman to the safe haven of southern Lebanon, Nadia loses her fetus. Her dream of turning trauma into triumph, through the rebirth of a new generation, is shattered forever when the doctors inform her that she will never be able to be a mother again. From now on, the homeland takes on the dimension of her adoptive child. This attitude stands in sharp contrast to that of her husband, who managed to find his peace of mind by creating an "internal homeland" within himself to which he would rather withdraw from the pains of the "larger homeland" proper.

Problems ensue, however, when the guerrilla leadership decides, yet again, to move their operations to the international arena. This time Nadia gathers the courage to disagree, argues for the need to learn from the history of past revolutions and to adjust the national struggle's parameters to fully include the agency of the forgotten feminine. She insists that revolutionary figures should learn from their past mistakes in order to avoid the loss of more fighters and the support of public opinion inside and outside the Occupied Territories. Determined to exercise her woman's agency even further, Nadia refuses to train young fighters to conduct plane-hijacking operations overseas. When hearing of her refusal, the leadership's punishment is swift and hurtful; they rumor her inability to continue serving in the revolution because of her familial obligations, and they ban her from contacting their camps or any of her old comrades. Sadly, her desire to alter the traditionally prescribed women's roles in nationalist movements from the victim/heroine dichotomy to a role of leadership in the national struggle is forcefully suppressed. Indeed Nadia's codification within the revolutionary apparatus echoes Deniz Kandiyoti's claims that in modern national configurations, "women are no longer excluded from the public arena, but subordinated within it" (quoted in Ofeish and Ghandour 2002, 131). Their limited role allows for little or no input in national reconstruction. Ultimately Nadia's ostracism pushes her to join her husband, who has decided to specialize further in the field of plastic surgery, in Paris, hoping to find solace from the homeland's problems in the diaspora.

Diasporic versus Homebound Journeys

Nadia's Parisian diaspora does not erase her painful memories of the homeland. Moreover, her attempt to find an answer to the thwarted Arab revolutionary practices in alternative Western revolutionary values, such as those of her French lover Frank, also fails miserably. To her dismay she discovers that, after Frank's long imprisonment in the Congo, he had returned to his Western roots, gladly accepting his newly assigned heroic status and restricting the level of his revolutionary engagement to writing his memoirs and lecturing about his previous struggle. Nadia's estrangement becomes immense after realizing that neither love nor her attempts to find solace in Arabic or Western revolutionary ideologies can bring her to forget the agony of the homeland. Forgetting the homeland is even harder for her, especially when she carries within her body a reminder of the homeland's pain in the form of a bullet wound that she received in West Germany during their last failed external operation. Once more, the intersection of the personal (the wound) with the political (the homeland's troubles) is evoked in the merging of the bodies of women and nation. In three letters to Frank that form the textual body of the novel, Nadia reflects on her inability to maintain her sanity amid the contradictions that permeate her life: past/present, political ideology/reality, war/peace, the homeland/diaspora:

> All I can think about now is my wound. I think bitterly that I am living in a time of war, and that peace (your favourite [*sic*] subject) is nothing more than a lie which man has to believe in so that he can go on living. I suddenly remember that I cannot go home—that I have buried my past in the fabric of those old walls. It is a past which torments me and which will not leave me alone whatever I am doing.

I remember, but I am trying to forget, and there is a present which exists only in my head. *I am alone and I have no weapons except the wounds which inhabit my body.*

I told you about it. I told you that there is a dagger within me, that somewhere in my body is a deep and lasting *rupture* which could kill me at any moment, that I have this open wound which is getting deeper by the day and the deeper it gets, the more important it becomes to forget.

The wound. The woman and the homeland banished in her head. Abu Mashour [*sic*]. You. The journeys of madness into the lands of *silence and exile.*

The wound. (11, italics mine)

Unearthing the buried past and negotiating its painful memories are crucial steps in the process of addressing the ruptured Arab self and ending its diasporic status. If left unattended, the wound's scabs will, as Gloria Anzaldúa aptly warns, hemorrhage and bleed, particularly at the point of border crossing (Anzaldúa 1987, 3). Indeed, any attempt to speed the healing by enacting a forced erasure of the traumatic events will result, as Nadia finds out, in failure and fractured selves. Hence the interplay between forgetfulness and intentional remembrance of trauma engenders healing of the wounds and breaks the wall of silence. The dualities and fragmentation that Nadia experiences are indicative of the war's effect on Arab citizens in general. However, these dualities are highlighted in women's war narratives because, owing to their alienation from the essential masculine paradigm, women are more prone to feeling the effects of this fragmented, shattered self. The issues of diaspora and displacement outside but, more important, inside the war-torn Arab countries stand out as a recurrent motif in female-produced war narratives. For example, Emily Nasrallah highlights this sense of fragmentation espoused in so many female war narratives, especially her fellow Lebanese writers who documented the sixteen-year civil war in Lebanon. Commenting on Nasrallah's short stories, Mona Takieddine Amyuni reflects on the scattered and fragmented portrayal of the author herself: "I become disjoined . . . my parts scattered . . . I am scattered in the corners . . . I have no throat, no vocal cords" (quoted in Amyuni 1999, 96). Likewise, the emphasis is also placed on displaying rather than hiding the "rupture" and the "wounds" caused by the war and the essentialist, binary paradigm within which they operate. Nadia, for example, displays her "wounds" as the true "weapons" with which she will diffuse the war myth. Despite its mythical nationalist image, war is not pretty, often not honorable, and it is really messy, really ugly. In this context, the depiction of fragmented, disfigured female selves exposes war's destructive machine. Thus, as miriam cooke points out, these authors see no need "to tidy up the mess of the war into neat and unchanging binary scaffolding of the War Story" (cooke 1999, 77).[4] If home is messed up, the responsible citizen's duty is not to hide the mess, but rather to expose it. Only this way can there be some hope of a reconstructive and transformative function, as women rewrite the meaningless, ruthless war saga.

Nadia's attempts to escape temporarily from the homeland's mess, to sweep its troubles under the carpet of forgetfulness in the diaspora, and to replace its warmth with the cold map on her residence wall are all met with failure. Stripped of all of its meaningful dimensions, the homeland turns into a buried maw'udah, a "corpse." Nadia comments, "Yes, the decomposing corpse of my homeland has been there for some time now. Every day, I open the wooden casket and take a look at the body. Every time I get that instant of joy and elation when I see that it has not completely rotted away yet. My homeland may be dead, but it has not rotted yet" (Na'na' 1995, 51). Activating the maw'udah's trope in the context of death and resurrection offers a nuanced framing to the old question of women's participation in state-building given that it highlights women's agency in resurrecting the dismembered nation. In this manner, women are transformed from erased sites of memory, from mere symbols of the nation to active agents of political change. The recasting of the normative association of country as a woman in this new light offers a reclamation of both entities as women claim full ownership of their image as icons of the nation and of their right to political activism. The urgency of Nadia's

4. For more on the history and dialectics of the War Story and its "dominant paradigm," see cooke 1996, 1–67.

individual involvement and subsequent homecoming decision is motivated by the promise of renewal and transformation, by the homeland's symbolic and physical resurrection. She decides to end her diasporic existence in Paris, and returns home to partake in the collective rebuilding of a national discourse that allows equal participation of all of its citizens, of all of the fragmented selves (including the feminine dialectic), that allows mobilizing the power of the populace within the homeland, and enacting the ethics of love. As a result of her ordeal, Nadia realizes that total detachment from one's homeland is not possible, nor is it desirable; that in addition to recognizing the existence of the national wound, one finds true healing by seeking actual presence in the homeland.

Additionally, Nadia's abandonment of the aggressive rhetoric of revolution and war stems from her new awareness of the hypocrisy of both Arabic and Western political theories as evident in her comrades' betrayal of her, and in Frank's commercialization of his own revolutionary ideologies and practice. Not long after his return from prison in the Congo, Frank turned back to his original French bourgeois roots and objectified his whole revolutionary experience to a mere exotic adventure to be written about and profited from in his publications. This discrepancy between "reality and imagination" prompts Nadia to wonder "why did I believe all the things which they taught me in school, and everything that the political parties told me, and the secret organizations? Why did I believe that heroism lies waiting in the hearts of men? Everything is just a vain grasping at shadows. Heroism is a big lie which we must believe in" (80). Nadia's brief experience as a militant fighter has taught her that true heroism does not lie in destructive practices, but in embracing new, reconstructive societal and political models that celebrate a life-giving ethos. It is rather her father, an "ordinary" man who led a "normal" life, who was the true "hero to bring nine children into this world and provide for them . . . It takes courage to live a humdrum life" (85). It is true that conflicts are essential at times to protect one's life and to affirm one's national identity. Nevertheless, Nadia comes to the conclusion that conflict should be resolved in a nonviolent manner. Construction of national narratives must also involve participation of all the fragmented national selves, including women and children, and not just male war-worshiping leaders. Indeed, the actual participation and physical presence of all the national subjects in the homeland's reconstruction are paramount. This realization is symbolized by the discovery of an insect in Nadia's Parisian apartment that is hard at work gnawing the map of her homeland, embodying the disarray of Nadia's "inner map." In the diaspora, Fadia Faqir contends, Nadia "loses her identity without gaining a new sense of wholeness, so the self begins to disintegrate since it can no longer handle or control the 'reality' around it" (Na'na' 1995, vi). The distortion of her identity is even more prominent when she confronts her reflection in diaspora's mirror. She sees the "naked" truth upon examining the ravages of time on her body, which, in turn, reflects the homeland's destruction. Her fears grow when she realizes that she might perish in foreign lands without writing her own narrative and contributing to the reconstruction of her country. Recounting this incident, Nadia states,

> I stood naked in front of the mirror and studied my face and body. I was greatly alarmed by the effects of time which could be seen creeping across them. It was worst around my eyes. I heard the sound of the insect mocking me. It seemed to be saying:

> "Beautiful lady, you're going to die. You're going to die and you'll never find your homeland."
>   Screaming wildly I lunged at the mirror and smashed it. I felt like the member of a devastated race . . . the remains of ashes. (86)

The superimposition of the country's map onto Nadia's body serves to highlight the urgency of women's belonging to the national narrative. Moreover, the distorted reflection of both woman and country in the Lacanian diasporic mirror is a pressing call for the remembrance of the dismembered, fractured self and for assuming female agency in national reconstructive projects. Ironically, Nadia's loss of identity is not free of its occasional sardonic moments. After her divorce, she receives a letter from her ex-husband reminding her of the need to make the divorce official in their prospective embassy in Paris. Nadia's initial response is amusement at patriarchy's insistence on preserving formalities, even when they mean nothing in the absence of the physical land within which these marital laws could take effect. She exclaims, "What embassy? What divorce? I don't belong to any country. None of my three passports—or is it four, I can't remember any more—have the name of my birth-place in them. It wasn't even my name, the name of the woman he had married" (125). On the one hand, Nadia's multiple passports indicate loss of a unitary identity on both the political and personal levels in the diaspora. On the other hand, it further affirms her refusal to subscribe to prescribed "imagined" and fixed national identities, in Benedict Anderson's sense, forced upon her by the dominant, oppressive powers in the homeland as well.

By sending Nadia on her homeward journey, Na'na' joins the ranks of other female war writers who believe that to be physically present in the homeland is essential to eliminating the glorification of war and its destructive, binary paradigm. The goal is still, however, to dissociate oneself from the axis of patriarchal polity. This can only be accomplished, Elspeth Probyn argues, not by abandoning the locale of the homeland (the local), but rather by working "more deeply in and against the local" (Probyn 1990, 186). The mission is to fight those destructive paradigms from within, to heed the voice of the "outsider within"[5] so as to reconstruct the Arab individual as a different hybrid—one who is capable of building a national discourse of antiviolence through embracing the stranger within. Observing the conflict from the comfort and psychological dissociation of a diasporic site runs the risk of objectifying the country and its war-torn victims in the same manner that Frank's revolutionary memoir views the Congo and its people as unwilling exotic subjects through his anthropological, orientalizing lens. Nadia's homecoming seems partially motivated by Frank's Western stance on her Middle Eastern plight. In a letter addressed to him before her departure, she unequivocally states her refusal to fit neatly into one of his Western war stories. Physical presence in the homeland both literally and literarily is paramount

5. I am borrowing this term from Patricia Hill-Collins (1986).

to engendering feminine national narratives that seek to redefine their agency in a mold different from the essentialist, masculine, war paradigm. Indeed, this physical presence reflects part of the ethics of love that has to be extended to one's own country even if it sadly entails sacrificing oneself for the chance to participate in the construction of a postwar, postmodern humanist nationhood.

In a similar fashion, Hanan al-Shaykh's *Beirut Blues* (1995a), originally published in 1992 as *Barid Bayrut*, chronicles the war woes of south Lebanon. The female narrator Asmahan, not unlike Nadia, writes her novel as a series of letters and insists on making Lebanon the site of her national struggle. Her stance is in sharp opposition to her male counterpart, Jawad, who insists on capitalizing on Lebanon's war tragedy with the detachment and voyeurism of a Western journalist and photographer. Unlike Asmahan's deconstructive, aural war narrative, which strives to condemn the destruction of war in the hope of rebuilding a better Lebanon, Jawad's scopic and photographic war narratives thrive on the pervasiveness of destruction and death. Elise Salem Manganaro aptly points out that Jawad's approach to his art is "almost like a vulture, his art thrives on the death of his subject." Indeed, Asmahan's accusatory finger points to him as such: the Lebanese are "specimens under your microscope . . . you regard us with a foreigner's eye. . . . You see us as folklore" (quoted in Manganaro 1999, 122). This counter-feminine national consciousness has to position itself in the homeland if it is to succeed in eliminating the hegemony of the essentialist, national narrative, and in ending the history of diasporic existence for these alternative feminine voices. Transforming the traditional, masculine dichotomies requires deconstructing systematic, institutionalized patterns of violence from within, and fostering the ethos of human love instead of religious or political sectarianism. The dialogue of guns has to be replaced with that of words, and theoretical aggrandizement of the war myth has to give in to the practicality and sanctity of peace. This goal can only be accomplished if women become active participants in the construction of a new, national, humanist, aural narrative, and not voyeurs from the sidelines.

Resorting to individual outlets such as opting for a diasporic existence does not effect the desired change because one risks a reenactment of the same system that often is transferred intact to the new host country. One also risks, as Nadia's diaspora demonstrates clearly, living on the margins of both the host land and the homeland, at once not being part of the dominant culture to which one is exiled and simultaneously failing to forget one's own country. Indeed, it is through observing Nadia's rough journey as she experiences the physical and moral plight of war that the reader becomes convinced of the necessity of pursuing a collective, active national involvement and a direct dialogue in the fight against dictatorial practices. The only hope lies in a direct engagement with a transformative, oral (rather than a military), action-oriented dialogue that promises to transcend these combative ethics and steers the nation in the direction of final reconciliation. These authors contend that to achieve a true transformative project, the national narrative should be told from different centers forever shifting so as to avoid a static definition of nationhood and the traditional, dominant war narratives that celebrate violence. Furthermore, this determination to parade traumatic atrocities of the war, to highlight the psychological and the physical state of decomposition caused by the ongoing battles, further proves the writers' intent of not forgetting the schism created by war's violence—a process deemed essential to undermining totalitarian concepts of nationhood. In his classic essay "What Is a Nation?" Ernest Renan argues that "the essence of a nation is that all individuals have many things in common, and also that they have forgotten many things" (Renan 1990, 11). The things that have to be forgotten, in Renan's opinion, are the crimes against and massacres of other minorities in the process of forming the concept of a unified, static nation. Renan reminds the reader that "it is good for everyone to know how to forget" (16), for the forgetting process is paramount to keeping the illusion of a so-called unity and hegemony of the modern nation as an "imagined community" (Benedict Anderson 1983). Building on Renan's claims, Homi Bhabha asserts the performative, institutionalized aspect of the act of forgetting: "To be obliged to forget—in the construction of the national present—is not a question of historical memory, it is the construction of a discourse on society that *performs* the problematic totalization of the national will" (Bhabha 1990a, 310–11).

By refusing to "perform" the act of forgetting, by jumpstarting national memories with the narration of the violence committed on the individual and the nation alike, Arab women war writers register their stance against the "totalization" of modernist nationhood construction. They stress the therapeutic element arising from the need to go back to the site of personal and national trauma so as to engender a cathartic reconciliation with the focus on survival as an ethical responsibility. By exposing this national trauma, they also ensure the reinstatement of the forgotten feminine voice long since lost in the process of exclusionary, masculine, national construction (both colonial and local). In addition, they further highlight the participation of other fragmented, forgotten racial and religious subjects in reconstructing the nation as a constantly vibrant, dynamic construct. The ultimate goal is to never forget the atrocities of the war resulting from divisive, hegemonic, colonial, or patriarchal definitions of nationhood and so to transcend divisive practices of colonial mapping. The writers' agenda is to ensure equal participation from all the multiple national subjects, and never to allow the sociopolitical, racial, or religious differences to once more erupt in destructive, totalizing wars. The feminine vision of a postmodern, national definition of citizenship is built on a dialogue of words rather than guns, and on the constant shifting and reshuffling of all centers of power so as to ensure equal participation of all fragmented and previously excluded national selves. miriam cooke uses this definition of the nation as perceived through the eyes of Lebanese "humanist nationalist" female writers. The nation is written, she asserts, "not as an ideological construct, despite its discursive nature, but rather as an individual sense of belonging and then of responsibility, which radiates out of multiple centers. It is first of all personal, it may be collective. . . . For those who are humanist nationalist, there is no single polity but multiple, fragmentary projects that are continually disassembling, but also reassembling and self-regenerating, because they foster, above all, survival" (cooke 1999, 82). Contrary to the deadly finality of war casualties and suicide missions, survival is the ultimate goal of female war narratives. However, accomplishing this seemingly everyday activity is not an easy task if the parameters of power remain unchanged. One may recall Nadia's aborted fetus, conceived within the violent patriarchal paradigms of power, and the loss of her hope of ever bringing to the world a new breed of Arab men who can transform the dialectics of violence. The fetus trope indicates the impossibility of survival if the current status quo is not shaken up by the same shells that it planted in the minefields of people's minds and bodies. Thus, engendering peace poetics has to entail first the recognition of the price paid by all warring parties in pain and misery. Second, it has to pledge a commitment of never forgetting this past troubled chapter from the life of the nation so as not to revert to its destructive, violent practices. Only then can a transformative survival project ever be possible. The urgency of women's participation in reconstructing the postwar "humanist" nationhood stems from a deep conviction in the feminine survival project, and in the healing effects of their encompassing narrative.

Arab women have long been part of the national struggle for independence and active participants in wars waged in the name of "the imagined communities" of a totalitarian concept of nationhood. The recognition of their participation, however, has always been erased from the written records, consequently from collective memory. Systematically their contribution to the national narrative remains locked in victim/heroine roles, and defined in patriarchal discourse. Recent engagements of female-penned war narratives and "militant fighters" in the national struggle propose a rejection of the essentialist concept of nationhood, of the master narrative of war, and of their co-optation as mere symbols in the victim/heroine dichotomy. Furthermore, they open up new avenues of reconstructing the nation from different centers and polities. Feminine war narratives challenge the prevalence, silence, hegemony, inevitability, and credibility of the patriarchy-manufactured war myth. It is a myth that claims war as a necessary rite of passage for nation-building, and insists on using women only as symbols of the nation but not as true agents in inscribing its postindependence narrative. Destabilizing the myth of the "war story" necessitates a constant reshuffling of the centers of power to allow fluidity and space for the emergence of a dynamic new nationhood—one built on the participation of all citizens. Women war writers expose the nihilism of the master war narrative, of the paradigms of patriarchal and institutional domination, and offer peaceful alternatives for conflict resolution and national reconstruction. At issue is women's right to participate in the construction of the national narrative away from the dominance of a destructive order, to prevent the erasure of their contribution, and to envision an alternative world order created with the aid of feminine agency—a world that finally reflects the true face of love and peace poetics instead of hegemonic practices.

6

Paradigms of Dis-ease and Domination

Hoda Barakat's *The Tiller of Waters*, *Disciples of Passion*,
The Stone of Laughter, and *My Master and My Lover*

Recent political disappointments in the Arab world have prompted Arab
thinkers and writers to contemplate the possible reasons for what they
dub the Arab "plight,"[1] the "disease" of a "disembodied 'Arab nation,'"
doomed to roam aimlessly and eternally "like the ghost of Hamlet's father"
(Nourallah 2006, 3). Some like Ghada Samman (1988) and Halim Barakat
(1993) have attributed this Arab malaise to a sense of alienation regulating
the relationship between individuals and the State. Samman remarks,

> Arab citizens often feel that the homeland departed and left them behind.
> History also departed, and authoritarian governments are engaged in
> the cover-up. . . . There is alienation at several levels of human rela-
> tions: between men and women, between men and other men at work,
> in politics, and in commerce. I would need ages to count the number of
> Arab "alienations." I invite every reader to dig in deep, in a moment of

1. Sociologist Halim Barakat recounts eight possible reasons for what he perceives
as "the plight of the Arab World," among them: "the prevalence of a reactionary religious outlook (Sadiq Jalal al-'Azm), the collapse of religious and moral traditions (Salah
Edin al-Munajjid), the ideological divisions among Arab nationalists (Adib Anssour),
repressive family socialization and child-rearing practices (Hisham Sharabi), the absence
of a scientific tradition and rational thinking (Constantine Zuraiq), the suppression of
creativity throughout Arab history (Adonis), the impact of alienating social conditions
(Halim Barakat), and a kind of disequilibrium in the Arab ego (Ali Zay'our)" (Halim
Barakat 1985, 25–48).

honesty and self-exploration, to add yet another word to the dictionary of Arab exile. (al-Samman 1988, 142)

Others have gone to the extent of claiming that "Arab subjectivity cannot be separated from a sense of trauma and failure" (Sheehi 1997, 54). While other women war writers, discussed in the previous chapter, highlighted the consequences of female alienation from the national narrative, by contrast Hoda Barakat exposes dominant, patrilineal practices that alienate and subjugate Arab males. From her diasporic site of Paris and within the literary corpus of her novels, Hoda Barakat joins this ongoing dialogue as she searches for answers to Arab society's malaise, locates its trauma in a systematic burial of past memories, and identifies various diseases in this "*ma'zum*" (troubled) society in crisis.[2] With each narrative construct, she highlights a series of crises ranging from the absence of historical memory and the consequent loss of cultural inheritance in *The Tiller of Waters* (2001) (*Harith al-miyah*, 1998b), to religious and ethnic violence in *Disciples of Passion* (2005) (*Ahl al-hawa*, 1993), to gender identity struggles and the enforced rules of masculinity in *The Stone of Laughter* (1995) (*Hajar al-dhahik*, 1990), to patriarchal master/slave paradigms of domination leading to destruction of self and of country in *Sayyidi wa-habibi* (2004b) (*My Master and My Lover*, not published in English). Each novel poses a complex question about the true meaning of the protagonists' relationship with history and with ancestors, uncovers the reasons behind the symbolic death of the predominantly male protagonists and that of the nation, and laments the forced conversion of the characters from peace to violence. With Barakat, we see a reversal of the Shahrazad motif in a manner that asserts female agency, and a transformation of the wa'd motif from the buried woman to the buried ancestral memories, and ultimately to the buried city/nation. In Barakat's body of work, the collectivity of her male characters masquerade in a Shahrazad-like fashion to tell the story of the city and the individual's burial in the sea of systematized violence and patrilineal paradigms. They too speak of a wa'd of a different kind, of

2. Personal interview with Hoda Barakat, Paris, Aug. 20, 2008.

the male who in these troubled societies suffers, as Barakat insists, from a "systematic wa'd" as well.[3]

Fabric, Fabulation, and Rhizomatic Narrative

The story of unearthing the archives takes on a new twist with Hoda Bara-kat's *The Tiller of Waters*. The protagonist, Niqula Mitri, resurrects both the buried city of Beirut, after its destruction during the Lebanese Civil War (1975–91), and the multilayered national history through his recount-ing of the story of the evolution of textiles in Bilad al-Sham (Greater Syria). It is with this author, known for her captivatingly alienated male protago-nists who stand at the edge of society and gender norms, that the story of the buried feminine narrative—that of the maw'udah—intertwines with the national narrative of destruction, dispossession, and domination. The motif of the buried feminine self awaiting resurrection and agency, which I discussed in earlier chapters, is transformed into the metaphor of the buried city of Beirut, which awaits the protagonist to unearth its multi-farious history. Niqula's personal and national (his) story is told from the midst of his fabric store's rubble, specifically from the ground floor that surprisingly remained intact despite the destruction caused by the war-ring parties in the civil war.

Unlike the upper floor, which contained the modern synthetic fab-ric lacking in durability and history, the ground floor houses the natu-ral fabrics of cotton, velvet, lace, and silk: fabrics that have an intimate connection with both Lebanon's and humanity's sociopolitical evolution. In recounting the history of fabric development, Barakat uncovers the story of humanity's manipulation and, at times, adulteration of natural resources. Hence each fabric represents a certain social ill, related to the kind of human interference needed for its production. For example, velvet represents the dangers of passionate desire; lace the threat of infatuation; and finally silk, although a natural product of the silkworm, has come to signify mankind's greed and manipulation of the divine intent, thereby

---

3. Personal interview with Hoda Barakat, Charlottesville, VA, Feb. 8, 2014.

leading to destruction for those who wage wars in the pursuit of wealth and power. The infatuation of power, of dominance, is similar to the lure of silk, the desire to indulge oneself in greed and dreams of rule and control. Only cotton, a complete product of the earth's plants, therefore needing no human manipulation, has continued to represent tenderness, warmth, and healing. These social diseases underline mankind's greed, struggle for power, and financial and political domination. Niqula's attempt to trace back the buried records of the demolished city intimately links history and fabric. He is able to access historical registers through his body's intimate involvement with fabric. Upon discovering the natural fabric intact, he is able to overcome the current war trauma by accessing his prewar memory, immersing himself in different fabrics. He states, "I would take off all my clothes and wrap myself in the length of fabric. . . . I would press it against my skin, against every part of my body, to resuscitate my own intimate memories of that particular fabric in every detail—to go back, as if re-reading this memory of mine, finding there the features and elements of this bolt of cloth, page after page . . . word by word . . . letter by letter" (Barakat 2001, 35–36). The organic pliability of fabric, its vertical and horizontal threads, endows it with the ability to register historical narratives from multidimensional angles. It shares this representational plentitude with women's various narratives, often polyphonic, multilayered, and intersecting. However, similar to some forgotten women's narratives, the fragility of fabric renders it ephemeral, forcing it to disintegrate without a trace. Perplexed, Niqula invokes the spirit of his fabric salesman grandfather: "Grandfather, did you grow so passionately attached to cloth because it will not be here when the archeologists excavate the traces of our disappearance? . . . Because its weave will disappear as quickly and easily as the life of cities like this one, though unlike them its patterns will not leave impresses in the earth's sediments, in the deposit of each successive layer, when the hurried diggers search for the residues of our passing" (66). The inherent anxiety behind the search for the missing trace reflects an acknowledgment of the importance of knowing the beginning in order to attain a happy ending. In her answer to my question of why most of her novels possess a melancholic ending, Hoda Barakat said that her "endings are despondent because they reflect societies and lives that did not accumulate knowledge, memories, or history."[4] Therefore, weaving, writing, and history are inextricably linked in this novel. Niqula is keen on reminding Shamsa, his Kurdish maid and lover, that "the first hieroglyph was one thread upon another. The first tablet written concerned the sleeves of garments," and the cotton chemise she is wearing acquired "its worked surface . . . from deep inside Egypt's tombs" (Barakat 2001, 60). The process of listening to the ancestral archives involves harkening to the *haki* (story) of a weaver who in his/her *hiyaka* (weaving) documents "the secret of life and peace, a secret forever menaced by the victory of death and war" (128–29). The new generation's role is to decipher the weaver's secrets: this "trustee . . . weaves the words of our ancient ancestors, the words that enrich the memory we inherit and that we enrich in our turn. And when the words of the grandfathers begin to be forgotten, the knots and threads in the weaving begin to come undone and the world ends in fragments, shapeless, a dust cloud in the nebula" (129). Hence Niqula's urgent mission is to preserve fabric's multifarious story in his own narrative of personal and national resurrection.

Niqula's return to the past reflects dissatisfaction with a present that has deceived him (9). The world he inhabits has absorbed the values of the modern industrial age. It is the age of a la mode, the *nouveautés*, and the synthetic fabric Diolen, when people's taste follows fashion slavishly and when buying is but an impulse and a passing whim. Merchandise is being sold for profit, detached from its history and memory. There is a "repetitive loss" and a systematic erasure of cultural memory that began with the introduction of fashion in the middle of the last century (40). In Niqula's father's opinion this cultural demise spreads to home furnishings as well: "That is also the story of this city's homes. Look at the drapery, summer curtains, upholstery on chairs, bedspreads and sheets, handkerchiefs. Every one a flimsy weave that does not last, cannot be passed down. Volatile fabrics that leave no trace or impact, like the folklore on national television" (142). The persistent commodification of cultural history, the adulterated mixing of fact and fabrication: all lead to

4. Personal interview with Hoda Barakat, Paris, Aug. 20, 2008.

the erasure of other ethnic groups' imprint, to the impossibility of weaving their narratives in the national Lebanese fabric. Recalling his father's and grandfather's historical accounts of the now war-torn Beirut, Niqula asserts that "Beirut's soil is composed of layer upon layer of lives that have passed on. Beirut's soil is not like the soil of other cities, living by the movement of the winds along their surfaces, shifts that shape their edifices but do not pierce deep inside" (32). Acknowledging the multilayered ethnic groups that formed the fabric of Beirut is the first step toward dispelling the myth of "pure" nationhood that conforms to a majority's national image over any other minority. Niqula's father's assertion that "this city is no one's country" reflects his refusal of the repressive, possessive, and essentialist form of modern articulations of nationalism, of real or imagined statehood (8). Some critics assert that "the survival of natural fabrics in the basement, and the burning of synthetic ones on the first floor could symbolize the conflict between the original or the ethnic and the imported and synthetic industrial. It is as if Niqula was also helping in rebuilding the city while it is being destroyed. . . . By telling Shamsa the story of the 'techniques that go into clothmaking,' Niqula is also 'planning and construct[ing]' Beirut once more" (Al-Hassan Golley 2003, 8). Indeed, the Crusoe-like way he goes about constructing his underground dwelling is indicative of the author's political commentary on the need to rebuild postwar Beirut from the viable remnants of detrimental civilization through an act of individual self-assertion (Barakat 2001, 62). Unarmed and isolated, in the grottoes underneath Beirut, from the rest of this modern destructive civilization, Niqula's recollections of his father's and grandfather's words act as memory triggers to make him face and overcome this national war trauma. He states, "I went on, bewitched by my memory of my paternal grandfather's words. A city that does not advance in time but rather in accumulating layers, a city that will sink as deeply in the earth as its edifices tower high. How many cities lie beneath the city, papa . . . grandfather . . . how many cities lie there to be forgotten?" (66). The history of Beirut as a city defies essentialist national narratives of the dominance of one sect over another; rather, that history demonstrates the coexistence of all minorities and their right to claim the city as part of their heritage.

In the process of accessing this lost memory, Niqula adopts the mission of educating Shamsa about Lebanon's history as well. His intent is manifested in the folds of his narration of the history of various fabrics: cotton, velvet, lace, and silk. His endeavor to combat death, to resurrect the traces of other cultures, which constituted part of the past fabric of Lebanon, endows him with a Shahrazad-like quality. Indeed, the mode and the purpose of his storytelling are identical to Shahrazad's. Niqula uses the delay tactic, ceasing his narration at dawn to entice Shamsa to come back the next day to hear its completion. As he weaves the story of fabric (hiyaka) with narration (haki), Niquila assumes Shaharazad's mission of healing the nation's memory from forgetfulness. Reenacting Shahrazad's healing mission, he sets out to redirect Shamsa's insatiable desire for silk and sex, for the visual and the sensual, to aural-oral desire, just as Shahrazad did to Shahrayar. As he warns her, "Look, . . . and then listen, and only then, touch. If you take the silk to your body now, all of this will become inaccessible to you and it will be impossible to tell you its story as I ought" (144). This role reversal represents an ingenious narrative technique on Hoda Barakat's part because it repositions the responsibility of healing the nation, and keeping its memories, from women to men, thereby relieving women from blame and placing the challenge of ending conflict solely on men. Embattled by devastating wars, it is modern-day Shahrayars (Arab dictators and warlords) who have to realize the dangers of silk, of power, and of their subsequent connection to greed, to death. Through his narrative, Niqula wishes to impress upon her the dangers of silk's acquisition and of greed. He insists, "you must linger for a while inside of what I have told you, what you have heard. Like the silkworm, you must fast a little, resisting the voracious appetite of your ears. Then the story's spinning will reach its culmination" (149). During their next meeting, Niqula notices her sudden weight loss and wonders, "Are you fasting like the silkworm, as I instructed you to do last time?" (152). Shamsa's response demonstrates her categorical refusal of his forced tutelage:

> No, said Shamsa. I no longer need to weigh anything. I no longer need to feel that I stand solidly on firm ground. I no longer like to eat. I have found something better. I will become as light as what I am wearing. I

might even try to fly. Like a butterfly. I wanted to tell her that before it flies a butterfly must rip its silk cocoon, must cut the filament. Everything that it has secreted throughout its life it must forget completely; when it becomes a butterfly, it must remember nothing about silk. To live the trivial, foolish, and rapidly fading life of butterflies, it must lay waste to its entire past. It must forget silk. But before I could open my mouth Shamsa spoke again. Isn't it better to wear this than to die of suffocation? Who knows, Shamsa? I answered her. Perhaps the worm is transformed into its own silk when it dies inside the cocoon. (152)

Interestingly, Shamsa rejects Niqula's (Shahrazad's) ethos of female self-sacrifice, of fixity of place, and of the maw'udah's predestined fate. Instead she embraces self-fulfillment and mobility. Their ideological duel reflects the challenges of memory recall, of historiography vis-à-vis the subject's gender and ethnicity. Secure in his presumed gender superiority and ethnic majority, Niqula maintains a belief in fixity, in Lebanon as a locale, as a consortium of past registers forming "imagined communities," in Benedict Anderson's sense (Anderson 1983). By contrast, as a woman and a member of a historically oppressed Kurdish minority, Shamsa insists on inscribing her own historical narrative of self and identity dislocation, of mobility and nonfixity. Early on in the narrative, Shamsa attributes her plumpness to her desire to anchor herself in the land and to find a country. She states, "I gain weight so that I may settle, so that I can feel the presence of a homeland. So that my dimensions will expand to occupy space" (Barakat 2001, 72). However, after attaining the silk's empowering knowledge, she starts to lose weight, acquiring agency and a voice to tell her story along the way. In a typical modernist stance she rejects Niqula's didactic role, inserts her own individual narrative of Kurdish dispossession and dislocation, and finally rejects his ethos of self-sacrifice as she embarks on her solitary journey of self-discovery. As she informs him of her Kurdish heritage, she asserts her people's aversion to "unclean wars," to soldiers, and to vengeance (73–74). Shamsa declares, "We [the Kurds] reside in our courage and freedom, in our solitude and in our free flight over lands owned by others, across borders barb-wired by identity papers and soldiers" (85).

Nevertheless, Barakat warns that pursuits of self-assertion are prone to moments of both utmost ecstasy and utter torment (162). It is the Icarus curse of flying too close to the sun,[5] to the well of knowledge; detachment from memory and from one's roots can present the utmost danger for the rebellious self. Niqula offers Shamsa an alternative vision, that of acknowledging her belonging to the land, to its roots, while simultaneously allowing her freedom through cultivating vertical and horizontal rhizomes. Rhizomes are the old roots transformed, renewed, and regenerative. Unlike Deleuze and Guattari, I do not associate rhizomes with an "agentless nomadism," but rather with temporal and geographic mobility, a phoenix-like capacity to resurrect past cultural inheritance so as to combat the war machine's erasure.[6] Hence rhizomatic narratives promise renewal, a new beginning, albeit in a new attire, coupled with the ability to connect, just like fabric, both horizontally and vertically to one's roots and cultural origin.

Niqula insists on approaching the story of silk with caution, for silk's utmost beauty conceals the curse of its pursuit and betrays the human greed that drove nations to wage wars for financial and political gain. Niqula warns Shamsa, "we must arm ourselves with special learning . . . so that we will not fall victim of its magic. For knowledge is dangerous to the uninformed who are unprepared to receive it. . . . from being an elixir it can become a deadly poison" (Barakat 2001, 126). It comes as no surprise, then, that "in all stories of silk you will find betrayal, evil, and abundant covetousness" (168). For, "when the thread's strength is joined unto its solidity the seduction of power knots itself firmly in place and so do the ruses of cunning and pain." Realizing "the lust for power" inherent in silk's acquisition, the ancients restricted its wearing to emperors and saints to "shield against . . . the illusions of might and the corruption they whet in individual minds and in society; against the possibility that

5. Coincidentally, Shamsa's Arabized name echoes the Kurdish version of it, Suryash, meaning the sun. See Barakat 2001, 82.

6. I thank Smadar Lavie for alerting me to the connection of rhizomes with nomadism. For more on this topic, see Deleuze and Guattari 1986. Also see Lavie 2010.

absolute categories might become muddled" (167). The silk's cautionary tale is a reminder of the need to preserve categories intact, of the buried city underground and the erased history of the various minorities in Beirut. Only by achieving the equilibrium of the yin and the yang, of the loom's warp and its weft, of past and present, is a cosmic, peaceful principle achieved. This calculated principle ensures that the weave's "'magical squares,' their chessboard-like arrangement in black and white, signals at once opposition and concord, and brings into harmony all of the contradictions: between femininity and masculinity, night and day, yang and yin. They become 'satanic' if they manifest any flaws, no matter how slight or innocent these may seem. Thus any blurring of unambiguous boundaries, drawn strictly between the ultimate examples of two pure categories, brings ruin down upon the order of things in the world and evil's curses prevail" (171). Niqula's investigation of the vertical and horizontal intersections that create fabric and culture is a way to mend the cultural tapestry that became unraveled, thereby exploding in destructive wars.

The novel does not offer easy answers, does not cast blame either on those wanting to preserve tradition (Niqula and his paternal ancestors) or those desiring to abandon it altogether such as Shamsa, who sees in delaying her gratification with silk, in anchoring herself to one lover and one place, and in identifying herself with the silkworm's fatal destiny only a suffocating ending that would prevent her from fulfilling her transformative potential of becoming a butterfly, of mobility, of soaring above tradition. Shamsa's fear is legitimized in the Chinese silk myth that highlights its traumatic death curse, particularly as it pertains to women.

> An ancient Chinese legend relates that in the beginning the worm that becomes a moth was a princess, murdered by her father's wife, jealous of her loveliness and filled with envy. Her killing, or her *burial alive*, transformed her into filaments or eggs. This filament, then, was not offered in peace or as the blessing of bounty, and as we approach it we must remember this. As expiation before the deed, recognition of an evil inherent in its discovery and production—and to repel the consequences of its temptation—the Chinese sowed the ancient silk road with sacred sketches offered up to the Buddha in more than nine hundred

and ninety grottoes dotted along a distance of eight thousand kilome-
ters. A merchant would stop at each shrine to offer his devotions and
supplications. (170, italics mine)

The myth recognizes the trauma associated with silk's production, and
highlights the importance of memory, the need to atone for past sins
before embarking on future endeavors. The silk myth brings to mind the
maw'udah's "burial alive" saga, and links acknowledging past traumas
with the ability to survive in the present. The lessons learned from uncovering the hidden traces of women's writings will propel future generations
to heed the call for women's agency and action. The narrative suggests that
survival depends on acknowledging the wisdom of the ancestors' legacy,
of amplifying their trace without allowing it to become a suffocating presence. In fact, the maw'udah's legacy is manifested, in this novel, on more
than the symbolic level. On one of his underground excursions, Niqula
happens to stumble upon the mummified body of an adolescent girl literally buried in an amphora. Something in her erect stature and in the way
she sat cross-legged gazing at Niqula reminds him of his departed lover,
Shamsa. Indeed, the amphora girl does not just represent Shamsa's forgotten narrative, but comes to reference all the untold histories and memories
of the entire Arab nation. In our interview, Hoda Barakat indicated that
she meant for the buried amphora girl to represent "the girl who never
reached womanhood, the city that did not become a country, the memory
that did not materialize into a present, the place that we do not have the
courage to face or to interact with, and the incomplete history that was
not reconciled, digested, or woven, therefore leading always to conflicting myths."[7] Barakat views this collective inability to process history's
lessons, to distinguish between what is myth and what is history, as one
of the diseases afflicting Arab societies and halting the development of a
unified national consciousness. Reflecting on the selective and fictional
nature of historiography. Barakat asserts that the amphora girl denotes
"our buried memories because authoritarian governments and the present

7. Personal interview with Hoda Barakat, Paris, Aug. 20, 2008.

have turned her into a mummy."[8] She states, "I come from a country and a region where there is no methodical or scientific documentation of memory. Therefore, history resembles myth; and myth resembles history."[9] This cultural amnesia and the inaccessibility of historical memories define the essence of the Lebanese Civil War's trauma. The Lebanese citizens' inability to go back to a cultural moment that predates colonial conquest and the modern nation-state, where all the conflicting ethnic and religious groups lived harmoniously, is partially responsible for the civil war's eruption. Niqula attempts to unlock this inaccessible past several times in the narrative by calling on his diseased father's spirit to offer him answers. For example, recalling his father's words, Niqula wonders, "What was it that we neglected to hear as we listened, as we offered ourselves humbly to [the ancestors'] legacy? Why did we extend our hands to cling to the cord that binds us to the generations, only to find the rope becoming a viper?" (Barakat 2001, 143). Additionally, Niqula's closing question, "Father, who killed me? Who killed me? For I did not die a natural death," posed in the final scene of *The Tiller of Waters*, resonates deeply in the readers' minds (173). It is an eerie reminder of the Qur'anic question, referenced in chapter 2, asking the maw'udah to identify her killer at doomsday. The buried female infant motif, discussed in earlier chapters, represented in this novel in the image of the trope of the amphora girl, has been successfully transformed to represent the buried city of Beirut, the absent father, and the forgotten cultural inheritance. Once more, I rely on Hoda Barakat's illuminating clarification:

> In my novels the absence of the father indicates a monumental individual crisis. Simultaneously, it marks absence of memory, of heritage, as if we are orphaned nations whose rituals of power accession and succession did not happen naturally. So unlike other societies, we did not advance forward. We destroy memory and walk towards the unknown. It is impossible that our perspective is either entrenched in the past to the point of Salafism, or rebellious to the point of complete

8. Personal interview with Hoda Barakat, Paris, July 13, 2011.
9. Personal interview with Hoda Barakat, Paris, Aug. 20, 2008.

erasure and departure. It is as if we are always building in the air, or on demolished ruins.[10]

The personal, feminine trauma, addressed by previous women diaspora writers, has morphed into the national trauma of the erased, buried city. From the buried maw'udah and the amphora girl, in Ghada Samman and Hoda Barakat, to the marginalized male citizen killed for the majority's failure to incorporate his narrative into the national consciousness, to the destroyed city and the lost country detached from its history and memory, Beirut's unique tale of dispossession transverses, vertically and horizontally, gender, ethnic, temporal, and geographic borders.

The history of textiles predates the modernist idea of nation creation with its imposed colonial borders. Thus, recounting Beirut's history through the story of fabric underlines the fictitious narrative of a hegemonic nation, built on a singular, authoritarian, colonial vision of the nation-state. I contend that Niqula's narration does not advocate "a single historical voice" as some critics have argued (Amin 2010, 110), nor is it a story of those who, in Homi Bhabha's sense, inhabit "the margins of the nation displac[ing] its center" (Bhabha 1990a, 6). Furthermore, it is not an alternative narrative professing a "counter history" (Terdiman 1985). Rather it is a rhizomatic narrative, calling for excavating the historical archives of Beirut, of going back to its lost memory, to its roots, so as to formulate rhizomes from whence can spring the reconstituted Lebanese narrative. Unearthing a historical registry that predates the nation-state's ethnic and religious division, and in its multiple rhizomes in a manner not so dissimilar to fabric's constitution both vertically and horizontally connected to ancestral roots, guarantees a reconstruction project that accounts for past memories and traces so as to overcome contemporary erasure and war traumas. At the end of the novel, despite the halted project of Niqula's resurrection of Lebanese memory and historical archives, despite the pessimistic ending foretelling his death and perhaps even

10. Personal interview with Hoda Barakat, Paris, Aug. 20, 2008.

Shamsa's demise, the reader is left with a glimpse of hope emanating from the anticipated gatherings of the deceased Lebanese souls in limbo. There the stage and empty chairs are set for a concert of the national singer, Fairuz, heralding the beginning of peace and national unity. Heeding the call for peace and correcting past generations' mistakes are still possible, if the country's youth can listen to the archives. Such is the advice of Niqula's father when he asserts, "No, it isn't the end of anything for someone of your age, because you will see enough to correct the mistakes and straighten out what has gone crooked. Nothing disappears quite like that, gone forever as it begins to decay" (Barakat 2001, 142). The trace lives on; it simultaneously marks the accomplishments and the mistakes of the past. Uncovering its vestiges and mapping the future guided by its light become the primary objectives for the new generation, and for Arab women diaspora writers.

Religious, Ethnic, and Gendered Violence

In *Ahl al-hawa* (*Disciples of Passion*) and *Hajar al-dhahik* (*The Stone of Laughter*), Hoda Barakat masterfully critiques societal norms that insist on gender, religious, and political partitions. In depicting the inner torment of a nameless, psychotic protagonist in the former and the agonies of Khalil's androgynous masculinity in the latter novel, she explores the extent to which a civil war's violence can extend to every societal and personal facet of her compatriots' being.

Disciples of Passion does not follow a natural progression of events; it starts with the protagonist's confession of murdering his interfaith lover and compels the reader to investigate the reasons behind the persistent personal and national madness. Therefore it is not surprising that the protagonist narrates the story from the asylum where he is trying to find the meaning of violence, of love, of madness, and of killing. The violence seeps from the background of the civil war to envelop the internal lives of the characters and the whole narrative. As its Arabic edition's back cover states, the novel is about people who reached "the point of no return, where fear is bigger than life and desire is the face of death."[11] After surviving kidnapping and torture in the Western sector of the city, the protagonist's sister Asmaa admits him to Dayr al-Salib, a sanitarium on the Eastern Christian side. The narrative alternates between his dazed and forced existence at the asylum and a lost past filled with moments of amnesia and sporadic clarity as to the nature of his multiple traumas. The protagonist attempts to piece together his memories to recreate a life whose specifics he is uncertain of, including a female partner whom he is unsure whether he killed or not. Violence dominates the atmosphere of the novel. It is there in the raw in the epilogue and the prologue of the narrative, and penetrates deep to the very core of each character. Retracing several landmarks on the path of violence during the war is, as Hoda Barakat asserts, an important step toward "processing and digesting the trauma of the Civil War."[12] The sixteen-year-long Lebanese Civil War had more than its obvious direct impact on the city and its inhabitants; thus in most of Barakat's novels there is a concerted effort to explore the "indirect impact" of the war on the marginal individuals who are not afforded space to exist beyond the parameters of power and violence.

Through a careful exploration of the dynamics of group belonging in ethnically and religiously divided communities, Barakat exposes the trappings of what Suad Joseph calls the "myth of extended kinship" that functions according to a paradoxical "care/control" paradigm. (Joseph 2000, 108). What is often referred to as the "kin contract" is a process through which sectarian communities have "systematically and simultaneously . . . nurtured and disciplined [their] members" and used this tactic "as a venue of state control" as well (Joseph 2000, 110). The male and female members of a particular sect are expected to conform to a set of rules that constitute the conditions of belonging to said clan. In return, the individual enjoys the protection of the group and access to power through the hierarchal familial, political system. The codes of belonging are particularly strict when it comes to the adult males of the group, who are expected to take

11. Barakat 1993, back cover of *Ahl al-Hawa*.
12. Personal interview with Hoda Barakat, Paris, Aug. 20, 2008.

arms, if need be, in defense of these unwritten rules. In the words of the protagonist in *Disciples of Passion*, "the rule was not made for those who die of love," "the mad," "the lovers, and the failed killers," but for those "sound and straight creatures of the Lord," who take arms in defense of their clan (Barakat 2005, 133–34). Individuals who do not conform face alienation, condemnation, and punishment.

For example the protagonist's interfaith relationship with a woman from the Western Muslim side of the city casts a doubt on the level of his commitment to his own Christian Maronite sect. At a checkpoint, a soldier asks him, "Why isn't a man of your height and weight out working? . . . You aren't working, and you are not carrying a weapon. So how do you feed your wife? How can you sleep with her? Or does she feed you and f—— . . . you big mule!" (103) His refusal to take up arms like the rest of his fraternal village youths undermined his sexual and social agency, exposed him to violence from the other side, and invited doubt in his masculine normativity and commitment to the group, which, in turn, will deny him protection. The androgynous protagonist of Barakat's first novel *The Stone of Laughter*, Khalil, is faced with a similar attitude when a "young armed man" looks scornfully at Khalil's "pale" body, his short legs, and his "housewife's shopping bag" (Barakat 1995, 33). The care/control paradigm disapproves of religious, ethnic, and gender border crossings, punishing and banishing those who transgress accordingly. The protagonist in *Disciples of Passion* is aware that his cohabitation with a woman from another religion, most likely from the enemy's camp, added to his clan's banishment of him. Sadly, he remarks, "No one visited us. It did not take Asmaa and me long to learn that people were distrustful of the woman who was with me. And we learned—Asmaa and I—that people wondered why I, a young man, had remained in the house rather than going off to fight for our people as the other hearty youth of my community had done" (Barakat 2005, 100). In the midst of a "fratricidal" battle, he feels that his "foolish . . . aversion to fanaticism and violence" left him vulnerable to the other camp's violence, that his love for a woman from the other camp "had stripped [him] of [his] final refuge and [his] own people." Lamenting, he declares, "[t]hat woman took my burial place from me" (103).

The pressure to conform to these sanctioned forms of dominant masculinity is exercised equally on all parties. For instance, the protagonist's Muslim friend in the asylum, Jaber, undergoes the same banishment from his community when refusing to fight on behalf of his group. Jaber explains to the protagonist that for the "noncombatant children" of the state who are "no good at war and no good at fucking women" (121), the space allowed them is the liminal space of the sanitarium where all categories of gender and status differentiation are canceled. Realizing his difference from dominant forms of masculinity, Jaber justifies his exclusion as such: "I am no longer of any use to my family and my clan because not only am I not turning out my children's bread, but I'm also incapable of carrying a machine gun even to guard the neighborhood" (121). In this exclusionary process, men are treated as children, and in their docility they physically start to resemble women as well.[13]

As *The Stone of Laughter*'s Khalil discovers, there is no space for ambiguous feminized masculinity in this combative society. He is painfully aware of his inability to belong either to the group of younger youth fighters "who have broken down the door of conventional masculinity and entered manhood by the wide door of history," or to the older men who are versed in "theory," and who "fasten their hold on the upper echelons . . . in politics, in leadership, in the press" (Barakat 1995, 12). Despite his several attempts to maintain a differentiated masculinity inside the confines of his private realm at home, the pervasive, public, outside world invades his whole being, and its marked violence obliterates his previously conceived feminine self. After being attacked by a group of militia men, he realizes that "when you leave the group you are truly orphaned" (102). Having "lost the delight at being outside sex," at straddling both sides of gender borders, he decides to step outside of his gender ambiguity and to perform masculinity by forgetting his feminine "voice," by adopting the "language" and violent ethos of the Father, by donning a mustache and developing broad shoulders, and finally by performing the ultimate

13. On the interrelationship between the feminization of males and their subsequent political exclusion, see Ghanim 2009, 198.

act of male aggression: raping his upstairs neighbor (142, 208–9). As he assumes ascendency in the fraternal order, Khalil substitutes for his earlier "feminine state of submission" (12) another form of surrender, that of "submission to [his] belonging to [his] brothers, submission to the glorification of life, to the general misery of life" (208). Ironically, Khalil's submission involves the selling out of both his body and his antiwar ideology as he finally submits to the militia's "big brother's" sexual advances, and becomes an arms dealer.

The cost of male indoctrination into normative masculinity is extremely taxing to the self that has to deny its femininity and, at times, is even lethal. Such is the case of the young martyrs, "sainthood's baby chicks, hatched by the machineries of tiny nations" (Barakat 2005, 108), duped into believing in a nation built on exclusive belonging to a combative ideology. Indeed, as described by the protagonist of *Disciples of Passion*, masculinity is a form of constant struggle that starts at the moment of conception, with the annihilation of the female chromosome in the human egg, and continues to adulthood. He asserts, "I remember what came before my lethal struggle to be a man, before my birth and after it, and then after I reached puberty" (82). In this context, performative masculinity becomes part of the variable traumas affecting males, engendering repeated violence as it enacts its gendered masquerade.

Furthermore, the confluence between religion and politics intensifies the crises of Arab societies because it bestows a divine legitimacy on the ensuing violence. As is customary with these strange bedfellows, the authoritative political leader becomes a mirror image of God the Patriarch in his religious and familial roles. Halim Barakat argues that, in some Arab societies, "there are striking similarities between religious conceptions of father and of God. Such similarities indicate that God is an extension or abstraction of the father" (Halim Barakat 1985, 44). Furthermore, "political leaders are cast in the image of the father and citizens in the image of children. Thus, God, father, and the ruler have many characteristics in common. They are the shepherds and the people are the sheep. Citizens of Arab countries are referred to as *ra'iyyah* (the shepherded)" (Halim Barakat 1985, 44). In *Disciples of Passion*, Hoda Barakat exposes the danger of such an association, and of venerating the divine, when she represents God as one who is partial to the strong majority against the dispossessed asylum minority:

> Those on the outside—they were the innocents who always do what the Lord commands of them, who obey Him in times of peace as in the civil wars. He did not tire of them, nor did He declare Himself as our portion, as the blessed lot of the lost sheep that were. He was not ours, not the Hope we could entreat . . . The ones outside, the blessed ewes, . . . [are] more lively, more voluble, more changeable. So the Lord changed his mind and his camp; the Lord sat down with them, sat among them like a father. And He left us. (Barakat 2005, 26)

What distinguishes Hoda Barakat's treatment of the political and religious paradigms of power is that, unlike other civil war writers, she holds both men and women responsible for manipulating the religious scene, thereby leading to its explosion in sectarian violence. Similar to men, women are equally implicated in fueling the war machine because they are the ones who incite the warriors and cash in the salaries of their deceased martyred sons (Barakat 1995, 198).[14] For example, Hanna in *Disciples of Passion* refused to bury her two fighter brothers until the men of the village brought her "two enemy corpses to witness the prayer for the dead and the burial from the edge of the hole dug for her brothers' grave" (Barakat 2005, 97). It was also Hanna who manipulated the iconic significance of the oil and blood, presumably emanating from the statue of the Virgin Mary to stir up more war sentiments among her clan. Surprisingly, Barakat suggests that the inability to cross religious and political borders is not gender specific, thus ascribing cyclical violence and a sense of cultural myopia to all involved parties.

Both novels are critical of official national narratives, of history, and of a society that views itself in the essentialist image of the imagined nation. The protagonist's need to be readmitted to the security of his clan, to "regain both capacity and force, . . . to be essential to someone—essential enough to erase the capacity to do without [him]"—is what drives him to

---

14. Also in my interview with Hoda Barakat on Aug. 20, 2008.

kill his Other: his female lover (116). Similarly, Khalil's statement that "it is death who is the father of the city" (Barakat 1995, 138) challenges essentialist concepts of nationhood, built on violence and death. He contends that "nationalistic sentiment feels pain if it is far from death and history, nothing makes history but death which loathes and despises laughter" (109). History's inherent danger, according to Ernest Renan, is exposing "the deeds of violence which took place at the origin of all political formations, . . . the essence of a nation is that all individuals have many things in common, and also that they have forgotten many things" (Renan 1990, 11). Recalling the site of traumatic violence that preceded modern national configurations is a crucial step toward dismantling the war machine. For that reason, the asylum residents and Khalil's androgynous self are reminders of prewar "civil communities that have been destroyed or have vanished" (Barakat 2005, 113). They are the "last civilians" whose presence conjures up memories of buried peaceful communities that predate history and nation.

The novels suggest that a society that creates partitions and maintains dichotomies engenders violence at the core of every citizen. Those who do not subscribe to the ethos of violence will be condemned to exile, for there is no space allowed for difference or dissent. For example Samaan, a friend of *Disciples of Passion*'s protagonist, is faced with deportation because he refuses to fight. Before departing on a self-imposed exile to Germany, Samaan declares, "I am not capable of being a killer. I tried, and I couldn't do it. I peed in my clothes, and my clumsiness almost killed me. I'll finish my studies in Germany. I'm not a fighter. Write to me, don't forget me" (53). The themes of remembering Arab communities that predate the era of historiography, of colonial concepts of nationhood, of dominant masculinity, and of violence engendering endless wars, are central to all of Hoda Barakat's novels. And so is the idea of reinscribing personal and national histories on the canvas of cultural memory. The protagonists in *The Stone of Laughter*, *Disciples of Passion*, *The Tillers of Waters*, and *Sayyidi wa-habibi* (*My Master and My Lover*) are acutely aware of society's demand to be part of a fraternal, tribal system and the consequent punishment for citizens who opt out. By exposing their traumas, Barakat highlights the dichotomous gender, political, familial, and fraternal partitions constituting the crises of Arab societies. The characters' desire to transgress these dualities, to reside in the generative liminal space of the in-between, simultaneously authors their suffering and their salvation.

Infatuation of Power

In *Sayyidi wa-habibi* (*My Master and My Lover*), Hoda Barakat exposes the intricacy and insidious interdependency of the power/love paradigm prevalent in familial, societal, and political daily relations in Lebanon. Along the way she also uncovers the fragility of the patriarchal "kin contract" and its foundational "care/control paradigm."[15] Readers follow the journey of the main character, Wadiʿ, and his playground friend, Ayyub, from childhood to adulthood as they unsuccessfully avoid being thrust into dominant fraternal circles that eventually lead to their demise. Their death suggests that in troubled societies, locked into perpetual crisis, "there seems to be no reasonable space allowed for small, marginal individuals to exist"[16] without being indoctrinated into the dominant power paradigm. Wadiʿ's failure to escape the grip of these ever-burgeoning, violent power circles, from school bullies to local militias and finally to global superpowers in his Cypriote exile, is a testament to the prevalence of these dominant modalities. The novel tracks Wadiʿ's trials and tribulations as he initially resists subscribing to authoritarian power structures, but ultimately finds the need to seek protection and to invest fully in the master/ slave paradigm.

Hoda Barakat's employment of this paradigm offers an interesting twist on the classic Hegelian master-slave dialectic in the sense that the master-slave/Tareq-Wadiʿ relationship in this novel does not appear to be built on "life-and-death struggle" (Hegel 2001, 632) among two dueling parties, but rather on love and the assimilation of what Suad Joseph calls the "patriarchal connective mirroring" process (Joseph 2001). Unlike Hegel's bondsman, who assumes his bondage position because his fear of

---

15. For a thorough analysis of these terms, see Joseph 2000.
16. Personal interview with Hoda Barakat, Paris, Aug. 20, 2008.

death acts as a "chain from which he could not break free in the struggle" (Hegel 2001, 632), Wadiʻ hands his "chain" freely to his "boss" and master, Tareq. Wadiʻ does not lose the self's fight for recognition as is the case with the Hegelian model; rather, the unique system of "patriarchal connective mirroring" renders the strife unnecessary to begin with. The relationship is not of two antitheses, but of two reflections, the self and its shadow; subscribing to the same authoritarian ideology. The reins of power are handed down not through strife and domination, but through love and adoration. In a typical Middle Eastern patriarchal connective mirroring relationship, the subordinate Other acquiesces to the power of the dominant brother because the subordinate is guaranteed to step into the master's role once the current patriarch's death renders him unable to perform his duties. In the meantime, all the subordinate (br)other has to do to gain the sought-after Hegelian "consciousness" of self is to wait for his turn on the accession line while practicing the rules of dominant patriarchy through the mirroring mechanism. This new formulation of the Arab patriarchal Other is distinctly different from Hegel's antithetical or later Lacan's distorted mirror image of the Western Other; rather, by virtue of the patrilineal, patrilocal, and patriarchal systems, the male Arab Other becomes a magnified reflection of the dominant self.

In this unique process, the master-self and slave-other become totally enmeshed as they both become absorbed in the fraternal authoritative fabric built on a mutual love-survival mechanism. As the slave-other develops a false consciousness through his investment in the survival of the master, individuation is never accomplished. Furthermore, the specific conditions of the Lebanese Civil War increase the need for the master-slave identity fusion, as the protection of fraternal orders becomes an absolute necessity for survival. There is no space for nonconforming individuals, as Ayyub's early demise, via assassination, attests.

Wadiʻ's desire to seek power by attaining a *muʻalem* (a boss, a drug, or a warlord) status stems from the background of his poverty, of his desire to replace his subordinate chef father with a stronger patriarchal figure. As an only child to an ordinary chef of one of the country's elites, Wadiʻ did not have access to the traditional protection of a large, extended family. Furthermore, early in his life he learned to despise his father's servile position and to value the patronage of those in power (Barakat 2004b, 171–72). The pressure to be part of a fraternal order so as to enjoy the group's protection started early on school playgrounds where Wadi', an exemplary student, had to drop out of school and to join a neighborhood gang to prove his leadership worthiness. His short-lived accession to a boss status is motivated by a desire to escape the "docile lamb" connotations of his name (*Wadi'* means docile) and a fear of being in the followers' position (171). He states that in his endeavor to assume "leadership positions," he had to keep at bay "the strong ropes that tie him down to the followers' position. It was exhausting to continue the pull towards the elite" (69–70). Indeed, the focus on the need to be under someone's protection for survival, on the buying and selling of souls, is made central at the beginning of the novel, as the first traumatic memory of Wadi''s childhood is his mother's statement "I beg you to buy me, people. Buy me Abu Wadi'" (Barakat 2004b, 7). In this context, the word "*ishtara*" (buy) denotes possession, placing a weak individual under a strong patron's protection, thereby enacting the psychodynamic, social structural, and cultural processes of dominant patriarchy. As he listens to his mother's entreaties while she waits to be picked up on her way to the dialysis session, Wadi' experiences the humiliation of poverty and realizes the importance of access to fraternal and political power. The novel leaves no doubt that the poor are the ones to be sold, and the powerful are the ones doing the buying. Hence there is no escape from a dominant master/slave paradigm that seems to be exacerbated by the political disarray of the civil war that often lurks in the background of Hoda Barakat's novels.

For the master/slave paradigm to function properly, there needs to be a justification for its existence and prevalence. Suad Joseph's "patriarchal connective mirroring" offers an excellent explanation for the paradoxical survival of such a dominant/subordinate model among senior brother/junior brother Lebanese familial power dynamics. She states that in this process,

> [t]he person experiences components of the self "in" the other which reflect back the self's alternating capacities for gendered and aged deference and authority. . . . It [the self] absorbs the emotionalities and

intentionalities of domination into complementary and constitutive components of subordination. The subordinate person comes to see components of the self in the patriarchal other. The patriarchal other is or comes to represent the authority the self has or will have in other relations. . . . The patriarchal other comes to represent to the subordinate self, the system of kin relations which underwrite[s] gendered and aged hierarchy and which evokes the care/control paradigm embedded in the kin contract. (Joseph 2001, 175)

Although Suad Joseph's model is meant to describe a particular power deference relationship among brothers of the same family, I argue that this subordinate deference mechanism is further-reaching and extends its application to the societal and political arenas as well. The canceling of the individual Other's sense of self is justified through the connective mirroring process because the Other gains accession to authority only through this identification process. With this framework in mind, the reader is not a bit surprised with Wadi''s description of his relationship to his future boss, Tareq, as that of the dog to his master,

Like a dog. I loved him just like a dog. . . . Despite their chatter, I will hand him my leash to direct me wherever he wants, as I happily wag my tail to prove my ecstasy. . . . You will be surprised at my power, the one that I regain now after it had dissipated. My submission is only for him, my obedience, pliability, and love. And to the others my sharp fangs, my wild barking, and instinctive, violent metallic jaws of death-like lurch, for the slightest of reasons, for whatever reason, for fancy. Only in this manner, things will be even. . . . Yes, exactly; I am the boss's dog, but your wolf, you scoundrels. Let us be absolutely clear, this is my jungle. (Barakat 2004b, 171–72, my translation)

The paradoxical master/slave relation is intriguingly empowering to the subordinate Other who is simultaneously demeaned to subhuman animal status, yet empowered via his association with the master's inner circle. The transformation of the dog trope to a wolf is consistent with Barakat's representation of a war-induced Lebanese societal decline to a jungle-like existence in all of her other novels, and is a reminder of Wadi''s elevated strength and status.[17] The connective mirroring process fuses master and slave to the point where they become reflections of the same patriarchal dominant self. The subordinate Other, in Joseph's estimation, "defers because the patriarchal brother *enables* the self. He defers because the patriarchal brother *animates* the self. The patriarchal brother becomes the symbol of the kin contract. He comes to embody the self as patriarch, self as power, self as authority. The br(other) becomes self and other" (Joseph 2001, 176, italics in original). The loss of boundaries between the two entities, between the master/self and the slave/other, is evident in Wadi''s assertion of his resemblance to Tareq: "I do not quite recall when I started noticing that I resemble him, or, perhaps, that he resembles me to a great extent" (Barakat 2004b, 15). The liminal space both parties inhabit allows for a fluid interaction given that both master and slave are invested in the survival and primacy of the paradigm.

Barakat reminds the reader of the invisible rules of male homosociability in *Sayyidi wa-habibi*, which mandate extreme wealth or excessive display of masculine prowess so as to be anointed with a leading position in the semipatrilineal power pyramid. If a male does not possess these qualities, his place in the masculine hierarchy will always be that of a follower. The limited roles that govern the formation and the performance of such masculinity forever inscribe the master/slave dichotomy, thereby finding no value in the male's individual sense of self. Several Arab social scientists and cultural critics have isolated the limited role of the individual, his/her "devastating condition of alienation" from the sociopolitical process, as the main catalysts for the failure of what Hisham Sharabi calls Arab "neopatriarchal" societies (Sharabi 1988; Sharabi 1977, 23, 27–64; and Barakat 1993, 271). According to Sharabi, neopatriarchy is a form of a "modernized," dependent patriarchy that mimics modernity; nevertheless, its "internal structures remain rooted in the patriarchal values and

17. The trope of wolves roaming the streets of postwar Beirut, gnawing at deceased human corpses, is a recurrent image in Hoda Barakat's *The Stone of Laughter* (1995) and *The Tiller of Waters* (2001), and is symbolic of Lebanon's demise into anarchy and destruction.

social relations of kinship, clan, and religious and ethnic groups. In a peculiar duality, the modern and the patriarchal coexist in contradictory union" (Sharabi 1988, 8). Furthermore, Adunis criticizes certain modes of Arab remembering and historiography that do not assert "individual memories" and experiences, but rather affirm historical and religious values instead. It is a system, he contends, that "organizes the past" rather than challenging it (Adunis 1986, 6). For these societies, "patronage based on impotence and submission" becomes the sought-after model, and, in turn, it "renders public institutions superfluous, [and] takes away the individuals' claim to autonomous right" (Sharabi 1988, 46–47). Since the adolescent male is programmed to build his societal and sexual function on his ability to relate to his male peers, in this manner he will not discern what it means to function on his own.

In her novels Hoda Barakat is highly critical of the vertical masculine relations that strip away the individual's free will, and, as I argued in my analysis of *The Tiller of Waters*, she endorses a sociopolitical interaction built on acknowledging both vertical and horizontal relations instead. In "ma'zum" (troubled) societies, the sense of belonging and citizenship suffers from wa'd, and is buried in alienating, dictatorial practices of the political elite. Thus more individual sense needs to be cultivated, and less belonging to the cult of the father/leader. Sharabi argues that the plight of such neopatriarchal societies stems from the prevalence of "vertical relations" that dictate the interaction between "ruler and ruled, between father and child" (7). Halim Barakat concurs with Sharabi that the trend of "vertical relationships" is the cause of the Arab sociopolitical malaise: "they continue to prevail and are regulated and reinforced by a general, overall repressive ideology based on *al-tarhib* (scaring) or *al-targhib* (enticement) rather than on discussion aimed at persuasion" (Halim Barakat 1993, 118, italics in the original). In fact, as a boss Wadi' resorts to public display of brute force to assert his dominant masculinity. He further announces his endorsement of the credo of "killing for killing's sake" and exalts the "cleansing," "cauterization" element of his ability to take someone's life. His violent behavior seems to register directly, "as points in a video game would," on his body in terms of taller stature, stronger muscles, and broader shoulders (Hoda Barakat 2004b, 90–91). As Samira

Aghacy puts it, Wadi''s "excessive virility . . . combining obscenity with aggression and brutality, is another way of regaining a lost masculinity and attaining power and control" (Aghacy 2009, 184). Indeed, his hyper-aggressive masculinity endows him with a god-like quality. Recalling Last Supper imagery, Wadi' professes his wish "to sit at the head of the table, to break and distribute bread to his [followers] . . . to start his ascendency to the realm of his Father" (Hoda Barakat 2004b, 94). He further justifies his killing spree by maintaining that "[he] is not a serial killer; for God cannot be a murderer when he obliterates people and cleanses humanity" (91).

Interestingly, Wadi''s assumption of the leadership position invokes the aforementioned interplay between sexual dominance/impotence and social submission. Explaining to one of his followers why he cannot sit on a pair of car tires, he states, "I do not sit on car tires to protect my testicles, because I use them. My woman asked me to pamper them and treat them in a manner befitting testicles of the royal kind. . . . I won't refuse her request, I do not dare; otherwise it is you, rat, who will find yourself pampering my testicles as my woman would. Then you will have to excel her abilities so as to make me forget her precious assets" (74). Wadi''s dominant boss position is secured through flaunting his active, sexual prowess vis-à-vis the others' (males and females) sexual submission and impotence. In this context, the master/slave relationship is further manifested in terms of the traditional active/passive roles of medieval Arab homoeroticism.[18] His ascendency to power is embodied in the penetrative, violent metaphor of "a polished dagger enter[ing] the night's belly" (74). The master assumes the ability to penetrate socially and sexually the borders of his followers. However, the confluence of these categories should not be confused with homosexual tendencies, for the potential of the alpha male to sexually dominate his followers does not necessarily entail a physical enactment of these powers. On the contrary, owing to the patriarchal connective mirroring, a process through which both master and slave fuse into one entity, the follower perceives the master's sexual prowess as an extension

---

18. For a detailed analysis of the active/passive dichotomy in Arab medieval homoeroticism, see Hanadi al-Samman 2008.

of his own, rather than a violation of his personal borders. Indeed, the convergence of the two identities is a testament to the everlasting endurance of the master/slave paradigm. As Hoda Barakat puts it, the ties of such "a master-slave relationship are even stronger than the love bond of a homosexual one"[19] because it is often endorsed by the psychodynamic, familial, sociopolitical, and cultural structures. Surprisingly some critics who have engaged in the analysis of this novel underplay the gravitational pull of this master/slave paradigm and the insidious cultural effects of its generational repetition (Hadeed 2013). Such privileging of the homoerotic underpinning of the homosocial relationship, despite Wadiʻs adamant dismissal of this reading at the outset of the novel, ignores the power of patriarchal mirroring and the cyclical dynamics that are at the crux of social and cultural dysfunction in prewar and postwar Lebanon.

The short period during which Wadiʻ achieved a muʻalem status and dealt with hashish trafficking as he enjoyed territorial and sexual dominion over his surroundings comes to an end when members of a militia put him on their assassination list. To protect his life, he has to flee to Cyprus, leaving his newly acquired wealth and strength behind. During his sea voyage, Wadiʻ experiences bouts of fever and delusion brought about by his hashish withdrawal, but also by what he perceives to be the incarnation of his father's docile spirit within his soul. His transformation is marked by an inexplicable fear, impotence, and an inability to communicate with his wife (Samia), his past Lebanese friends, or his current Cypriot acquaintances (Barakat 2004b, 133, 143–46). It is as if once he is out of the master/slave paradigm, Wadiʻ is unable to function in homosocial settings outside of its parameters. His growing fear does not subside until he reenters the system again, this time, however, in the role of a slave follower. He finds another young muʻalem (Tareq) to take him under his wing. For a short duration, he enjoys the sudden infusion of power and sexual virility that being the second in line of succession avails him. However, Wadiʻs final loss of self and subsequent disappearance occurs when he discovers the illusory and elusive aspect of the power paradigm (182–83).

19. Personal interview with Hoda Barakat, Paris, Aug. 20, 2008.

Wadi''s "patriarchal connective mirroring" process is totally shattered when his imaginary line of succession to the patriarchal order is broken up by the discovery that his boss is but a small link in the chain of local fraternal and global colonial powers. After his sudden disappearance, a wistful Samia comments on the potential cause of his disillusionment, which, in her estimation, springs from Wadi''s discovery that he is but "a small and solitary player at the margin of margins; that his insignificance was the only reason behind his survival, not his alleged extraordinary intelligence, maneuvering, or hiding skills" (190–91). In addition, with the breakage of the "kin contract" and the care/control paradigm comes Wadi''s realization that no matter how hard he tries to grasp power, he cannot reach the top of the pyramid because foreign and external powers are the ones who truly control the sociopolitical and economic environment. The break occurs when Wadi''s boss is humiliated in front of his own boss, in a never-ending reenactment of the subjugation process until it finally stops at the superpowers' door. Wadi' implicates the superpowers in Lebanon's strife when he states that "the shadow which suddenly jumps from behind his back and slaps [him] on his nape is not necessarily Lebanese. It is a gigantic, vicious and deranged shadow with an enormous power" (145). The paradigm of domination is a monstrous, consuming machine that no longer conforms to the time-honored patrilineal, patrilocal, tribal models with invisible local and foreign players secretively guiding and feeding its endless voracious appetite.

Wadi''s breakdown is because of the shattering of the patriarchal connective mirroring system and a disequilibrium in the care/control paradigm. After realizing that his "boss" Tareq used him to be the façade and the sacrificial lamb for his illegal secretive arms deal, the care element of the traditional care/control paradigm is erased. Tareq represents a new system of masters who practice their dominion over their followers by professing a superficial veneer of care and diplomacy. However, despite the change of the master's attire from feudal, to capitalist, to political, to drug and warlord, to global, he is as pernicious as his previous predecessors. What further undermines Wadi''s faith in the power pyramid and ultimately usurps his desire to go on is his discovery that Tareq himself does not occupy a coveted master possession in the master/slave system.

Hence, he cannot offer Wadi' the protection he desires. According to Hoda Barakat, "the repetitive chain of master/slave, master/slave continues forever, and it is a demeaning, humiliating system."[20] The pervasiveness of this master/slave paradigm is quite obvious in Tareq's recounting of what transpired among himself, Wadi', and Tareq's boss prior to Wadi''s disappearance. Tareq informs Samia that he explained to Wadi' the context of the boss's humiliating outburst, which was directed at Tareq. He asserts that this is but a normal process in the hierarchal pyramid of power: "I told Wadi' that this is life and he should not worry for me, for my boss's boss has a boss as well. This is life for those who decided not to be consumed haphazardly or sell themselves cheaply. I had to learn this the hard way from my father whom I buried forever, deep in the ground with these hands. I buried the educator who preferred his cancer and pride over me, his only son" (Barakat 2004b, 183).

Hoda Barakat identifies the social and political crises that held Lebanon in their grip as rooted in the patrilineal, neopatriarchal mirroring system keen on burying individuality. Furthermore, just as she did in *The Tiller of Waters*, she underlines a generational crisis related to the advent of modernity that seems to consume, to erase, to bury all the traces of the ancestors' moral ethos and replace them with a code of violence, greed, and opportunism. Tareq's father, for example, the old-fashioned schoolteacher, opted to decline a warlord's offer to send him abroad for cancer treatment because his morals forbade him to accept favors from hands soiled by the blood of fellow Lebanese citizens. Tareq's refusal of his father's "antiquated" ideals (182), his symbolic patricide, represents an evolution of the infanticide motif of the maw'udah, which I discussed in earlier chapters, from the buried feminine self to the buried city in *The Tiller of Waters*, to the buried ethics and ethos of the care/control kin contract along with the disappearance of honor and compassion in *Sayyidi wa-habibi*, to gender identities torn asunder by the violent modalities of war in *The Stone of Laughter* and *Disciples of Passion*. What renders the highly cherished "care/control" paradigm dysfunctional in this narrative

---

20. Personal interview with Hoda Barakat, Paris, Aug. 20, 2008.

is the absence of the care-love aspect of the equation, thereby creating an imbalance allowing fear and force to dominate the sociopolitical domain. As the titles suggest, terror and adoration are the only two feelings emanating from such a master/beloved duality. Neither of these extreme affects, however, is conducive to nation-building because one relies on paralyzing terror, the other on undeserving adoration of the leader, both canceling the role of rational judgment and individuals in the choice of national leadership. From his diasporic standpoint, Wadi' recalls past events and is able to reflect critically on a more innocent time, during his childhood, that predates his acculturation to power paradigms. He fondly remembers Ayyub, his childhood friend, who attempted to chart a peaceful space of his own, outside the militias' killing machine, and yet was obliterated by the same violent modalities he despised (142). Furthermore, Wadi' laments his compatriots' "interrupted knowledge" of their own warring history, their inability to escape the repetitive maser/slave paradigms and to benefit from collective modes of national remembrance (124–25). Without this synthesizing approach to history and national memory, Barakat warns, one runs the risk of loitering in exile's airports, waiting for eternity, for a happy closure to "an impossible novel" (191), and for a homeland that increasingly grows out of reach.

7

Border Crossings

Cultural Collisions and Reconciliation
in Hanan al-Shaykh's *Only in London*

Innaha London ya 'Azizi (2001) (*Only in London*, 2002), the product of
Hanan al-Shaykh's decades-long residence in London, is her attempt to
examine the possibilities and difficulties of mapping out a hyphenated
Arab identity at the liminal seams of diaspora. Shortlisted for the Independent Foreign Fiction Prize in 2002, the novel explores the negotiations
between identity's fixity and changeability, borders and borderlands, difference and hybridity, ultimately demonstrating how, as Susan Friedman
puts it, "routes produce roots and routes return to roots" (Friedman 1998,
167, 178). Unlike other diasporic narratives that introduced characters
yearning to return to their homelands, these particular émigrés are settled
physically in the diaspora but unsettled emotionally. They learn to negotiate the gains and losses of hyphenated identities, and to appreciate flexible citizenship, thereby forsaking homeland longings and engendering
new belongings articulated through the "dialogic" relationship between
roots and routes. In al-Shyakh's narrative, the diasporic Shahrazad celebrates mobility as she continues to find meaning in rediscovering familial
attachments, and in unearthing cultural artifacts that connect dynamic
borders of the homeland and the diaspora.

The novel depicts the lives of three Arab individuals: the British-Iraqi
Lamis, the Moroccan Amira (originally Habiba), and the Lebanese closeted homosexual Samir. These characters are leaving frustrated projects of
a personal and financial nature behind in Dubai, heading to London with
dreams of resettling and making a fresh start. Amira, who usually sells her

escort services to Arab men on Edgware Road in London, is disappointed at the knowledge that her services in Dubai are no longer needed because of the competition of blond and skinny Russian women entertainers. The transvestite Samir leaves a wife and five kids behind, and hopes that in London he can finally be free to come out of the closet. Nicholas, the British citizen, is the only one whose trip from Dubai culminated in success and satisfaction after he brokered the sale of rare Indian artifacts to a wealthy sheikh in Oman. But the novel's portrayal of how "routes produce roots" centers on the story of Lamis. Following her divorce from a wealthy Iraqi husband in London, whom she was forced to marry at a young age, Lamis had returned to Dubai to live with her immigrant parents and to start a dried flower arrangement business. However, after facing the trouble of having her shipment of dried poppies confiscated as contraband at the emirate customs' office, Lamis abandons the whole project of replanting her roots in the Arab world and returns to London. Most of the Arab characters in the novel have gone to London to seek freedom: from abject poverty (Amira as well as her Egyptian dancer friend Nahid), destructive wars in their home countries (Lamis), or restrictive sexual norms (Samir). However, this imagined freedom is crushed when the characters fail to escape from the Arab internal/British external, minority/majority cultural paradigms that lock their identities in the fixed molds they initially sought to demolish. Notwithstanding the book's focus on the characters' lives in the diaspora, the novel opens with its major characters suspended between heaven and earth in a turbulent plane heading from Dubai to London, thereby emphasizing the troublesome Arab world they left behind and the uncertainties awaiting them in the diaspora, the fictitious and divisive nature of borders, and ultimately the characters' desire to soar beyond them.

Crossing Ethnic Borders

After her divorce, Lamis embarks on a mission of self-actualization that involves opening the door to the London that "her ex-husband and his mother had closed . . . in her face" (Al-Shaykh 2002, 23). Her plan for accomplishing this drastic affiliation shift involves immersing herself fully in everything English while simultaneously cutting off her Arabic attributes. Emphatically she declares, "This is going to become my country. I've stopped living a temporary life" (19). She devises a long to-do list, intending not only to secure a job and her own apartment, in order to ensure her financial and personal independence, but to "learn English properly," "make friends with some English people," totally abandon Arabic food, and "stop wearing black kohl on [her] eyes" in order to achieve total assimilation into English culture (19). This drastic departure from her Arabic heritage is a double-edged sword: although it promises a transformation akin to that of "a snake shedding its skin," it also comes with the insecure feeling of vulnerability and nakedness, for "without kohl [Lamis's] eyes were naked" (20). Stripping the layers of her Arab identity proves to be a painful process articulated most explicitly during her English accent lessons. Lamis's English teacher warns that the price of abandoning her mother tongue would be noticeable not only in changes in her pronunciation, but also deep within her personality as well (53). However Lamis is determined to proceed with her assimilation project as she unequivocally declares that London, rather than Iraq, which she left when she was twelve years old, is indeed her "first home" (53). With this goal in mind, Lamis starts a regimented English course bent on taming her tongue and cleansing her memories of Arabic attachments, including Arab friends, places, and even food. The teacher's orders are that Lamis should find English friends and "keep away from anything Arab, even in [her] mind. [She] should stop eating Arab dishes, because subconsciously [she will] be saying their names" (54). Lamis follows these rigid rules with moderate success; however, her frustration builds up at the insistence of the teacher that, after leaving her class, she should not even "think one sentence in Arabic" (179). The experience of divorcing Arabic words, food, memories, and even her son's name from her mind proves to be excruciating. Acting as a chameleon is not without its dangers, as the experience of losing one's skin, of being exposed, defenseless, is excruciatingly painful. Increasingly this forced decontamination of the Arab within threatens her own existence every time she is banned from uttering her name or that of her son, whose name, Khalid, with the guttural sound "kh," is unmistakably Arab. Tearfully Lamis confesses to her teacher, "my memory's all in Arabic. As if I'm a parrot. Don't parrots ever lose their memories?" (180). Lamis's impassioned plea identifies the inherent danger of dissociating the diasporic subject from his/her homeland longings and belongings, of erasing the recurrent memories that will inevitably lead to the symbolic dismembering of the immigrant body. It is not surprising, then, that the English tutoring sessions resemble a "torture chamber" where all of her five senses are assaulted as "the English teacher hurls one whip after another on her mouth, ears, larynx, eyes, and nose" (Al-Shaykh 2001, 265). Interestingly this passage, which addresses the forced dismemberment of the racial gendered body forced to conform to the dominant English culture, is missing from the English translation of the novel. By changing her physical appearance to conform to diasporic foreign dimensions, the immigrant body demonstrates the problems of its containment and of performing majority-style citizenship on its racialized and gendered terrain. As a result of this exclusionary practice, the desired citizenship in this culture becomes a mirage, both untenable and oppressive. For example, the English teacher's insistence on suppressing Lamis's childhood memories backfires when one of the most pronounced of Arabic letters, the *R*, returns with a vengeance. It is significant that, in Lamis's imagination, the letter *R* is characterized as a child running wild in the fields of her memories. "It is the 'r' thought Lamis. I have to stop it from jumping on my tongue like a child jumping over a rope. I should make it stay back in the darkness of my mouth, lay it down as if I was preparing it for sleep. But it catches me unawares and runs off like a thief afraid of the barking dog" (Al-Shaykh 2002, 94). Indeed, Lamis's attempts to reinvent the way she speaks, dresses, and wears her makeup eventually lead to her cultural stripping, to a state of nakedness and absolute vulnerability—one that she initially feared upon abandoning her traditional kohl and with it her Arab heritage.

Lamis's difficulty in coming to terms with the strict British pronunciation rules of the English language finds its echo in the disappointing experience of attempting to make English friends. At a party in Nicholas's house, she attempts to engage in meaningful conversations with some of his British friends. However, she becomes frustrated on discovering that most of them are interested in her as the token Iraqi refugee whose persona and narrative are expected to comply with their preconceived models of Arab identity. For example, when she tells one interlocutor that her migration to London was a response not to Saddam Hussein's oppressive regime, but rather to her arranged marriage to a wealthy Iraqi, he loses interest in maintaining the conversation. Another guest speaks to her in classical *FusHa* Arabic, and even corrects her own Arabic grammar as he proceeds to ask about the number of Iraqi immigrants in London (Al-Shaykh 2001, 227). Ironically, Lamis discovers that she has to play into their orientalist perception of Iraq in order to maintain their interest. Performing the token Iraqi role, "Lamis felt like a geography book and history book rolled into one. A thought crept into her mind and nudged her increasingly low self-esteem into the abyss: Nicholas thinks of me in the way these people do," she laments (Al-Shaykh 2002, 154). As her ethnicity is reduced to a flattened map that the English can draw, control, and decipher per their specifications, Lamis is stripped of any personal dimensions and feels "as if a television screen had been installed between her and the other guests: they were the viewers and she was the correspondent from Iraq, not there to be talked to or argued with but to deliver information" (155). Their exotic view of her, as if on "a television screen," inhibits dialogue and mutual connectivity. Despite these initial setbacks, Lamis "force(s) herself to try to construct a bridge between herself and them." However, after observing the ease with which Nicholas's ex-girlfriend, the Dutch Anita, takes charge of the conversation, her mediocre English pronunciation notwithstanding, Lamis concludes that her alienation from the mainstream culture has nothing to do with her mastery of the English language, but everything to do with the fact that she is not European. Frustrated, Lamis realizes that her quest to acquire an English identity is hindered by her inability to assimilate into the English culture. In desperation, "Lamis found herself suddenly wanting very much to be confident and European" (158), as she mistakably thinks, at that point in the narrative, that to assimilate into the British society, to effectively cross the boundaries of ethnicity, one has to leave one's own cultural identity behind.

Amira's boundary crossing is similarly doomed to failure. Amira had first come to London to escape from abject poverty and familial, sexual exploitation in her native Morocco. With no education or financial security to rely on, she has been forced to lead a life of prostitution in the Arabic ghetto of London's Edgware Street. As she approaches middle age, she is acutely aware of her weight increase, of her dwindling list of clients, and ultimately of her dire need to reinvent herself. Although she has serviced Arab clients in the past, her upward mobility project would involve leaving "'little Arabia' as the English call Edgware Road," and living in "the real London" of Bayswater Road in the midst of the Hyde Park and Marble Arch districts (34). Consequently, Amira's transformation involves crossing class boundaries as she decides to impersonate the character of a Gulf princess to lure high-end clients who harbor the fantasy of sleeping with an Arab princess. Amira's plan is based on her belief in the permeability of identity borders in the diaspora as opposed to their rigid parameters back in the homeland. For in the diaspora, "nobody asked princesses for their identity documents. Everything was possible when you were abroad. You could recreate yourself with a name and parents of your own choosing" (113–14). The fact that she is cut off from her poor familial roots, with no social system to dispute her claimed royal ancestry in the diaspora, means that she can perform flexible identity transformation and appear "quite authentic" in her ruse (113). Her masquerade is complete with the deployment of the Western Cinderella fairy tale model, the hiring of three female assistants to act as her entourage, and a driver. In her attempt to convince the girls to join her, Amira tells each girl, "Right, Cinderella. I'm not promising to help you marry Prince Charming, but I'll show you the way to his wallet, on condition that you listen to what I say, do as I tell you, and keep it a secret." So Amira the fairy godmother, who was also Amira the Princess, hired the English driver instead of the dog-coachman, a Rolls-Royce in place of the pumpkin, and three companions as her retinue rather than coach horses (114–15). This fictitious coupling between Amira/Cinderella and Amira/the Arab princess has to come to an end when, after a short period of success at her ruse, Amira is beaten brutally by the bodyguard of a real prince offended by the way she has dishonored his family name. Despite Amira's belief that the diaspora would be the perfect ground for transgressing the limitations of her impoverished background, her own perception of what constitutes a truly Arab and/or English identity betrays the barriers that she was not able to transcend, for she is guilty of reinforcing the same stereotypes that she sought to demolish. For example, upon hiring a driver, she insists on his possession of what she considers a "pure" English identity that, in her estimation, excludes all other ethnicities. With great conviction, she demands, "I want an English driver. Not Indian English, Arab English, African English, Chinese English, Polish English, Scots English or Irish English. English one hundred per cent with a cap and jacket" (114). Amira's driver preference reveals the impossibility of her own attaining such an identity. Ironically, Amira's belief in the exclusivity of English identity hinders its attainment despite her several attempts to be sheltered under its coveted umbrella.

The fates of Amira and Lamis pose the dilemma of diasporic identity affiliations built on exclusive mimicry of the dominant culture. The Arabic Shahrazad may take on Cinderella's identity, but the proposed transformation, as in Amira's impersonation of a Saudi princess identity or Lamis's adoption of an exclusive English identity, remains illusory at best because it is not built on a true dialogue between the two cultures, but rather on superficial changes springing from the redeployment of colonialist conceptions of self and Other (114–15). This masquerade has already proved ineffective for Lamis, whose ex-mother-in-law's recounting of an Arabic version of the Cinderella story is a constant reminder of Lamis's inability to leave her poor background behind. It offers a concrete proof of the transient and shifting parameters of identity transformation, particularly if it does not stay grounded in its cultural roots (122). This illusory aspect of the transformation rings particularly true in Amira's case. Indeed, this is no ordinary fairy tale with foreign identities fractured to the core by exclusionary binary oppositions, thereby adding to the dilemma of their othering (32, 113). Samir will similarly fall hostage to essentialist constructions of blond ambition and supreme Anglicized identity. Lamis alone will be able to go beyond these restrictive identity binaries, but not before she fully learns what is entailed by the crossing of borders.

Crossing Gender and Sexual Borders

In one of her interviews, al-Shaykh states that in *Only in London* she meant to talk about "a society which curbs freedoms to the extent that even after departing from it, its citizens are still haunted with confusion and schizophrenia" (al-Abtah 2004). Her statement highlights the persistent, traumatic haunting of the homeland state's repression, and the potential for what James Clifford calls the construction of a "disaggregated," "dia-sporized," identity (Clifford 1997, 271). Both the comic and catastrophic aspects of such an identity are portrayed in the character of Samir as he attempts to cross the boundaries of gender.

The reader first encounters Samir on the plane in the opening scene along with the other three characters: Lamis, Nicholas, and Amira. Imme-diately both comical and catastrophic sides of his persona are evident as he frantically searches for some sleeping pills to appease a smuggled monkey (Cappuccino) whom he was fooled into transporting illegally across borders for financial gain. The monkey that he hid in a carry-on basket is symbolic of his closeted homosexuality—the real reason behind Samir's migration to London. In London Samir believes that he can prac-tice his homosexuality openly and be free to cross-dress and sleep with blond British youths without any societal reprisal. To Samir, "London was freedom. It was your right to do anything, any time. You didn't need to undergo a devastating war in order to be freed to do what you wanted, and when you did do what you wanted, you didn't have to feel guilty or embar-rassed, and start leading a double life and ultimately end up frustrated. God must have started up the war in Lebanon so that people would leave him in peace, Samir had thought" (Al-Shaykh 2002, 149). In Lebanon Samir's transvestitism led his mother to send him to a mental institution twice during his childhood. Ironically, it took a civil war for Samir to wear what he wanted once more, "telling his wife that if he disguised himself as a woman he could avoid trouble at checkpoints and buy bread more quickly" (149). The juxtaposition of the Lebanese Civil War's traumatic atrocities to the comical aspects of Samir's transvestitism (purple boa and red boots) highlights the conflicted, schizophrenic nature of his diasporic existence, particularly as it intersects with his repressed sexuality. Despite the attempt to escape from his restrictive Arabic background, his limited knowledge of English prevents him from forging true sentimental homo-erotic relationships with his British partners. Sadly, Samir is readily aware of this estrangement as he laments the loss of "true love" and the intimate connections he had forged back in Lebanon, and compares them with the cold, business transactions conducted with the English youths: "this was true love, not blond hair or blue eyes" (237). Furthermore, this language deficiency creates a multitude of farcical instances of semantic failures and miscommunication between Samir and his prospective clients (90–93, 247), thereby forcing him to further restrict himself to the ghettoized Arab district of Edgware Road.

Like Samir in his attempted gender border crossing, Lamis believes that her divorce gives her the license to embark on a journey of self-realization and sexual fulfillment. In the past, she had come to know her beauty and her sense of self through seeing her reflection in other people's eyes. However, she never had a true connection to her real self or body. For example, as a child, Lamis often looked at her reflection through different bodies of water and mirrors, only to be discouraged by her maternal grandmother, who warned her that if she continued with this narcissistic preoccupation, the looking glass would snatch her soul away (21). After she meets the English Nicholas, she continues to see herself through his eyes, as she discovers sexual ecstasy, body awareness, and fulfillment via his mediation. For the first time in her life, however, Lamis is encouraged to explore her body and reflection in "the mirror of reality": "'Oh, there is nothing to hide, nothing.' And, as if for the first time since she'd been wrapped in a blanket as a newborn infant, she found herself standing completely naked in front of the mirror of reality—Nicholas—and feeling like a child who, upon seeing herself for the first time, becomes aware only by degrees, with a few moments of doubt and fear, that the image in the mirror is really her" (127). During the span of their relationship, Lamis's body blossoms, its existence affirmed through her awareness of its sensual awakening. Her exhilaration at having united with her forgotten body prompts her to be uninhibited, even articulating its presence in front of "Anita's camera lens and enjoying what it demanded of her, fascinated by this revealing of her body in its natural state, not wanting to arouse or be aroused, but alive, moving, sitting, uncovered" (194). Her husband and family had never acknowledged the presence of her body. Consequently Lamis comes to associate her sexual liberation with embracing the English and denial of the Arabic sides of her identity.

For example when Lamis wants to make love to Nicholas, she is motivated by her desire to get close to everything English, to inhale "the English smell" intimately (102). With Nicholas she was able to experience her first orgasm, as she fantasizes that she is Cinderella who will be whisked by the English prince charming from her Arabic environment (103). Unfortunately, Lamis's reflection in Nicholas's "mirror of reality" seems to be distorted, in true Lacanian fashion,[1] by his own biased *houri*/harem view of Arab women, the equivalent of the Western virgin/vamp binary. Despite his professed knowledge of and empathy with Arabic culture and Islamic artifacts (82), Nicholas's perception of Arab women as "chameleon-like" reflects his own orientalizing gaze, to which myopic view he remains hostage. His inability to understand how Arab women could be uncovered and fasting at the same time (46–47) suggests that Nicholas is in need of his own border crossing. Nicholas's fascination with Lamis stems from his static image of the "oriental" woman: exotic, timid, and docile. For that reason, when Lamis demands and insists on her sexual satisfaction, he walks out enraged, yelling, "you're like an animal . . . Stop it! Stop it!" (203). This belief in the so-called "bestial" nature of Arabs is shared by Stanley (Nahid's English husband), who protests the emaciated state of Egyptian donkeys by telling his wife, "you're savages" (220). When Lamis refuses to perform the function of the docile sexual object and insists on her sexual agency, Nicholas turns her into the threatening, emasculating vamp as demonstrated in a succession of drawings superimposing her face on his sketches of the Devedasis women in the infamous southern Indian temple of Khajuraho (242), and on a carnivorous "Venus flytrap" plant. With shock Lamis examines the picture that he drew of her:

> It was a drawing done by Nicholas of a woman's face in profile, a cone-shaped cactus ending in a strange, almost terrifying green flower with its mouth open greedily: a Venus flytrap. She picked out the drawing and looked at it with a shock of recognition. It was her face. She froze; the woman stared back with a hard expression in her eyes. A man's penis

---

1. For a thorough overview of Jacques Lacan's "mirror stage" theory in terms of its relationship to the child's psychological development of selfhood, see Lacan 1977.

extended from her head round into her mouth and the face had swal-
lowed most of it. Lamis threw the drawing down and ran out of the
room, but it pursued her. (210)

In her quest for sexual freedom, Lamis's sexuality appears to be threatening to Nicholas in a manner not so dissimilar from Arab men's apprehension toward the excessive display of female sexuality. When she refuses
to live up to his romanticized image of Arab women's timidity, Nicholas
portrays her as "a Venus flytrap," capable of emasculating him with her
vagina dentate attributes. Gayatri Spivak reminds us that this monstrous
representation of the "native informant" emerges from an imperialist
stance intent on constructing the body of the "Third World Woman" as a
static signifier (Spivak 2009, 375–77). Not surprisingly, Lamis's discovery
of Nicholas's patriarchal and orientalist viewpoints prompts her to strip
Nicholas of his intermediary role despite his subsequent apologetic admission that the Venus flytrap is "a shy plant" and not an "evil carnivore" after
all (271). Ultimately, the static vagina dentate motif, also seen in autobiographical fictions I discussed in chapter 3, joins that of Shahrazad and the
female buried infant (maw'udah) as recurring images in Arab women's
diasporic literature—vestiges denoting the intersection of the threat of
women's sexuality with that of their discourse and mobility.

In ascribing this intermediary role to Nicholas, al-Shaykh joins the
ranks of her fellow diaspora women writers in this study, such as Samman,
Na'na', and al-Neimi, whose heroines are initially aligned with foreign
Others on their way to personal fulfillment, later surpassing those Others as they acquire full personal and political agency. The question of the
foreign Other's mediation between the heroine and her multiple cultural
positionalities is posed earlier in *Only in London* when Lamis views the
English gynecologist as the liaison between her body and her husband's.
She reflects on how the doctor's "English hand plunging inside her, acting
as a mediator between her, her offspring and her husband" (Al-Shaykh
2002, 17), was able to forge a connection to her body in ways that her husband could not. Likewise Nicholas becomes the medium between Lamis
and the carnal knowledge of her body. However, as she acquires agency at
the end of the novel, Lamis no longer needs a foreign male's mediation to

connect her body to its cultural roots. Like other diaspora characters such as Samman's Zein, Na'na's Nadia, and al-Neimi's unnamed heroine (discussed in chapter 8), Lamis is able to shed the guardianship of the foreign instructor/lover as well as the haunting of past ghosts. As she negotiates the thorny boundaries between her Arabic and English identities, Lamis finally succeeds in going beyond Nicholas's guardianship. She will come to see Nicholas as the bridge that connects her with London and Oman, but it is up to her to transcend the static identity definitions of the Arab-English binary and to start the journey of reconnecting with Arab roots on her own terms.

Stretching Identity Borders

The defining moment for Lamis's reintroduction to Arabic language and culture is her encounter with the text of a thirteenth-century manuscript in the "Oriental and India Office Collections" at the British Library. The textual body of the manuscript engenders her own cultural embodiment as she recognizes the letters with ease, feels the intergenerational connection with its writer, and comes to rediscover her affinity with Arabic language and ancestral heritage. The temporal and spatial separation of the manuscript from its Arab homeland reminds Lamis of her own estrangement, but also brings to mind her pride in Arab civilization, history, and the scholarly writings of her grandfather. She reflects,

> Although the manuscript was so old, reading the Arabic, she saw that the language was still as it had been hundreds of years ago: she read the sentences with the greatest of ease; her heart pounded with affection of her language. So it was true, then, the picture that they'd painted at school, of the way Arab civilization flourished in the past—here was a proof of its long history. She thought about the hands that had turned these pages, and felt a sharp bang of regret that, when she'd been in Dubai, she'd thought that being Arab was an obstacle in her life. (125)

Arab history is conjured up in the manuscript, resurrected like the maw'-udah from ancient tombs, diffusing and discrediting counter-orientalist

narratives that demonize Arabs, portraying them as subhuman. Unearthing this ancestral archive connects Lamis with her forgotten Arab heritage, fond childhood memories of her grandfather, and the importance of
writing as a trace to preserve cultural records. With affection she recalls
how, to safeguard himself from oblivion, her grandfather would recite
the following thirteenth-century verse taken from a Damascene manuscript: "My hand has written so many books; my hand will wither but the
books remain" (125). It is only after reconnecting with this forlorn Arabic
manuscript in the British Library that Lamis revises her original goals of
assimilating to the British culture. She still keeps rearing her son and finding love and a job as top priorities, but now she has serious reservations
about the need to speak English without an Arabic accent (194, 275–76).
Following the path of her grandfather and father, Lamis views the Arabic
language with their eyes. Quoting the poet Adonis, her father had stated,
"*The alphabet seemed to me like a homeless child with no place to live, even
though it was kept cased in a museum, and I began to follow it in its wanderings, so I could take it in my arms*" (227, italics in original). Increasingly,
she embraces aspects of the Arabic culture as she envelops Arabic letters
with her eyes and fingertips: "she held them affectionately, fingering the
words. Had she really once considered substituting these for others and
doing away with her heritage, no longer seeing, hearing or speaking, and
consequently ceasing to breathe?" (274–75). As Lamis touches the Arabic
words, the manuscript acquires a certain sense of corporality and connection to the feminine body that is seeking identity location, not unlike
the manuscript itself, despite its diasporic locale. Lamis's actions liberate
the subaltern body from its static identity positions imposed upon it by
both imperialist English and native postcolonial Arabs alike. Henceforth
her body is no longer the marker of postcolonial subjectivity; rather it
assumes its own agency, belonging, and multiple affiliations. Suddenly
she realizes that her earlier project of abandoning her Arabic identity and
language for the sake of an English one is a mirage because she cannot
escape the mold Londoners cast her into, nor can she erase her cultural
history and memory, both of which are exclusively Arabic. She recalls how
in one of his letters her father lamented the fact that, because of their war-
torn country, she had to "grow up without roots" (228). However, after the

reincorporation of the manuscript in Lamis's body, she embodies both her Arabic language and her culture. Consequently Lamis realizes the importance of not severing her linguistic and cultural roots, the value of memory recall and of making recurrent shuttle journeys back to the homeland.

However, the expatriate's return to sites of trauma at home is always fraught with danger. Lamis's father's story of eloping for fear of persecution during the Saddam era bespeaks the difficulty of tending the unhealed wound that reopens at every site of border crossing, the pain of their uprooted existence, and the challenges of living between borders, albeit in another Arab city such as Dubai (234). As I noted in chapter 1, this perpetual tension, according to Avatar Brah, defines "the *concept* of diaspora [which] places the discourse of 'home' and 'dispersion' in creative tension, *inscribing a homing desire while simultaneously critiquing discourse of fixed origins*" (Brah 1996, 193, italics in original). This tension generates anxiety and fear of return that may engender identity erasure or death.

Therefore Lamis's initial refusal to join Nicholas in Oman is not surprising, for it reveals the ingrained fear of return of many exiled Arab citizens. From previous personal misfortunes, they come to a realization that recrossing the impermeable borders of the homeland is a "terrifying experience," rife with danger (183). Likewise Lamis is "afraid to travel with [Nicholas], even as a tourist, to any Arab country" (184). Indeed, as her son Khalid often reminds her, she is afraid to shed her tortoise shell and live on the edge (215). The question of home and the dilemma of whether or not to return to it are closely related, as Avatar Brah suggests, to the "process of inclusion and exclusion," to the individual's "political and personal struggles over the social regulation of 'belonging,'" and ultimately to the tension between "roots and routes" (Brah 1996, 192). Indeed, Lamis's challenge is to adopt what Brah calls a "multi-axial locationality" (1996, 205) that would collapse the rigidity of the geopolitical, cultural borders in order to avail Lamis of the opportunity of recrossing in a shuttle-like movement of to/from—the equivalent of Friedman's "intercultural *fort/ da*," between the homeland and the diaspora (Friedman 1989, 154). In the context of the new diasporic consciousness that celebrates both negative and positive aspects of diaspora as well as the porous borders that facilitate multiple journeys and identities, home is redefined and its spatial limits stretched to include the new transnational citizen forever determined to claim roots via multiple routes and reinvigorated rhizomes. Toward the end of the novel, Lamis learns to stretch the edge of her comfort zone, of the dividing borders of both her home country and adoptive country, to be comfortable in assuming multiple identities and positionalities without relinquishing her Arabic heritage or any of her personal freedoms.

In so doing, she invokes the legacy and the shrewd example of Elissa, "the Phoenician princess who founded Carthage in spite of her brother's opposition. Like her, she wanted to stretch the boundaries. When Elissa's brother grudgingly granted Elissa a piece of land no bigger than an oxhide, Elissa asked her followers to stretch the fibers of skin lengthways and widthways, widthways and lengthways, until she'd finally outwitted her brother: her kingdom reached right to the seashore" (Al-Shaykh 2002, 55). Similarly, Lamis's ability to stretch the limits of her identity belonging mimics Elissa's success at creating a space of her own that originates in the homeland, but stretches beyond its borders to increase and enrich geopolitical and personal boundaries. This newly envisioned relationship to space follows Doreen Massey's "dynamic concept" of place that is "constructed out of a series of changing social relations, extending from the local to the global, which will always 'stretch beyond that "place" itself'" (quoted in Linda Anderson 2007, 272). In this sense, old roots are reinvigorated with rhizomatic horizontal and vertical affiliations, thereby celebrating the liminal spaces that enrich both sites. This "contrapuntal" condition defines the very essence of diasporic living in Edward Said's estimation, and gives it "positive" effervescence and constant renewable energy (Said 2000, 186). Similar to Said's reflections on the positive, "contrapuntal" living experience of the exile that affords a welcoming "plurality of vision" (Said 2000, 186), James Clifford views the "transnational networks" forged within and outside the homeland as a crucial unifying phenomenon of diasporic discourses. He argues that "diasporic discourses reflect the sense of being part of an ongoing transnational network that includes the homeland not as something simply left behind but as a place of attachment in a contrapuntal modernity" (Clifford 1997, 256). In this new articulation of diasporic experience, the center of the expatriate's experience shifts from the homeland to within each individual in his/her respective locales.

So citizenship becomes flexible, multidimensional, thereby stretching and erasing geographic borders. In this sense, to put it in Aihwa Ong's words, diasporic limits are stretched, manifesting themselves in "flexible citizenship" modalities (quoted in Clifford 1997, 257).

The process of decentering the concept of home and adopting a flexible citizenship mode of belonging necessarily leads to celebrating marginal spaces. In the past Lamis believed that living on the margins of two contrasting cultures was a negative state of lack; however, after serious soul searching involving answering questions related to the extent of her contribution to her new adopted place, "apart from [sheer] confusion," she realizes the positive potential of her liminal space (Al-Shaykh 2002, 262). Seeing London, her apartment, and the apartment of an old neighbor (Rose Dunn) anew from atop the British Telecom (BT) communication tower gives Lamis a bird's-eye view on the value of her diasporic locale and political role within it. She states, "Here, where I'm looking now, Rose Dunn is sitting with her stooped back, and I'm allowed to look: because I'm not from here. I can swagger about wherever I please. Like an eagle circling I can alight on any spot I choose and declare that this is where I'm going to settle down. Not like Rose Dunn who lives directly over the place where she was born" (263). Lamis comes to appreciate the value of her marginal locale, which guards her against fixity of geography and convictions, and affords her the mobility to be constantly on the move in a state of travel and flux. Unlike Rose Dunn, who has access to only one language and one place, Lamis is bilingual, and claims belonging to two cultures and multiple perspectives. From this privileged positioning, she welcomes both positive and negative dimensions of the diaspora, both gains attained in her adoptive country and the loss of her homeland. James Clifford argues convincingly that "diaspora consciousness is constituted both negatively and positively" (Clifford 1997, 256), hence it "lives loss and hope as a defining tension" (1997, 257). In the same manner Lamis comes to value the ability to dwell, to contribute to London, and also to depart, to travel back and forth at will between her adoptive country and the Arab world. Lamis's capacity to move freely *through* the borders that separate home from diaspora ultimately *transforms* them into hybrid sites of identity regeneration where both attachments and detachments are acknowledged and cherished.[2] From atop the BT tower, Lamis is able to reflect on her own life and to see herself from a different standpoint, from a detached, self-critical perspective. Invoking Virginia Woolf's *To the Lighthouse* (1927), she states, "the tower guides me like a lighthouse, as if I'm a lost ship" (263). At last she is able to position herself within London's spatial grid in a meaningful way, retaining her connection to both her Arab belongings and her English surroundings. Fortified with this detached perspective, "she saw herself in the bedroom, looking out at the tower, and looking back from the tower to the bedroom. There she was, a pebble stuck in midstream, no longer carried along by the current" (Al-Shaykh 2002, 265). Lamis's earlier confusion and exclusionary visions led her to paralysis and inaction. She comes to learn that fixity is to be guarded against, and fluidity of movement from/to the ever regenerative sites of home/diaspora, dwelling/travel through a constant process of attachment/detachment is what she needs to articulate her newly empowered diasporic consciousness.

As an expatriate Lamis has to learn, in Edward Said's words, how to achieve "independence and detachment by *working through* attachments, not by rejecting them" (Said 2000, 185, italics in original). *Only in London*'s ending suggests that those who heed this golden rule can negotiate a fulfilling existence in the "interstitial space" between home and diaspora (Bhabha 1994), whereas those who insist on fixity end up in perpetual loss. Unlike Lamis, who was able to create a fluid balance between fixity and flux, the other characters insist on adopting an unyielding identity positioning, thereby failing to achieve this equilibrium. The drastic solutions based on the denial of one's identity have catastrophic endings for Amira, Samir, and Nahid. Amira's masquerade as a Saudi princess ends up in bodily violence at the hands of the prince's bodyguard. Likewise Samir's obsession with transient sexual encounters with English blond youths

2. In her definition of the term *diaspora*, Avatar Brah invokes both the Greek origin of the word *dia* meaning "through," and *speirein* meaning "scatter," as well as the *Webster's Dictionary* definition to conclude that the term *diaspora* refers both to a "dispersion from" and to "multiple journeys" (Brah 1996, 181). For more on the relation of this definition to the contemporary development of the concept of diaspora, see Brah 1996, 178–210.

culminates in the loss of his compass and monkey, Cappuccino, the source of his livelihood as an entertainer (Al-Shaykh 2002, 250). Finally, Nahid's marginal existence as a prostitute in London leads her to a series of familial rejections. Her alienation is complete when, even after her death, the English soil of her adoptive country spits her body out of the grave because of the pouring rain "as if God doesn't want to take Nahid back" (240). However, for Lamis, the plot completes its circular motion in the closing scene as the reader sees her sitting peacefully inside an aircraft returning to the Gulf of Oman. However, this circular journey is by no means a repetitive, Sisyphean task, for this new Lamis is comfortable with her Arabic roots and confident of her total control of her routes. In her new way of belonging both to London and to the Arab world, Lamis discovers the value of unearthing and holding on to her culture's archives. She is determined not to let her past be divorced from her present; rather, "the past [can hold] the present in its grasp" (266), and she can continue the journey of self-discovery, wandering in perfect harmony and wonderment.

8

Unearthing the Archives, Inscribing Unspeakable Secrets

Salwa al-Neimi's *The Book of Secrets,*
The Proof of the Honey, and Poetry Collections

Like most of her contemporary diaspora women writers, Salwa al-Neimi straddles the forever elusive line between homeland and diaspora, past and present, belonging and vagrancy. A poet recently turned novelist, she shares the journalistic experience of al-Shaykh, Barakat, Naʿnaʿ, and Samman; their insistence on writing in Arabic despite their diasporic locals; and their aspirations for a cultural change in the Arab world resulting from a sociopolitical deconstructive project. Increasingly, this dissecting project entails a critical analysis of the present but also an excavation of the past to identify traumatic moments that should be revisited and triumphant ones that should be resurrected. In this spirit, the return to the literary and folkloric tradition signals contemporary Arab writers' intent to access and listen to the historical and literary archives. It is an attempt to be both a "producer as well as a consumer" in the "global political economy of knowledge" (Prasad 1992, 59).

In al-Neimi's poetry and prose, unearthing the feminine body of the maw'udah and her erased verbal expression inevitably leads to the deployment of a revitalized Shahrazad trope, and to the resurrection of a more secure premodern period worth harkening back to. By engaging her Arab local and Western global interlocutors in what Gayatari Spivak calls a "planetary" discussion (Spivak 2003, 73), al-Neimi manages to dispel Middle Eastern and Western stereotypes that historically contributed to the erasure of Arab women's bodies and discourse. The collectivity of al-Neimi's heroines, both in her short-story collection *The Book of Secrets* (*Kitab al-Asrar*, 1994, which has not been published in English), and in *The Proof of the Honey* (2009), set out to transform Shahrazad's authorial role. They are intent on shattering the circle of oral or "secretive writing," thereby regaining Shahrazad's agency and authorship (Al-Neimi 1994, 95). For example, in her short-story collection al-Neimi offers different vignettes of a woman's life during early adolescence and middle-aged womanhood, reflecting in the process on controversial topics such as: abortion, honor killing, the institution of marriage, Arab women's political agency or lack thereof in their own cultural liberation project, and issues pertaining to their authorship.

Not surprisingly, and in congruence with the rest of the Arab writers in this book, the intersection between women's procreation and literary creativity is central to the first story of *The Book of Secrets* entitled "Abdomen," thereby highlighting tradition's stifling effect on both activities. The scene opens in a dark room as the nameless heroine lies, eyes wide open, bleeding and awaiting the successful completion of her illegal abortion operation. Through a collage of past and present events, the reader follows the process through which the heroine had an abortion-inducing plant inserted into her womb, by a shady doctor, in order to get rid of an out-of-wedlock pregnancy. The heroine's own seeping blood reminds her of another nameless Bedouin woman slain by her brother in an honor-killing ritual intended to cleanse the family's honor after her illegitimate pregnancy. The nameless heroine admits that, although no one seems to remember the name of this unfortunate girl, she "used to name, to see, and to hide her in the heart of [the heroine's] own secretive stories" (Al-Neimi 1994, 10). The issue of *"wa'd al-fadhiha"* (burying the scandal) takes central stage, acts as a stark reminder of the wa'd motif, as the connection between woman's sexuality and her erased identity and forgotten story is solidified (14). Underscoring the connection between the heroine's spilt blood and her hidden story, the heroine states, "This is my blood. I stretch my hand and hold the drops before they fall on the sanitary towel. I will catch them in my finger and with them write my name on my forehead. I may even write dates and numbers to commemorate this historical day" (16; all translations from stories and poems not published in English are mine). The protagonist's inability to bring forth a living fetus and to expose the duplicity of traditions as they relate to women's sexuality is indirectly related to her exclusion from public speech and the writing realms. Historically, female writers' lack of access to traditional cultural means of creativity forced them, in Susan Gubar's estimation, "to experience their own bodies as the only available medium for their art." Thus certain metaphors often associated with the feminine body, such as wounding and bleeding, become salient signifiers for the way through which a female artist experiences her own creativity, literally, as "a painful wounding," and as "bleeding into print" (Gubar 1982, 78). The "Abdomen" heroine's act of writing her name on her forehead with her aborted illegitimate fetus's blood delineates women writers' initial need to express taboos with their blood. More important, as the Palestinian poet Laila al-Saih reminds us, it bespeaks the urgency to "transfigure[e] blood into ink" (cooke and Rustomji-Kerns 1994, xxi, 16). There is an acute necessity to revisit the crying wound, the traumatic site of honor killing, burial, and erasure in order to transform death into life, pain into pleasure, and women's unrecognized, "illegitimate" writing into the legitimate public space that avails them of the opportunity to pen their own history.

Indeed, revisiting the trope of the confined, consumed feminine body is a crucial departure point for al-Neimi, who views its systematic confinement as symptomatic of the cultural and political erasure that plagued and continues to contaminate contemporary Arab societies. For that reason, invoking the maw'udah's buried infant trope in her poetry collection *Ajdadi al-Qatalah* (2001) (*My Murderous Ancestors*) and the image of honor killing in *The Book of Secrets* functions in Paul Connerton's estimation as "acts of transfer" (1989, 39), as necessary steps in the present on the path of revisiting traumatic sites of the ancestral past, so as to contest and to overcome their debilitating effects. For example, the issue of the consumption of the female body is addressed at the beginning of the aforementioned poetry collection in a poem surprisingly entitled "Happiness" in which she declares, "Every wolf I dreamt of / Devoured me" (2001, 7). This short poem highlights the importance of dreams, of recurring nightmares, and the haunting of both male and female ancestors. In her poetic repertoire, al-Neimi distinguishes between the haunting tactics of male

versus female ancestors. For instance, male ancestors enact their haunting in the persistence of their suffocating traditions, while female ancestors haunt to remind the female subject of their forgotten story, to act as
traces of the erased female body. Despite the author's temporal and spatial
distance from the Middle Eastern locale of her ancestors, their possession
of her mind and body continues unabated. Her liberal and romantic diasporic site of Paris cannot offer much relief when she is tormented by the
following discovery: "Under my bed / A graveyard!" (2001, 78). Her initial
reaction is that of surprise and bewilderment: "Why do the corpses keep
on coming, / Granting me their gifts," she asks (74). However, the initial
apprehension soon dissipates into an acceptance of this unique gift: the
ability to converse with the ancestors. As a result of this interaction, the
female subject learns how to embrace the chance to be an instrument of
change, a model for future generations. Therefore the focus of her mission
becomes the change that the ancestral female spirits inspire her to com-
mence. Consequently, the rest of this poem calls for changing the present
of the embattled women back in the homeland. Al-Neimi asserts,

> I left them behind
> Swallowing their screams and their loaf of degradation
> (Won't they ever satisfy their hunger?)
> I dance around the fires of their history
> Like them, defeated.
> My words explode,
> A bomb
> And they fly around me like shrapnel
>
> In my dream, my wounds heal and I stay without their traces
> (I stay without history!)
> The wound is healed with words,
> The wound reopens with words,
> The story never materializes into a story unless we proceed to tell it.
>   (74–75)

The possibility of eliminating all the traces of the wounds in the diaspora,
of "build[ing] new countries for [her]self" without harkening back to the

shrieking voices of her female ancestors is not a feasible option (73). Hence there arises a simultaneous desire to heal and to reopen the wound for fear that its healing will erase the trace of women's struggle, thereby keeping younger women from realizing the history of the older generations' plight. Revisiting the wound through narration ensures the everlasting presence of the trace, its value for posterity as a reminder to never again allow restrictive social norms to suffocate feminine expressions.

Throughout her literary corpus, al-Neimi does not single out men for their part in women's subjugation; rather she places some of the responsibility on women as well. In a manner similar to Ghada Samman's "Guards of Silence" segment in *The Impossible Novel* (chapter 3) and to Reem's epiphanies in *The Square Moon*'s "Thirty Years of Bees" (chapter 4), elderly women are portrayed as the staunch guardians of tradition. Similarly, in *The Book of Secrets* the heroine's mother emerges as one of these traditional mothers who indoctrinate their girls to restrictive, societal roles. For that reason, the heroine's physical pushing of her mother in the story entitled "I Used to Resemble You" represents a symbolic refusal of these inherited values. Furthermore, her poem "Commandments" in *My Murderous Ancestors* is an important example bespeaking her rejection of this confinement. In a surprising sociolinguistic twist, al-Neimi associates the prohibitions on women's expression with the grammatology of the Arabic language (the language of the Father) and with her mother's complacency in enforcing conventional, restrictive rules. She states,

> As they taught me,
> I color rivers blue and valleys green,
> As they taught me,
> I use the nominative case with the subject, the accusative case with the
>   object,
> And the genitive case with the object of prepositions,
> As they taught me,
> I speak in a hushed voice,
> (And it would even be better if I never speak)
> As they taught me,
> I construct my life in the passive tense,
> As [she] taught me! (Al-Neimi 2001, 21)

The transfer of the accusatory finger in the refrain from the patriarchal, plural masculine "they" to the matriarchal, singular feminine "she" is an acknowledgment of the role some matriarchs have played in keeping the restrictive traditional values alive. Hence it is necessary to acknowledge the wound caused not just by patriarchy, but also by a certain brand of matriarchy that is in compliance with the status quo. In the abovementioned story, the daughter references the importance of revisiting childhood wounds before any healing can take place. She tells her mother, "I do not want you to die before realizing the depth of the wound that I learnt to forget, even as it seeps death into my being. A wound that I hid carefully so that you won't see it even in a moment of weakness" (Al-Neimi 1994, 87). Once reconciliation is accomplished, however, the heroine is encouraged to go past the wound's trauma. Only the fading memory of the scar, its trace, remains. For that reason, the new generation of women, represented in the young daughter of the heroine, only bears the slightest of genetic associations with their mothers or grandmothers. Luckily they do not resemble their foremothers in their life history, for they stand to have a better future than their predecessors. The heroine of "I Used to Resemble You" asserts, "the resemblance stops here. I want it to stop here. I hold my daughter's hand. She does not resemble me. She did not meet you, nor did you her. As I embrace her, I smell her fragrance. I tell her beautiful stories about her distant grandmother in her Damascene home. 'You have my mother's scent,' I tell her as I embrace and breathe in her smell. Surprised, she laughs. My daughter does not resemble me, she did not meet you, nor did you her, she has your scent and I inhale it within" (91). The process of memory and rememory are at work here in the allusion to the scent metaphor. Fortunately, the new generation of women is capable of transcending all the impediments that caused their foremothers to stumble. Maternal memories of past oppression linger as a scent, but luckily the daughters do not have to deal with their oppressive presence.

The process of transposing personal memories of violence onto the map of cultural memory, despite acts of deliberate forgetting, has a unifying effect, for it brings about a welcome future reconciliation. In a poem entitled "Wall" from her collection *Inna 'Ataynaka* (2004) (*We Bequeathed unto You*, not published in English), al-Neimi describes the potential healing and unifying dynamic of the process of forgetfulness and memory recall in this manner: "I live with forgetfulness / and write from memory / Does the poem unite me?" (2004, 7) This interplay of memory and forgetfulness, of presence and absence, is essential to the reconstruction of adult identity in diaspora, to revisiting childhood sites of pain and empowerment. The painful and beneficial aspect of memory recall is further highlighted in a poem called "Dr. Hyde" from al-Neimi's poetry collection *Dhahaba Alladhina Uhibbuhum* (1999) (*Gone Are the Ones I Love*, not published in English). Memory, in this poem, is viewed as a burden, as an unwanted inheritance among generations of women who accepted their conventional role as the sacrificial lamb. However, revisiting the traumatic site of women's bodily consumption helps the protagonist to understand the process of their ostracism from the religious and the written domains, and further propels them to shun their Christ-like sacrificial role. She states,

> I came from there,
> Carrying my memory on my back, as an African woman holding her
>   baby (I thought that I would uproot it easily like a loose baby
>   tooth.)
> Turn the light on and look at me:
> Under my skull,
> are two crossed bones.
> . . . .
> I came from there,
> Generations of women reside in me,
> Granddaughters, mothers, and grandmothers,
> Break like a tree trunk,
> under the wood-cutter's blows.
>
> I came from there,
> Where childhood was,
> And bread was a tree.
> I swallow my mother's sacrifice:
> This is my body; eat it.
> This is my blood; drink it.

My father gives allegiance to his seventh Imam in a corridor,
And I do not belong to this world.

When night falls,
My words breed like stars.
They alone are what I was given for a body,
(And what I have accepted.) (1999, 16–18)

It is interesting to see that al-Neimi, who is the product of a Christian mother and a Muslim Isma'ili father, is equally critical of women's sacrificial roles in both religions. She does not shy away from using both Christian and Muslim scriptural images and phrases in order to critique as well as to reconstruct new feminine roles. The word "there" in the verse "I came from there" indicates not just the spatial site, but the symbolic site of women's cultural traumas of physical and literary wa'd as well. Female survivors must temporally and physically transgress this painful memory. The focus is on the transformative value of women's words in redeeming their erased physical and textual body, and on carving their own feminine discourse within religious hermeneutics.

Similar to her association with memory, a woman's relationship to her body is perceived as a "burden" as well. Al-Neimi reflects on the way her heroine in "A Nap" experiences her body, stating, "I am still afraid of my body, I carry it as a burden upon burden" (1994, 41). Once again the last phrase, "*'ab'an 'ala abi'*" (burden upon burden) is reminiscent of the Qur'anic expression "*wahnun 'la wahn*" (travail upon travail), which represents the divine edict for man to honor his parents, for "in travail upon travail / Did his mother bear him" (The Holy Qur'an 31:14). The referenced burden in al-Neimi's narrative is a reminder of the recurrent haunting of the buried feminine body; its interfacing with the Qur'anic burden, however, marks a moment of transformation in which the burden, through its recognition by the divine, is lightened, perhaps even eliminated. In this manner, al-Neimi's association between the woman's body and childbearing through the Qur'anic trope of "burden" places the feminine body in the center where it not only asserts its presence, but demands divine reverence. Time and again, one of the problems outlined by al-Neimi's poetry is Arab women's inability to record their own history; she affirms, "My body is deprived of its history" (2001, 43). As a way to weave in feminine history with official history, she relies on the help of friends in high places. This friend would be none other than the voice of God, manifested in the plethora of Qur'anic verses embedded in her poetry. Al-Neimi enlists the divine as she incorporates the feminine voice in the cultural narrative, thereby ensuring an unparalleled and immediate admission of her diction into the political and public domains. She jump-starts textual and cultural memory through incorporating Qur'anic language in her poetry, as in her *Inna 'Ataynaka* (*We Bequeathed unto You*) poetry collection, where verses taken directly from the opening verse of *al-Kawthar* (the Abundance) *Surah* in the first verse "*Inna 'Ataynaka al-Kawthar* / To thee have We granted the Fount (of Abundance)" garner the divine's support in empowering the feminine voice (The Holy Qur'an 108:1). In her assimilation of divine phrases and metaphors, al-Neimi attains not only recognition in the public written language, but access to a higher authorial voice by incorporating the divine author par excellence in her diction.

Furthermore, the technique of embedding Qur'anic terminology in her poetry and fiction (*al-tadhmin*) is a two-pronged approach that serves the purpose of honoring the scriptural archives and further legitimizing the nuanced changes the author is proposing to the way her compatriots perceive women's bodies, love, and human relationships. For example, in her story "The Angels," al-Neimi employs the Qur'anic lexicon—in particular, the refrain "*fa bi ayyi ala'i rabbikuma tukadhdhiban*" (Then which of the favors of your Lord will ye deny?) (5:13)—to reflect on the fleeting nature of romance within the institution of marriage. To say that this nuanced interpretation of the divine refrain was not the original intended meaning of the surah is an understatement. Indeed, *Surat al-Rahman* (The Merciful), where this phrase is repeated thirty-one times among its seventy-eight verses, uses the dual case and contradictory thematic pairs to reflect on the transient nature of humans and created things, thereby highlighting the permanence of the Almighty God. Al-Neimi's employment of the expression, however, invokes the same divine phrase to assert the transience of marital love and the permanence of erotic desire realized only through women's awareness of their bodies (Al-Neimi 1994, 27). Similarly, her rewriting of the Prophet's hadith "*la yakhlawana rajulun bi-imra'ah, fa inna al-shaytan thalithuhuma*" (Satan is often the third [attendee] in the secluded company of a man and a woman) reflects her critique of a marriage that has lost its intimacy, when she adds the words "except for couples" to the well-known hadith.[1] Adopting this stylistic technique is in congruence with the rest of her poetry, where she surprises the reader with the use of the highly poetic and sublime Qur'anic lexicon when least expected. For example, in a poem entitled "Infatuation" al-Neimi repeatedly uses the most recurrent Qur'anic phrase "*tajri min tahtiha al-anhar*" (Gardens beneath which flow rivers) in order to create a parallel feminine paradise of desire in diasporic locales (2004, 83).[2] Through the process of intertextuality, Qur'anic diction and sometimes biblical themes are woven into daring allusions in complementary yet surprising ways. The result is an epistemology of the divine conceived and redefined in a feminine diction and matrix.

In addition to reclaiming a space within the religious discourse, Arab women's agency depends on their political participation as well. Ultimately, political awareness and the ability to advocate for one's own rights are necessary to achieve independence. However, al-Neimi contends that part of the problem is "women's ignorance of their own causes, a fact that inflicts them with schizophrenia, which, in turn, causes them to adopt ideologies incompatible with their rights" (1994, 37). For example, in "Stratagems," the heroine introduces the reader to the various "tricks" that she uses to stay invisible, to evade expressing her thoughts in public. In a gathering during which she patiently endures listening to her male colleagues' "past and future accomplishments," she discovers that she has

---

1. This particular hadith is narrated by the second caliph, Umar ibn al-Khattab, and subsequently ibn Umar, and further authenticated by al-Turmudhi. See Ibn Batta al-Akbari n.d., 123, http://www.alsunnah.com.

2. The phrase "*tajri min tahtiha al-anhar*" (Gardens beneath which flow rivers) is one of the most recurrent phrases in The Holy Qur'an, occurring thirty-four times in the following surahs: 2:25, 2:266, 3:15, 3:136, 3:195, 3:198, 4:13, 4:57, 4:122, 5:12, 5:85, 5:119, 9:72, 9:89, 9:100, 13:35, 14:23, 16:31, 20:76, 22:14, 22:23, 25:10, 29:58, 39:20, 47:12, 48:5, 48:17, 57:12, 58:22, 61:12, 64:9, 65:11, 66:8, 85:11, 98:8.

"no glories" of her own to boast about, so she states, "I do not open my mouth, my words remain solely mine" (Al-Neimi 1994, 95). Her remark bears an eerie resemblance to Hamida Naʿnaʾ's heroine, Nadia, and her inability to voice her opinion in front of her male comrades.[3] Al-Neimi's heroine dubs this form of "erased language" as "parallel discourse" and wonders: if the "motive behind writing is to break isolation, then what is the motive behind swallowing our words? What do we try to break? What do we try to mend?" (97). With this line of interrogation, al-Neimi explores the pitfalls of "parallel discourse," of women's exclusion from language, from public enunciation, which finds its hospitable articulation only in the secretive, confined space of orality. Despite the assertion of some critics as to the empowering value of this oral discourse, "as a parallel oral narrative to the written discourse" (Mehta 2007, 63), the fact is that the housing of this oral discourse in the private walls of women's secluded boundaries prevents oral narratives from proper embodiment in text in the public arena. Consequently, the protagonist finds out that her engagement in the public sphere is a must for self- and national actualization. In light of the heroine's inability to express her thoughts and stories orally, in the public space, her writings take on an empowering mission as they become the avenue to affirm her presence in the text. She states, "I do not have stories: real or imagined. I do not have public words. How do we defend ourselves? It becomes a habit to narrate them [my stories] to myself. I do not have stories to tell. Is it deficiency in life experiences or in imagination? Perhaps, it is both. Luckily, there is writing: Cautiously, the words bloom through me in a hesitant smile" (Al-Neimi 1994, 102). Orality's wall of "parallel discourse" is finally demolished as words are manifested through the heroine's body of writing. Only through the act of writing will she be able to communicate and inscribe her presence into history and the public domain. This perception is an invitation for women to transform their expression from the hidden realm of orality to the public domain of the written. Herein springs the need for transforming the

---

3. See, for example, Naʿnaʿ 1995, 38–39, and my discussion of Nadia's lack of empowerment in chapter 5 of this book.

figurative Shahrazad from the oral to the written, the literary to the political, and the local to the global.

Throughout her lyrical and prose writings, al-Neimi advocates for embodying the body into text. Consequently, the body becomes an important locus for the deployment of narrative. Within its boundaries, we witness feminine resurrection from burial and honor killing, to agency through sexual fulfillment, "embodiment within the text," and presence through narration and writing (Mehta 2007, 16). Ultimately, the journey of the female body from oblivion and secretive enunciations to sexual and verbal articulations in *The Book of Secrets* liberates not only Arab women but Arab men as well. It further leads to her next emancipation project, mainly liberating the body of desire for the entire Arab culture. Al-Neimi's call for the resurrection of the body takes both personal and cultural dimensions; it ranges from inscribing the feminine in the public discourse to resurrecting premodern archives and Arabs' erotic literature, in an attempt to rescue their identity from Western erasure, as in her renowned novella *The Proof of the Honey*.

Reinscribing the Body's Language on the Arab Cultural Map

Al-Neimi's excavation of premodern erotic literature has resulted in the bestseller *Burhan al-'Asal* (2007) (*The Proof of the Honey*, 2009).[4] Her previous engagement in liberating the feminine body from symbolic wa'd in her poetry has led to the resurrection of the Shahrazad trope, and burgeoned into a determined effort to liberate the Arabs' cultural corpus from the stronghold of local traditional practices and Western hegemonic misconceptions. Surprisingly, the novella starts by conjuring the same nightmares that haunt the heroines of *The Book of Secrets* except for one single distinction. The heroine's role in *The Proof of the Honey* evolves from that of the victim to that of the murderer, the witness and reporter of traumatic events. She states,

---

4. Citations in the text are to the English edition unless otherwise noted.

My recurring nightmare took the form of one unchanging scenario: there was a corpse hidden somewhere and I was the murderer. I had hidden the corpse carefully and I lived in terror of its being discovered. I would scheme in vain to prevent the others from seeing it, but sooner or later they would. The nightmare was set in those moments that preceded the discovery of my crime, of the corpse, of all my hidden secrets. I would open my eyes in the darkness, trembling with terror. "The skeleton's in the closet," as the proverb says. I didn't need an expert to interpret these dreams. (Al-Neimi 2009, 23–24)

Indeed, the transformation of the feminine subject from the victim's role of the maw'udah to the perpetrator of the murder indicates the sense of intergenerational trauma (discussed in chapter 2) and the responsibility for divulging the "hidden secrets." In other words, if the contemporary female writer does not assume her responsibility in uncovering the crimes committed on both the feminine and the national body, then she would be just as guilty of perpetuating the cycle of violence. Of interest in this pioneering work is the transfiguration of the feminine body into the national one to the extent that resurrecting the "corpse" of the maw'udah ultimately leads to the reclamation of the erotic cultural corpus of the nation. Consequently, the shift from incriminating the local culprits to the global ones reflects al-Neimi's commitment, similar to previously discussed Arab diaspora writers, to infuse the political in personal criticism. The novella in question demonstrates the myriad transformations that Arabic literature has undergone, as of late, on both the inter/ intratextual levels. Despite its diasporic locale of Paris, the novella insists on framing its debate within the context of Arabic medieval and classical historiography. Al-Neimi's exploration of the premodern erotic corpus is an attempt to capture the essence of Arab identity that was lost because of colonialist and orientalist approaches to Arabic literature, an attempt to bring the Westernized Shahrazad home.[5] While her addressees in the

---

5. See my earlier discussion, in the introductory chapter of this book, on the estrangement of Shahrazad from her cultural Eastern roots in Western representations that solely

previous short stories and poetry collections have been solely Arab citizens and predecessors, in this novella she adds the contemporary Western Other to her mélange of interlocutors. In this novella she argues for the right of desire to exist unbridled for both men and women and, despite her diasporic site of Paris, she declares that the Arabic language is the most suitable medium for expressing the body and Eros (Al-Neimi 2009, 21). Her excavation of the open erotic manuscripts of the premodern period is a return to an era that predates the atrocities of modern-day wars, to the playfulness and sarcasm of the *zurafa'* genre (literature of entertainment), to the fluid Islamicate identities that accompany a confident Arab self,[6] secure in its dominance of its territories and of itself. She is determined to resurrect the Arabs' corporal lost memory, to articulate the female body's desire to inscribe its experiences in writing, and to reject the role of the native informant.

From the outset, the body takes center stage when the narrator declares, "some people conjure spirits. I conjure bodies. I have no knowledge of my soul or of the souls of others. I know only my body and theirs" (13). The nameless narrator's relationship with the French Thinker constitutes the axis around which the plot of *The Proof of the Honey* is spun. For despite the narrator's fondness for reading medieval Arab erotica and for experiencing fulfilling sexual relations, before meeting him she keeps her reading hobby a secret and never dares to proclaim it through writing to the public. She divides her own personal history into two periods: the "first *jahiliyyah*," the age before the Thinker, and the age of "Sexual Renaissance," her time after knowing him (31). Her decision to write about their sexual encounters marks the close relationship between her writing and her sexual awareness, or the inscription of desire into writing. She states that "all the rules are erased. I listen only to my own voice. The voice

---

glorified her feminist framing in the frame story without acknowledging the symbolic aspect of the Arab heritage in the rest of *A Thousand and One Nights*.

6. See the explanation of Marshal Hodgson's "Islamicate" coinage in Babayan and Najmabadi 2008. The editors of the collection explain that the term "'*Islamicate*' was intended to highlight a complex of attitudes and practices that pertain to cultures and societies that live by various versions of the religion Islam" (ix).

of my desire, my rare desire" (15). When the Thinker comes into her life, she describes the release of their sexual energy in imagery reminiscent of *A Thousand and One Nights* as the unleashing of the genie from the bottle. However, at this point, her interest both in the Thinker and in reading classical Arab erotic literature remains secretive. Thus she continues to live her private and public lives in parallel lines. She states that "the Thinker came along and . . . in the hollow of our bed, I told him about my secret readings. The two secrets—him and my readings—mingled and merged into a single torrent" (19). Throughout her readings of this erotic literature, the narrator is astonished at the ease with which literary predecessors have dealt with the sexual aspects of the body, at the integration of the corporal with the religious, the spiritual with the cosmos. For example, in one excerpt she reads that the benefits of coitus are that "[i]t calms anger and brings joy to the soul of those whose natures are ardent. It is also a sure treatment for the darkening of the sight, for the circulation, for heaviness of the head, and for pains in the sides such as blind the heart and close the gates of thought" (18). It is known that those who abstain from it suffer from "psychological and physical disease? Madness, dejection, and melancholia all at once?" At this juncture, the narrator adds mischievously, "God protect us and let us not refuse sex!" (19). Similarly, the narrator praises the ease with which the ancients used erotic vocabulary, and laments its disappearance from the linguistic repertoire of spoken and written Arabic. She states that "forbidden words brought to life a history of sexual repression and of the resistance to that repression. Ironically, I never used such words myself, even in my innermost thoughts—they were only to be read, never spoken or written" (21). It is as if modern Arabic language underwent castration that created inhibition, sexual hang-ups, and distancing from its rich history at a time when such sexual subjects were still treated as part of science, of theology, and of the believer's harmony with the body, the soul, and the cosmos. The novella's informed narrator connects this transformation, or what she calls "sexual misery," to the process of translation. Oddly enough, the translation she references is not one from Arabic to a European language; rather it is from "Arabic to Arabic!" For example, she points out the disappearance of the use of certain words such as *nikah* or *nayk*, both synonyms of the words "coupling" and "to fuck." She reminds her readers that these words were widely used from the ninth to the fifteenth century in sociological and scientific manuscripts such as al-Suyuti's *Al-Idah fi 'Ilm al-Nikah* (On Clarifying the Science of Coition), which was rendered into *Al-Idah fi 'Ilm al-Jima'* (On Clarifying the Science of Intercourse), despite the disruption of the internal rhyme in the title by substituting the word *jima'* for *nikah* upon reprinting the manuscript in contemporary times. Indeed, this linguistic disharmony comes to the fore when the medieval essayist al-Jahiz, whom the narrator quotes at length on several occasions, critiques certain contradictions in personal and cultural mores regarding sexuality in his writing. On this prevalent hypocrisy, al-Jahiz elaborates, "Some of those who are given to asceticism and abstemiousness feel disgust and shrink back if the words 'cunt,' 'cock,' and 'fucking' are mentioned. Most men of this sort turn out to be as lacking in knowledge and magnanimity, nobility of soul and dignity, as they are rich in falseness and treachery. These words were invented to be used. It is nonsense to invent them if they are then left to go to seed" (110). In fact, the tendency to censor these words has amounted to a prohibition in our modern times. Al-Neimi's previous focus on resurrecting the buried feminine body, in her poetry and prose, takes on a whole new dimension in this novella in which erasure of the language of desire in contemporary Arabic culture seems to mirror the annihilation of the feminine self. Thus resurrecting the medieval language of erotica serves to unite the cultural body and soul, males and females together in perfect harmony. The author "blames the masters of modern Islamic thought for imbibing [Western] values." The author views this reality as "a paradox" with the unfortunate consequence that "Arab society today has interiorized all the Western notion of sin and guilt associated with the body."[7] Upon rewriting the Cartesian famous motto in Arabic as "I fuck, therefore I am," the narrator's computer exercises censorship by underlining in red all the conjugated forms of the verb *fuck*. She asserts that "the computer

---

7. See, for example, "Has Sensuality Deserted Muslim Lands?" *France 24*, May 29, 2008, http://www.france24.com/en/20080529-sensuality-Arab-erotic-literature-proof -Honey-Salwa (accessed Jan. 12, 2010).

will not admit to knowing such a word! It, too, is programmed for dis-simulation. This computer is a shrinking violet! Or to be more precise, a eunuch of a computer" (Al-Neimi 2009, 110). She then concludes her reverie by asking the following poignant questions: "Who castrated the language? Who castrated the computer? Who castrated me?"[8] With these rhetorical questions, the narrator seems to advocate a return to the body so as to retrieve the Arabic language's connotative ability and virility, and to save it from "castration."[9] Indeed, the process of burying the premodern texts, and truncating the efficacy of the Arabic language, resulted from the influence of imported puritan values during the colonial experience. We are reminded by Khaled El-Rouayheb and Joseph Massad of a time in the medieval Arabic era when sexuality was more fluid (El-Rouayheb 2005; Massad 2007). Likewise, discussions of sexual matters were part of an established zurafa' literature genre that harkens back to a more stable and secure time in Arab political and cultural times.[10] The time in ques-tion is the era before the advent of colonialism and the importation of the European colonizers' Victorian cultural mores. Along with the atroci-ties of colonialism comes a new violence—one associated with translation and arising from the erasure of the ancestral language from modern-day articulations.

In fact the subject of the violence of translation, of how it consumes its primary text-subject, is one raised by several Arab critics, such as Anton

8. This series of questions is mistakenly translated in English as "That has castrated the language. That castrated the computer. That castrated me" (Al Neimi 2009, 110). Therefore the in-text quotation does reflect my own translation of the original Arabic text, and the author's focus on resurrecting the Arabic language and on finding the cul-prit. See al-Neimi 2007, 118.

9. The issue of "castrating" the Arabic language has also been raised by Joumana Haddad, founder and editor-in-chief of the Arab world's first erotic glossy, *Jasad*, which debuted in December 2008 and is published quarterly. In several interviews, Haddad dis-cusses the magazine's goal to "unlock" erotic taboos, free the "castrated" language, and return to the "openness" of the Arab erotic literature of the tenth century. See "Jasad: Sex, Fetishes, and the Erotic in a New Arabic Glossy," *Muslima Media Watch*, Feb. 9, 2009, http://mislimahmediawatch.org/2009/02/09/jasad-sex-fetishes (accessed Feb. 10, 2009).

10. See my discussion of this particular issue in Al-Samman 2008, 274, 308.

Shammas, who views translation not as a "border crossing," but rather as "cannibalism" (Shammas 2003, 124–25). Similarly, 'Abdelfattah Kilito, in agreement with al-Jahiz, sees that in the process of translation one language is always apt to cause *daym* (harm) to the other language (Kilito 2008, 23). Ultimately, the novella's endeavor to right the wrongs committed on the Arabic language by resurrecting the buried language of Arab erotica conjures the wa'd motif, and promises to regain some of the lost fluidity and harmony of Arab linguistics and of desire. Of the Arabic language the narrator proudly declares, "No other language could excite me that way. Arabic, for me, is the language of sex" (Al-Neimi 2009, 21). According to the narrator, modern attitudes toward sexuality are the unfortunate outcome of a "castrated upbringing" (22). She wonders, "Why was it possible for me to take pride in my reading of Western and Eastern pornography while hiding the fact that I was reading al-Tifashi? How could I proclaim my passion for George Bataille, Henry Miller, the Marquis de Sade, Casanova, and the Kama Sutra and make no mention of al-Suyuti and al-Nafzawi?" (22). These rhetorical questions remind Arabs residing in diaspora, and women in particular, to take an intellectual detour to the cultural canon on the path of seeking their physical liberation, for the seeds of said deliverance do not reside in an imported Western feminist ideology, but rather in listening to their long-forgotten Muslim and medieval archives. In fact, the narrator's use of the traditional texts does not stop at erotic Arab premodern literature, but also includes the Prophet's sayings, the teachings of his wife 'Aisha, and philosophical statements of Ibn al-'Arabi and al-Jahiz as well. For example, on the importance of foreplay before intercourse, the narrator reminds the reader of Prophet Mohammad's saying, "Let not one of you fall upon your folk as a beast does, but let there be between you a messenger—the kiss, and conversation" (30).

The process of acknowledging the body's desire, of releasing it from the private to the public realm, is an interesting one, for, at first, the narrator needs the aid of her foreign partner (the Thinker) to express it in writing. By the end of the novel, however, she acquires full agency and is no longer in need of the West's interference in reclaiming her own heritage. At the outset, the narrator keeps the joys of these texts to herself; later the Thinker encourages her to bring the history of these erotic manuscripts to light by writing about them. It takes the direct request of her supervisor, the director of the National Library in Paris, however, to make this written transformation official. The director informs her of a joint conference between New York University and the Bibliothèque Nationale entitled "The Hell of Books," dealing with controversial books. For this reason, he asks her to prepare a study about erotic Arab literature to be presented first in New York and then in Paris. The narrator's motivation behind writing the study was to introduce Arabic erotica literature not just to a curious American or French audience, but also to the Arabic reader who seemed to have forgotten his/her rich classical heritage. She hopes to jump-start her compatriots' memory about the fluidity of the concept of sex, and the harmonious integration between body and soul in early Arabic culture before the insertion of Western taxonomies during the Arab world's colonial experience.

The fact that these two Western entities—the Thinker and the American/French conference organizers—provide the narrator with the impetus to write and cajole her into playing the role of the native informant casts a shadow of doubt on the authenticity of her project of unearthing Arabic erotic manuscripts. Undoubtedly, the narrator's initial response suggests her understanding of the dangers embedded within this double agency, and projects uneasiness with her prescribed informant's role: "I pictured myself reading one of my favorite passages from one of those books in a loud voice in front of a gathering of scholars. Would I be transformed into a doctor of eroticism? A pornologist?" (42). Her rhetorical question expresses her anxiety about reproducing the same old orientalist portrayals of the Middle Eastern odalisque forever ready to engage in bawdy pleasures. Realizing her hesitation, the library director insists, attempting to highlight the native informant's unique role in facilitating cultural understanding between the Arab world and the West: "Are you aware that the Americans have become interested in everything Arab and Muslim since September 11th? What do you say?" Interestingly, the narrator's witty response underscores the Americans' disingenuous motive behind this newly found desire to seek knowledge of the enemy. It further reframes this desire as sensational and consumptive, part of the need to strip the Other of his/her private and protective layers. She states, "I might find some points of convergence with the Americans if they started to show an interest in the Arab science of coition" (45). Ultimately, however, the narrator's decision to participate in the conference is indicative of her desire to be part of knowledge production in order to ward off the West's hegemony over her own narrative. Madhava Prasad explains that the "postcolonial nightmare" occurs when the native subject becomes part of the apparatus of power and knowledge production, owing to mobility or relocation to a site of knowledge production, and suddenly realizes that s/he has been misrepresented, appropriated, and consumed (Prasad 1992, 58). Accordingly, Prasad defines postcoloniality as "the historic moment in which the coveted 'private' realm is created as the zone of 'non-interference' that is off limits to the 'public'" (59). In its engagement with the most private of privates, *The Proof of the Honey* goes beyond colonial and postcolonial binaries to revel in the security of bygone Arab cultural moments. The heroine's intention to open up the "coveted private" zone, to engage both Arab and foreign interlocutors in the discussion, ushers an end to the "postcolonial nightmare." Hence the need to retreat to postcolonial defensive moments as a means of protection against the colonial intrusion is thereby eliminated. Indeed, the novel invites its intended audience (the Arab readers), and in turn its indirect Western readers (by virtue of the work's various translations), to explore the forbidden realm of the body and sexuality. Excavating the archives of the corporal cultural past engages the heroine in a process of remembering at the end of which the Arab body, soul, and civilization reunite, thereby regaining confidence and autonomous presence. The return to the specificity of the private Arab cultural realm is a regenerative act that propels the narrator to action, and is in congruence with Arab women writers' project of heritage reclamation. Toward the end of the novel, the narrator acquires her private, narrative, and cultural agency by shunning the Thinker's influence, thereby regaining her authority: "I read what I have written and it occurs to me that I have made the Thinker into an allegory. I have recreated him, but not in my image. I said, 'Be,' and he was. He was just as my words shaped him. This image belongs to me; it has nothing to do with him . . . the Thinker was a writer's device, a ruse, and that he never existed at all: that is why I had to invent him. . . . *The story is mine*; he is only the subject"

(138–39, emphasis is mine). At the end, when the French library director informs her that the Americans canceled the conference because of "security reasons," she feels relieved at not having to play the role of the "native informant" ever again. Still, she remains grateful that had it not been for this project, she would not have had the motivation to bring these books back to life. She states proudly, "What mattered was the book. And the Thinker I had created. I would publish the study: what need had I of the apologetic director, or the Americans and the French cowering in terror of the bogeyman of terrorism?" (141).

Furthermore, the novel is critical of old Western propaganda that portrayed an exotic Middle East as evident in Flaubert's narrative and in nineteenth-century paintings, and of new post-9/11 misconceptions that proclaim "Islamic fanaticism" as the reason behind an austere "sexless Arab society." For example, the narrator mocks a novel by an unspecified French writer who proclaimed after spending two weeks in Egypt, "there is no Sex in Egypt!" "There is no Sex in Islamic Society" (67). These proclamations engender the following response from the narrator: "Gone are the Nubian maidens the writer had encountered in the nineteenth century . . . in their place are women wearing hijabs. The cultured traveler is traumatized to find that Flaubert's Levant, the Levant of 1847, has vanished. All that is left is September 11th and the days of Islamic jihad" (67). Taunting the stereotypical narrative, the narrator's comments suggest that "Jihadist" mentality is the outcome of contested East-West colonial encounters, and the West's desire to propagate and control Middle Eastern cultural narratives. "In either case," she asserts, "blind propaganda prospers in ignorance, whether real or feigned" (68).

In its narrative structure, the novella borrows from medieval structural techniques; thus it is divided into eleven "*abwab*" (chapters) that function as chapters. Thematically, it also builds on the tradition of *A Thousand and One Nights* in the sense that the female narrator's narrative, not unlike Shahrazad's, is strongly tied to her body and its sexual encounters. She admits the following to the reader:

> What I found interesting were the two alternating motifs—the bed and
> the story. In my life, one has led to the other, and vice versa. In my life,

they have been intimately linked, and I oscillate between the two. In my life, I have been addicted to beds and stories. Every man is a story and every story a bed. I don't want to lose the bed. I don't want to lose the story . . . The *sarir* is for pleasure. *Sarir* is from *sirr*, or "secret." Two words which have the same root. Desire is secret. Pleasure is secret. Sex is secret. Sex is the secret of secrets. That is why in my mind it remains linked to *sarir*, even if I do it in a lift. (97)

Sarir (bed) and *sirr* (secret) are also linked by virtue of alliteration and assonance to *sard* (narration), which makes the affinity of this holy trinity to the heroine of the *Nights* an infallible one. However, unlike Shahrazad, whose narrative agency is limited to the internal frame of the *Nights* and whose sard and sarir activities are strongly determined by the nexus of sex and death via the threat of decapitation and the surrender of her narrative to the external narrator of the *Nights*, the sexual encounters of *The Proof of the Honey*'s heroine remain free from the threat of death and erasure, literally or literarily. Additionally, her ownership of her sard remains fully intact. Her decision to divulge the secret of her body's sexual desires does not lead to her surrender of her authorship rights. On the contrary, it leads to the recognition and publication of her work. Unlike King Shahrayar, who ordered the conversion of Shahrazad's stories from the oral to the written format and safeguarded them in the secrecy of his safe, the female narrator in this novella authors her own written sard, thereby maintaining narrative agency after divulging the sirr (secret) of her corporal ecstasy. In a triumphant outcry at the end, she declares, "the story is mine; he [the Thinker] is only the subject" (139).

Another point of departure from the corpus of the *Nights* is the invocation of the legendary character al-Alfiya (literally a woman of a thousand times), who was mentioned by al-Jahiz as one of the most learned sexologists of her times. Hailing from India, the land of the *Kama Sutra*, she was known to lecture, in a detailed scientific manner, to men and women on the sixty positions of intercourse and on the maintenance of erotic attraction among couples. The narrator informs the reader that the myth about al-Alfiya started with her name, which she was given because "she had slept with a thousand men" (130). Al-Alfiya's story brings to mind another legendary female character who had presumably slept with a hundred men and kept a collection of her lovers' rings as proof of her escapades: the mistress of the demon in the *Nights'* frame story (Haddawy 1990, 8–10). As those who are familiar with the story know, the maiden who was abducted on her wedding night and imprisoned in seven chests at the bottom of the sea decides to take revenge on the demon who was the cause of her misfortune by cheating on him with a hundred lovers. She managed to exact her revenge while the demon was taking his siestas on a deserted island. She threatened the men that she would cry rape if they did not succumb to her wishes. Consequently, the men obliged and made love to her lest they face a certain death at the hands of the enraged demon. In contrast to the demon's mistress, whose sexual encounters are based on deceit and duress—hence her casting in the frame story as an example of treacherous, untrustworthy women—al-Alfiya's sexual encounters are considered to be necessary to the attainment of her scientific knowledge. She is praised by al-Jahiz as a scholar "who speak[s] only of what [she] know[s] from personal experience, and who will only teach knowledge acquired through the direct observation of real phenomena" (Al-Neimi 2009, 129). The narrator herself anoints her as "a glorious heroine of women's liberation" (129), and concludes the segment on her person with the following lamentation: "how could al-Alfiya ever imagine that her legitimate [granddaughters,] centuries later, spread over five continents, would not even know her name, when she was the first, the pioneer?" (131). Unearthing the archives of this forgotten mother, and of Shahrazad's motif, will prove to be a rebirth of the buried body of desire that modernity has shrouded in secrecy and in contempt.

Despite crediting al-Alfiya with a pioneering role in foregrounding an Arab erotic education, al-Neimi refuses to espouse any feminist agenda to her project. In fact, her work purposefully stands at the opposite side of advocating a feminist, queer, or postcolonial stance. On the contrary, the novella asserts itself as a testament to pure desire and espouses a genuine interest in male and female corporal pleasure, long lost and stigmatized in contemporary Arabic culture. After quoting a premodern erotic text advocating for the hastening of the marriage of virgins lest they be plagued with a certain "constriction in the womb," resulting in "delirium and melancholia in the brain" and eventually "madness," she declares, "if I were to say that in front of a militant feminist, she'd declare war on me and accuse me of submitting to male chauvinist ideology" (128–29). Furthermore, the novella breaks ranks with the current trends of Arab sexuality studies that associate female medieval sexual desire with tribadism, and female homosexuality as a whole with presumed dominant queer tendencies in what have been dubbed by Western historians as "*Islamicate*" societies (Babayan and Najmabadi 2008). Indeed, the heroine asserts on two different occasions her unequivocal heterosexual desires (Al-Neimi 2009, 21, 82–84). Despite the fact that the narrator mentions the story of Hubba of Medina, known to be the most renowned same-sex lover of women of all of Arabia, still her focus is on resurrecting the pleasure associated with heterosexual desire that has long been occulted in modern times (83).

Contested and Contaminated Reception

Upon its first publication in Beirut in 2007, *The Proof of the Honey* received varied reactions from Arab literary critics that fanned the fires of its immediate popularity and instantaneous banning from the markets of most Arab countries with the exception of Beirut, Abu Dhabi's book fair, and the North African countries of Tunisia, Algeria, and Morocco. The book broke sales records that even Naguib Mahfuz himself did not achieve in his heyday (120,000 copies by its third Arabic edition), and was the number one seller on Arabicbook.com for several weeks. In addition, its translation rights have been sold to eighteen languages, half of which are already in print in European markets (Aslan 2008). Despite this unprecedented success, it was banned by Damascus Book Fair 2007. Those who critique its use of erotica do so on the basis of its use of explicit language that places the novella, in their opinion, in the ranks of sensational literature that relies on the linguistic "shock factor" to increase its sales. The Egyptian Hasan Talab, for example, adamantly "rejects 'exhibitionist literature' whose sole intent is stirring base desires and reaping fame and profit" (Hasan 2009). Others see that the novella is promoting a return to "sexual *salafism* (traditionalism)," which surprisingly they equate to "Islamic *salafism*" (al-'Isa 2008). They argue that both trends have a lot in common, and are connected to marketing ploys keen on increasing profit through the sales of erotic books or the engaging charisma of quick-to-rise, world-famed TV Muslim preachers. Some critics insist that this unabashed naming of body parts and sexual acts is bad enough for male writers, but even worse when women do it bluntly.[11] Still, there are a considerable number who hail the book as one that started a "sexual intifada" and a "sexual revolution." The Arab poet and columnist Onsi El Haj [Unsi al-Hajj], for example, praises the agency of *The Proof of the Honey* as "more striking than any other argument and more subtle than all these mystical, exotic, oriental, postcolonial studies working hard to prove to the West that the world it now considers as its opposite, if not its enemy, has not only been free, but still is, and will continue to be." El Haj goes on to reflect that the novella has "no trace of feminism, no social vindication," and that by "freeing itself from any desire to defend, to show, the book aspires to be and is, in fact, more than plain rhetoric" (El Haj 2007). Apparently al-Neimi's disavowal of feminism several times in the text affirms El Haj's observations. Other Arab critics, such as Rayyan Al-Shawaf, find the novel's engagement with premodern texts "fascinating," but lament the fact that "Arab intellectuals and artists feel compelled to justify their controversial works by depicting them as continuing an illustrious Arab tradition—as al-Neimi has done." In his opinion, the tendency to hide behind tradition points the accusatory finger to the "burdensome weight of history and heritage in Arab societies" (Al-Shawaf 2010). Other critics celebrated the novella's delving into the traditional sexual archives, proving that a return to historical registers may not be as "burdensome" as al-Shawaf suggests (Bin Hamzah 2009). *The Proof of the Honey* is a novella that starts playing to the obedient tune of the native informant of Arabic erotic history, but ends up shunning that role and internalizing

11. These comments emerge in reference to a new comedy show called *LOL* (Laughing Out Loud), often a staple on the Lebanese OTV channel that is owned by the Christian militia leader Michel Aoun. The show features explicit sexual jokes, among others, narrated by two women and two men. Reactions to the show have been mixed, with audiences often critiquing the "audacity" of women speaking explicitly about sexual matters in public.

the resurrected knowledge, a more relaxed premodern Arab heritage at ease with itself and its surroundings. The author resorts to an Arab tradition that predates the moment of a Victorian embrace of such notions as the vilification of the body and the concept of Original Sin, rooted in Protestantism.

Upon its translation into a number of European languages, and into English in 2009 as *The Proof of the Honey*, it was met with critical refusal to read the narrator as anything but a native informant. Salwa al-Neimi's gender and diasporic location, coupled with the novel having been written in Arabic, resulted in sensationalist, sometimes orientalist, covers, replete with quotes of critical acclaim taken from leading book review sections of newspapers and magazines. While the covers of the Dutch, French, and English editions highlight the exotic, featuring a naked female torso reclined in a backward, odalisque position, the cover of the Portuguese translation shows a veiled Muslim woman. This is an old contradiction of orientalism; as Peter Ripken points out, "the veil and the *houri*, . . . two clichés of the Arab female identity, are flipsides of the Orientalist coin. The dual image of the submissive/sexual woman of the harem is a conjoined fantasy that one could argue continues to appeal to Western readers."[12] Indeed, critics noted that Arab erotic literature written by men does not sell as well as that of the erotic literature written by Arab women.[13]

"Uncovering" the veiled world of Muslim Arab women is one of the recurrent tropes in the orientalist fantasy of the harem. Writing from the perspective of an Arab woman living in the West, Fatima Mernissi compares the fantasy of this Eastern harem with the reality of what she dubs the "Western Harem" (Mernissi 2001, 29–42, 208–20). The fact that both the author and the narrator of *The Proof of the Honey* are Syrian women living in Paris leads to a misreading by Western and Arab readers alike,

12. See, for example, "Salwa Al Neimi's Proof of the Honey," *English Pen World Atlas*, Jan. 13, 2009, http://penatlas.blogspot.com/2009/01/salwa-al-neimis-proof-of-honey.html (accessed Jan. 12, 2010).

13. On this topic, see "al-Mar'ah al-'Arabiyyah wa-al-Jins min al-Haramlik ila al-Ibahiyyah," Maktoobblog.com, Oct. 4, 2007, http://www.Maktoobblog.com (accessed Jan. 10, 2010).

with a predilection for conflating the author and the narrator and reading *The Proof of the Honey* as a testimonial, autobiographical novel that "exposes" the secret desires of Arab women. In several interviews, Salwa al-Neimi insists that her narrator's sexual liberation is the result of invoking Arab and Muslim heritage (Bin Hamzah 2009). In this manner, she echoes Muslim women's liberation scholars who argue that enjoying sanctioned sexual pleasure is compatible with the Muslim faith (al-Hibri 2000, 58; Kahf 2003; 2007; 2008). Nevertheless, some Western audiences insist on viewing the novella in a feminist and anti-Muslim framework (Merrihew 2009), despite the narrator's repeated disavowal of feminism (Al-Neimi 2009, 128–29) and the book's project of reviving the fluid, sexual tradition of the premodern period.

Western readers herald *The Proof of the Honey*'s author for her pioneering spirit as the first Arab woman to explicitly address sexual topics.[14] For Arab readers the issue is not only one of al-Neimi's choice of sexual topics, but also her use of explicit language denoting sexual organs and acts. To those readers, al-Neimi's response is that "[her] own battle is to be free within the structures of Arabic language itself."[15] Al-Neimi is reclaiming erotic language, to reinscribe the body on the contemporary Arab cultural map, to use the erotic language of premodern periods against its subsequent occultation and demonization in modern times.

The return to tradition in al-Neimi's poetic and prose articulations in both their traumatic and erotic manifestations is a concerted effort to go beyond the fragmentation, the contestation, and the binaries of postcolonial and feminist frameworks toward the assuredness and certainty of a more stable Arab self. It is accomplished by activating the iconic tropes of wa'd and Shahrazad, by transforming them to allow the diasporic female

14. This claim has to be disqualified because there was another novel, of a dubious origin, reportedly written by an Arab woman in her forties, living somewhere in the Maghrib region, who wrote her novel of erotica under the pen name Nedjma in French in 2004 (Nedjma 2005).

15. See Salwa al-Neimi's interview "Veus Unides: Salwa Al Neimi," June 22, 2011, on YouTube regarding this topic, which was accessed at http://www.youtube.com/watch?v=gVmS8dlu3UU (July 25, 2012).

subject to witness trauma and to author redemption. In *The Proof of the Honey*, excavating the literary archives has meant pursuing an endeavor of combating local and global contamination and subsequent misrepresentation. Indeed, listening to the archives holds the key to unlocking long-lost narrative and sexual nuances, and to relocating diasporic desires of longing and belonging onto the Arab World's cultural map. Unearthing the premodern archives of narration—a process that goes beyond the assimilative, imitative phase—involves, in Matt Richardson's opinion, an active "listening to the archives"[16] and engages the present in a conversation with the past. This return to intertextual historicity in contemporary Arabic literature works against the tendency of Western publishing houses to assign Arabic texts value and lucrative translation contracts based on their approximation of Western literature and the time-worn "exotic," "repressive," and "violent" images of Arab culture. Rather, resurrecting the Arabic canon in this manner places the interpretive power back in the Arabic text itself, where al-Neimi asserts "the proof of the honey is the honey itself."[17] Indeed, the proof of the novella's value springs from within the Arabic tradition that it aspires to revive from the diaspora. This revitalization project brings the diasporic author's journey full circle back to the homeland, where absence is replaced by presence, and where routes ultimately lead to one's roots.

16. On the application of this strategy to African American queer literature, see Richardson 2013.

17. See "Interview with Salwa Al Neimi" on YouTube, Dec. 7, 2009, http://www.you tube.com/watch?v=A1YeYKDY4Rk (accessed July 25, 2012).

Postscript

From Trauma to Triumph

The main thrust of *Anxiety of Erasure* has been to examine the double obsession with Shahrazad and wa'd al-banat—literary and physical annihilation—as a regenerative and creative force in the writings of contemporary Muslim and Christian Arab women living in diaspora. These women use their engagement in diasporic locales and societies to reclaim their voice not as exiles, but as continuing participants in their homelands' intellectual life, exemplifying Avatar Brah's assertion of the traumatic as well as the triumphant aspects of diaspora (Brah 1996, 193). My engagement with the literary output of these writers has demonstrated the value of nonfixity, of multiaxial critique. Throughout this book, I have argued the benefits of the therapeutic effects resulting from resurrecting forgotten histories as well as the reactivation of collective memories of the maw'udah and of Shahrazad.

In their literature, the personal nightmare of wa'd has been transformed from the feminine to the collective Arab population, which is prevented from voicing its dreams of freedom and dignity owing to the prevalence of authoritarian regimes determined to bury Arab people's aspirations and, in turn, the whole Arab nation. Indeed, the systematic activation of the wa'd motif in demonstration banners and virtual Facebook and Twitter revolutionary pages, of almost every country undergoing the exhilarating changes in the ongoing Arab Spring and its aftermath, is a testimony to the powerful call for justice that the maw'udah's image evokes in the Arab collective imagination. In fact, on April 10, 2012, a caricature representing the souls of the sixty thousand martyrs and four thousand assassinated Syrian children haunting the bedside of that country's leader, Bashar al-Assad, went up on the Syrian revolution Facebook page. Recalling the Qur'anic iconic question of the maw'udah: "*wa-idha al-maw'udatu su'ilat bi-ayyi dhanbin qutilat*"[1] (When the female infant, buried alive, is questioned / For what crime she was killed), the caricature caption reads "*bi ayyi dhanbin qutilna?*" (For what crimes were *we* killed?). The transformation from the Qur'anic singular feminine "she" to the plural "we," in the revolution banner, highlights the embodiment of the feminine traumatic pain in the collective consciousness of the nation. Indeed, recent diaries of the Syrian revolution penned by the Syrian writer Samar Yazbek demonstrate fully the extent of the wa'd trope's assimilation into the national imaginary. The reactivation of the wa'd in Yazbek's *Taqatu' Niran* (2011) (*A Woman in the Crossfire: Diaries of the Syrian Revolution* [2012])[2] is but one example of the survivability of the feminine traumas into the national ones. Yazbek's book revives the maw'udah's voice and poignantly points the accusatory finger toward Assad's brutal regime and its systematic practice of killing its own people.

The manner in which she engages with the three main components of the wa'd's archetype—the threat of the Other, identifying the culprit(s), and resurrecting the maw'udah's voice—is crucial to the success of her oppositional narrative. The book chronicles the first four months of the Syrian revolution from March 15, 2011, to July 8, 2011, and records in painstaking detail the political chaos of the State and the status of the demonstrations in Dar'a (the birthplace of the revolution), Damascus, Homs, Hama, Baniyas, and Jableh as well as other Syrian towns and villages. Yazbek's material comes from her own experience in demonstrations and compulsory visits to security police offices as well as from direct testimonies of activists, political detainees, and martyrs' family members. In addition to gathering witnesses' testimonies, she maintains her involvement with the revolution's Coordination Committees on the ground and is vocal on her Facebook page in support of a free, democratic

---

1. The Holy Qur'an, *Surat al-Takwir*, 81:8
2. All references are to the translated version unless stated otherwise.

Syria. However, using her public persona as a prominent 'Alawite writer in this oppositional manner does not set well with the authorities, and she is quickly summoned to meet one of the high-ranking security police officers. She is led blindfolded to his office where he hurls insults (*cunt*) and slaps at her (Yazbek 2012, 82). His anger is compounded because, as an 'Alwaite and a supporter of the revolution, she has "betrayed the ties of blood and kinship" and brought about "shame" (*'Ar*) to the 'Alwaite clan (83). Their ensuing interaction is worth mentioning, in this context, as it reactivates important components integral to the wa'd story.

> "We're worried about you," he said. "You're being duped by Salafi Islamists if you believe what they're saying."
>
> "I don't believe anyone," I said. "I went out into the streets time after time and I didn't see any Salafis. I saw how you kill ordinary people and arrest them and beat them."
>
> "No," he said, "those are Salafis."
>
> "They weren't Salafis," I told him. "You and I both know that."
>
> "If you keep on writing," he said, "I'll make you disappear from the face of the earth."
>
> "Go ahead," I said.
>
> "Not just you, but your daughter as well."
>
> In that moment, my heart stopped beating.
>
> Sitting down behind his desk, he said, "Put the knife down, you lunatic. We're honorable people. We don't harm our own blood. We're not like you traitors. You're a black mark upon all Alawites." (84)

Yazbek's stance in support of the revolution against Bashar al-Assad, a member of her own clan, brings to mind the fear of the feminine element in bringing the enemy home. In other words, in initiating an intimate, political encounter with the Other, she dishonored the whole sect. If we recall the wa'd stories I discussed in chapter 2 of this book, the threat of enduring the 'ar of the daughter's betrayal was the main reason behind burying her in the sand. In fact, in the Arabic version of *A Woman in the Crossfire* the officer declares, "You're 'ar upon all Alawites" (Yazbek 2011, 104). The officer's threat that if Yazbek does not desist he will "make [her disappear] from the face of the earth" is a euphemism for the burial and the disappearance of thousands of political dissidents in Syria's modern history, dubbed "the disappeared," who were summarily arrested, never to be heard from again. Indeed, his desire to silence her voice by ordering her to shut down her Facebook account, and to never publish articles in support of the revolution in *al-Quds al-'Arabi* journal, is akin to a symbolic wa'd.

Throughout the book, Yazbek narrates how the whole sect treated her as a traitor, how her own family and friends disowned her, how they turned her own daughter against her, and how she was banished from her birthplace of Jableh, never daring to visit it again after the regime distributed pamphlets calling for her head there (35, 81). Yazbek's tactic in diffusing the regime's accusation of her so-called betrayal is turning the accusatory finger to Bashar al-Assad himself, calling him time and again "murderous president," "a murderer," "a butcher" capable of committing massacres worse than Tamerlane, and a "cartoonish Frankenstein" (140, 193, 152, 164). Her inclusion of the chants of Dar'a women who held a banner stating, "*Anyone who kills his own people is a traitor!*" redefines treason and points out, in a manner not unlike the maw'udah's voice in the above-mentioned Qur'anic verse of *Surat al-Takwir*, who committed the crimes of killing and who is the real culprit in the country's demonic demise (153, italics in original). Furthermore, the questions that she raised throughout the diaries diffuse the regime's official narrative of Salafi "infiltrators" killing the Syrians. She includes the testimony of an activist during the early days of the revolution, who insisted that the youths organizing the demonstrations came from all the ethnic Syrian rainbow (Sunnis, Christians, 'Alawites, Kurds, and Druze); they were not religiously inclined, but that they had to resort to launching the demonstrations from the mosques because they were the only places citizens were allowed to assemble in this martial-law State (237). At one point she wonders, "where are all these murderers coming from?" (47); at another, "who is killing the soldiers and the demonstrators?" alike. Her account of the strange physiognomy of some snipers, coupled with the unusual manner in which they groomed their beards, incriminates the regime in importing Iranian Revolutionary Guards and Hezbollah agents to help kill their own people—a fact that became self-evident in the second year of the Syrian revolution when both

Iran and Hezbollah publically admitted their military and logistic support of the Assad regime. Yazbek remarks, "I stared into his [the sniper's] eyes, which were like every other murderer's eyes that have appeared these days, eyes I have never seen before in Damascus. How could all those murderers be living among us? . . . The man's complexion was dark and his features hinted at a kind of foreignness we were all starting to wonder about" (54). Clearly it is not the transgressive woman or the revolutionary activists who are bringing the foreign Other to Syria; rather it is the duplicitous regime. Yazbek's accounts do not spare the security police and the regime's gangs (known as *al-shabbiha*)[3] from incrimination either. Almost all of her witnesses indicate that al-shabbiha were the ones shooting soldiers in the back of the head when the latter refused to shoot unarmed demonstrators, and that they were the ones who instigated *al-fitna al-ta'ifiyyah* (sectarian feud) in Syrian villages of mixed ethnic demographics. Another aspect of Yazbek's oppositional narrative is her redefinition of the term *hijab* (the veil), which in the regime's narrative takes on a sinister, derogatory connotation. In Yazbek's exposition, however, it is not the veil of the covered women that Syrian citizens should be weary of; rather it is the security "veil" that acts as a wall preventing citizens from interacting with each other, from the freedom of movement, and from seeing the truth. This oppressive security veil "grows and grows until it becomes an entire country" (46). In fact, the dismemberment of rebellious Syrian cities by several security checkpoints, cutting them off from electricity, water, food supplies, Internet, transportation, and other communication methods, all while continuing the aerial bombardment of them, renders those cities dead. In besieged Dar'a, for example, Yazbek remarks that "the land is being surrounded, buried/*ardun maw'udah*" (30), and that "Damascus was a ghost town" (31). In defiance of the regime's isolationist tactics, Yazbek increases her efforts to connect the activists through a network

---

3. *Al-shabbiha* are hired gangs often recruited by the Assad regime to terrorize citizens. Their name is derived from the expensive black cars they drive (called *al-shabbah* [the ghost] in Syrian slang), and is thus indicative of their ability to kill, to make ghosts (*tashbbih*) out of people by making them literally "disappear" in a ghostlike manner.

of Coordination Committees (187, 219). Moreover, she insists on documenting Syrian women's role in launching and supporting the uprising. Women of all walks of life, ethnicities, and religious affiliation were part of the struggle and active members in the "Syrian Women in Support of the Uprising" initiative, which specialized in delivering assistance to the wounded and to martyrs' families (150). Yet despite Yazbek's moderate success in mobilizing the women's committees, the trauma of the buried cities weighs heavily on her soul, and she feels its effects in her own body through the affects of fear, anxiety, insomnia, vomiting, and madness. Increasingly, the dismemberment of Dar'a al-maw'udah (buried Dar'a) is felt in her own body, which she experiences as "a disintegrating corpse" (81). In this instance, the personal wa'd is conflated with the national one as the transgressive female writer assimilates the persona of the maw'udah to become the poster image of a resurrected, revolutionary dialectic.

Resurrecting the Maw'udah's Body

In their efforts to contain her, the security police placed Yazbek under close surveillance. The repeated threating phone calls and summons of the high-ranking officer were meant to intimidate and break her spirit. In every visit, she was taken to the torture chambers where political dissidents are tortured and humiliated. She was forced to see their wounded bodies oozing blood and pus as they hung lifeless from the ceiling of their cells. Their piercing screams haunted her at night, giving her constant insomnia. She copes during those trips to the prison's underworld by pretending that she is a fictive character, and that the humiliation she is enduring is actually happening to someone else. She states, "I would pretend I was a character on paper, not made of flesh and blood, or that I was reading about a blindfolded woman forcibly taken to an unknown location, to be insulted and spat upon because she had the gall to write something true that displeased the tyrant. At this point in my fantasy I would feel strong and forget all about how weak my body was, about the vile smells and the impending unknown" (Yazbek 2012, 90–91). This dissociative technique unites her on a symbiotic level with the body of the maw'udah, indeed, with the body of the buried nation and its people.

Through this unification she is able to experience their traumatic history in her own body, a process that forever replays and assimilates this intergenerational trauma in her own being. When she attempts to write down the testimonies of the tortured detainees, her body trembles as it experiences the same pain endured by her compatriots. "My fingers started trembling," she reports, "a condition I know all too well. Rarely can I finish recording a testimony without winding up crying or shaking. Rarely can I write down the words coming from the mouths of the tortured without them washing over me as though it were happening for real. What sort of torture is this?" (120) As the security police's surveillance increases its grip on every aspect of her life such that she cannot leave her house, or communicate with others via the Internet or in person, Yazbek starts to view her body as a buried corpse demanding its right to be heard. The corpse refuses to be silenced and gains power through the transfer of trauma as Yazbek documents the stories of the tortured prisoners and the martyrs in her writing. She draws strength from their stories, and her narrative witnessing takes on a poignant slant as she becomes the voice of the voiceless, those like the revolution's singer Ibrahim al-Qashoush whose lifeless body was dumped in the Orontes with his throat cut, who are literally deprived of the agency to tell their stories. Her inclusion of the lyrics of his song in her text is a resurrection of his voice, indeed of the countless disappeared Syrian citizens (216). In the same vein, the testimonies she documents on stealing the martyrs' bodies, on the selling and buying of their body parts, incriminates the regime even further in atrocious crimes against humanity (125, 232). She is haunted daily by the corpses of the tortured, and her responsibility toward documenting the stories of the witnesses takes on an added urgency when they become martyrs themselves in subsequent demonstrations. Corpses dominate the scene in this morbid tale, and before long this revolutionary writer starts to refer to herself as the living dead, "*al-maita al-akthar hudhuran*" (Yazbek 2011, 101); she is a "dead woman, yet still present somehow" (Yazbek 2012, 81). She understands the importance of reviving the dead cells and regenerating her body through narrative witnessing (Yazbek 2012, 104). The voice and the body of the maw'udah compete for presence, for reunification, for rebirth in her person. Yazbek remarks, "the paper woman in my fingertips told me, 'Bloodshed or humiliation, it's either one or the other.' I told her to shut up and just leave me alone for a little while, like a corpse calmly fighting against its own decomposition" (134). Writing becomes the means for the corpse's regeneration, and resurrection will occur through writing the testimonies of the revolution witnesses. Only through this narrative witnessing can the body of the victims be resurrected and can the maw'udah's voice, both that of the woman and the country, be heard from underneath the rubble. To protect her daughter's life, Yazbek had to leave Syria and live in exile in London. *A Woman in the Crossfire* would go on to win the 2012 PEN/Pinter Prize awarded to "International writer(s) of courage" and the Swedish Tucholsky Prize in the same year. In 2013 she received the Oxfam Novib/PEN Award to recognize writers who have been persecuted for their work. In light of the descent of the country into a brutal civil war, owing to the apathy of American and European administrations that allowed Iran, Russia, and other militant groups such as the Islamic State of Iraq and Syria (ISIS) and Hezbollah to hijack and divert the revolution from its peaceful course, the value of Yazbek's diaries in documenting the early months of the Syrian uprising is insurmountable and in reminding us that "[t]his is the people's revolution of dignity. This is the uprising of a brutalized people who wish to liberate themselves from their humiliation. That's how the uprising in Syria broke out. I saw it among the people I first interviewed, before I was prevented from moving between the Syrian cities and before the security services and the *shabbiha* and the Ba'thists placed a bounty on my head wherever I went" (218). Yazbek's reappropriation of the maw'udah's transgressive behavior in her ability to exercise her free will and mobility, and in seeking forbidden encounters with unwanted others, allows the writer to be incarnated in the archetype's image. Using the maw'udah's divine right in naming those who have committed crimes against humanity, Yazbek identifies the criminals who have buried Syria and condemned it to the spiraling hell of civil war. Her courageous actions landed her in the "crossfire" and caused her to be burned by enemy and ally fires alike, but as she hastens to remind us, "Fire scalds. Fire purifies. Fire either reduces you to ash or burnishes you. In the days to come I expect to live in ashes or else to see my shiny new mirror" (Yazbek 2012, 258). Yazbek's final words are hopes for the Phoenix, for Syria's resurrection from the ashes to write glorious chapters of dignity and freedom for all of its citizens.

Shahrazad: Revered, Rejected, and Resurrected

While there is little dispute about the traumatic cultural memories invoked by the buried maw'udah's voice and body, it is with Shahrazad, however, that Arab women writers love to disagree. Some, like Hanan al-Shaykh, have found in her character the ultimate queen of narrative, the eternal muse: Shahrazad's stories "take [al-Shaykh] back to the origin of [her] writing." It is "as if," al-Shaykh asserts, "contemporary women [novelists] are uniting with Shahrazad, claiming *A Thousand and One Nights*, telling her 'sister Shahrazad, we are still writing, adapting, and showing your stories on stage.'"[4] Following the practice of the "as if," which Rosi Braidotti claims is a useful "technique of strategic re-location in order to rescue what we need of the past in order to trace paths of transformation of our lives here and now" (Braidotti 1994, 6), Shahrazad's narrative is resurrected through al-Shaykh's play *One Thousand and One Nights: Modern Plays* (2011). However, other writers have vehemently rejected her "character" because, in their opinion, her idealized representation is "a conspiracy against Arab women in particular, and women in general" (Haddad 2010, 142). Joumanah Haddad, for example, finds that Shahrazad's "compromising" and "negotiation skills" thwart "women['s] resistance and rebellion." Haddad relishes the act of Shahrazad's symbolic killing in *I Killed Scheherazade: Confessions of an Angry Arab Woman* (Haddad 2010, 142–43). By contrast, other Arab diaspora women writers celebrate

---

4. Hanan al-Shaykh's promotional introduction to the stage production of *One Thousand and One Nights*, directed by Tim Supple, at the Luminato Festival in Toronto in June 2011. See festival site promotions at http://www.luminato.com/2011/1001nights.
Also see al-Shaykh and Supple 2011.

Shahrazad's newfound access to publication and mobility. For example, in Mohja Kahf's poetry Shahrazad is on the move, "back / For the millennium and living in Hackensack, / New Jersey." She "want[s] publication" and "teach[es] creative writing at Montclair State" (Kahf 2003, 43). Undeniably the contemporary Shahrazad is mobile, global, revolutionary, and in print. She left her fixed position behind the walls of Shahrayar's palace and embarked on several journeys that emboldened her to finally own both narrative and body. She is free to explore relationships with foreign lovers and others, but also to transcend the limitations of these entanglements in order to soar beyond Arab and foreign guardianship (Samman, Na'na', al-Shaykh, and al-Neimi). In modern Arabic literature, her character burgeons and morphs into other characters that combine both traditional and modern dimensions. For instance, the creation of "Dunyazad" and "Aufuqzad"—respectively meaning "child of the world" and "horizon"—symbolically references the trope's transformation from the limitation of her namesake, "of the city," and the expansion of contemporary literature's horizon to go beyond Shahrazad's initial feminist concerns (Suleiman 2006). In an anthology of contemporary Arab-American fiction entitled *Dinarzad's Children*, for example, the editors highlight their choice of the title to give presence to the forgotten voice of Shahrazad's sister, Dinarzad, who, but for her role in initiating Shahrazad's narrative in *A Thousand and One Nights*, has remained silent ever since (Kaldas and Mattawa 2004, ix, xiv). If Dinarzad were to speak today, the editors of this collection of Arab-American fiction post-9/11 pose the question, what would she say? In my opinion, the need to dislodge Shahrazad from a fixed feminist role, to transform her contemporary descendants to a position more befitting their multiple locales and hybrid identities, their local and global aspirations, and their revolutionary tactic, is a primary feature of contemporary, particularly diasporic, Arabic literature.

Ultimately, the writers' relationship to their female predecessor is a mixed one, simultaneously grateful for her contributions and resentful of her co-optation. Their bond with Shahrazad is not a blind one, for it speaks of a promise to transform the trap of her orality and locality into an active sociopolitical written project that eventually uplifts not just the women writers themselves, but their diasporic countries as well. Whether rejected or revered, Shahrazad takes many forms as she puts on the mask of the forgotten literary mother whose inspiration and/or erasure is a catalyst for the writers' insistence on retrieving and transcribing her orality into text, and inscribing her absence into presence. Shahrazad surfaces at different moments in their narratives. Her bodily presence forever reminds them of her literary absence and warns them against oppressive powers' co-optation of their authorial voice. In this nuanced literature, Shahrazad's resurrection is a classic case of what Susan Friedman describes as "the 'talking cure' suggest[ing] the dynamics of an analogous 'writing cure'" (Friedman 1989, 146). Orality is transformed into print where everyone can access the forbidden and the repressed through writing. Writing, insists al-Neimi, forces "words to be, to exist. I have to put experiences in writing so as to know that I lived them."[5] Writing and survival are inextricably linked; with writing, the voice of the maw'udah regains its buried corporality and acquires presence.

Indeed, resurrecting the lost literature of the forgotten mother, through the insistence on writing, is a primary goal in the literature of contemporary diaspora Arab women writers. With their insistence on commemorating their experiences in writing, our writers defy Shahrazad's orality and reinscribe her presence into the image of the literary mother. In fact, Samman's Zayn in *The Impossible Novel* regains her authorial voice only after discovering her literary mother's memoirs and unpublished written words. Likewise, al-Shaykh's penning of her mother's oral memoirs in *The Locust and the Bird* reconnects the severed ties between mother and daughter. Additionally, the forgotten trace of the mother finds its resonance in the theme of the absence of the feminine in constructing national narratives in Hamida Naʿnaʿ's and Hoda Barakat's novels. Specifically, the resurrection of the mummified amphora girl in Barakat's *The Tiller of Waters* articulates buried memories of national coexistence and peace poetics. Similarly al-Neimi's determination to unearth significant Arab manuscripts celebrating love poetics, to revive them in the text of *The Proof of the Honey*, speaks volumes to the urgency of employing a parallel

---

5. Personal communication, Sept. 12, 2011.

project of resurrecting and listening to the archives. It is this desire to acquaint oneself with cultural memories as well as with the unknown and the unclaimed literary corpus of the forgotten mother, with the inaccessible history of her erasure, that propels the creative act of listening to Shahrazad's and the maw'udah's voices.

At the hands of contemporary diaspora women writers, the Shahrazad of today is not interested in liberating women from real or imaginary veils; rather, she is determined to demolish the walls of local and global oppression that silence Arab females and males alike. While visiting the Occupied Territories in Palestine in 2008, Hanan al-Shaykh remarked on the "tragic" consequences of the "Apartheid Wall" erected by Israeli forces to separate Palestinians from their farmland and the rest of their families. She asserted, "I was shocked by the reality of the wall . . . shocked by the tragic life it ensues in al-Khalil [Hebron] and Bethlehem. I cannot believe that the world remains silent in the face of such ugliness, in the face of such imprisonment" (al-Shaykh 2008). The heroine of her subsequent play *A Fly on the Wall* (2008) concurs: "Today they cut my house in half; tomorrow they will prevent me from talking" (al-Shaykh 2008). In a similar vein, as I noted above, Samar Yazbek refers to the Syrian regime's checkpoints as "walls" and "veils" cutting neighborhoods off from each other and preventing people from voicing their resistance. Suddenly the silenced voice of the jahiliyyah's maw'udah is connected with the oppressed voices of the Palestinians in Israel, the Syrians under the Assad regime—indeed, with all the subjugated voices of Arab citizens living under the rule of local authoritarian regimes. Though the jahiliyyah's form of the physical feminine wa'd is not explicitly articulated by all Arab women diasporic writers, yet it is evoked as a recurring myth in the symbolic suffocation and limitations placed on the freedoms and free speech of Arab citizens of both genders in their literary output. In answering questions I posed to al-Neimi regarding the prevalence of dead corpses hiding under the heroine's bed in her poetry collection *My Murderous Ancestors* (2001) and in her prose, she stated, "Despite the fact that the idea of wa'd did not come to my mind upon writing, we might see it as a concept that sheds light not only on Arab female writers, but also on male writers as well. Perhaps, the fact that we are deprived of our countries, inside and outside, is indeed the contemporary form of wa'd."[6] The process within which Arab women diaspora authors articulated the atrocities of the wa'd for women has evolved to encompass the buried cultural *turath* (tradition) and memories of love poetics in al-Neimi, the state of buried freedoms and citizens in Samar Yazbek, individual will and the buried city of civil war-torn Beirut in Barakat's novels. Contemporary wa'd in most Arab countries is no longer directed at the victim's feminine gender, but employed by tyrannical regimes intent on burying, with equal brutality, the voices of freedom and calls for democracy coming from both male and female citizens alike. In fact, Arab Spring's revolutionary activists' most notable statement, both in public squares and on Facebook and Twitter, is *"innahum yurriduna wa'd al-thawrah"* (they [dictatorial regimes] are trying to bury the revolution). The bodies of iconic victims of the Tunisian (Mohamed Bouazizi), the Egyptian (Khalid Said), and the Syrian revolution (Hamza al-Khatib, Zainab al-Husni, and the children of the Hawla, Qubayer, al-Qusair, and Douma massacres) attest to the survivability and the ongoing brutality of contemporary wa'd.[7] Yet Arab women

6. Personal communication, Sept. 12, 2011.

7. Iconic victims of these Arab Spring revolutions have faced a horrific death at the hands of their respective countries' security police forces. Mohamed Bouazizi of Tunisia burned himself alive on December 17, 2010, to protest the state of his dispossession and police humiliation. Khalid Said of Alexandria, Egypt, died in detention on June 6, 2010, as a result of torture inflicted upon him by Egyptian security forces. Similarly, Hamza al-Khatib of Dar'a, Syria (a thirteen-year-old boy, died April 29, 2011), and Zainab al-Husni of Homs, Syria (a nineteen-year-old girl, died July 27, 2011) were tortured, mutilated, castrated (in Hamza's case), and dismembered (in Zainab's case) by brutal Syrian security forces during the Syrian revolution. Finally, on May 25, 2012, in the village of al-Hawleh (a suburb of the city of Homs, Syria), 110 people were bombed by the Syrian regime's tanks and more than sixty children died, some reportedly slaughtered by the regime's militias. Ten days later in the village of al-Qubayr near Hama, June 6, 2012, another massacre was committed when the regime's security forces executed another eighty-six villagers, most of them women and children. Not to be outdone, the regime's use of chemical weapons in the Damascus suburbs of Ghouta on August 21, 2013, represents yet another chapter of contemporary wa'd. Hundreds of infants and adults were suffocated by the regime's use of sarin gas.

diaspora writers are engaged in their own empowerment project, which entails surviving Shahrazad's orality and traditional and contemporary forms of wa'd. Through their preferred mode of the epistolary genre, the writers' literature can be viewed as constant open letters to the homeland, as their targeted audience was always their compatriots back home. Thus these diasporic narrations do more than just reclaim personal and public spaces for Arab women. Rather, they reclaim the nation for all its citizens by calling for an immediate restructuring of individual Arab identity and cultural and national politics to usher in a new dawn for the nation and its alienated citizens.

In Kahf's *E-Mails from Scheherazad*, Shahrazad reminds us that "Where I come from, / Words are to die for" (Kahf 2003, 43). The new virtual Shahrazad articulates the duality of death and discourse, which used to govern the rules of Arab women's authorship but offers diaspora as an outlet for new beginnings and for rhizomatic returns. It is through the experience of her diaspora that the female diasporic writer promises to transform this legacy of erasure, to heal what Edward Said called the state of "unhealable rift" and the "condition of terminal loss" (Said 2000, 171). Arab female writers of the diaspora attempt to heal the traumatic wound of death and exclusion, to overcome the rift caused by forgetfulness and fixed histories. In this process, the "condition of terminal loss" is transformed into presence, as death is erased through resurrection and life is affirmed through survival.

This book has been a testament to the resilience of Arab women in the face of internal and external adversity, a reminder that in their case a personal quest for self-affirmation can and must involve the political task of national rebuilding. Against all odds, these courageous women, reviving the maw'udah's voice, espousing and redefining the mission of Shahrazad, have not shied away from shouldering responsibility for the homeland left behind—a homeland that, no matter how long or how far their spatial and literary journey, is always their final destination.

Works Cited ❧ *Index*

Works Cited

'Abbas, Ihsan, and Muhammad Yusuf Najm, eds. 1967. *Al-Shi'r al-'Arabi fi al-Mahjar: Amrika al-Shamaliyyah*. Beirut: Dar Sader.

'Abd al-Ghani, Mustafa. 1985. *Shahrazad fi al-Fikr al-'Arabi al-Hadith* (Shahrazad in Contemporary Arab Thought). Beirut: Dar al-Shorouk.

'Abd al-Razzaq, Fawzi. 1981. *Adab al-Mahjar: Bibiliugraphiyyah lil- Dirasat al-Naqdiyyah wa-al-Maqalat*. Special issue entitled *Arab Writers in America: Critical Essays and Annotated Bibliography*. In *Mundus Arabicus* 1:45–179. Cambridge, UK: Dar Mahjar.

Abdo, Nahla. 2002. "Women, War and Peace: Reflection from the Intifada." *Women's Studies International Forum* 23, no. 5:585–93.

al-Abtah, Sawsan. 2004. "Hanan al-Shaykh: Sarahtu Abi bi-Anani Ada'u al-Hijab fi Haqibati wa La 'ala Ra'si." *Al-Sharq al-Awsat*, no. 9530, Dec. 31. http://aawsat.com/details.asp?section=19&article=274487&issueno=9530.

Accad, Evelyne. 1990. *Sexuality and War: Literary Masks of the Middle East*. New York: New York Univ. Press.

Adunis. 1986. *Al-Thabit wa-al-Mutahawwil: Bahth fi al-Ittiba' wa-al-Ibda' inda al-'Arab*. Vol. 1. Beirut: Dar al-Fikr.

Aghacy, Samira. 2009. *Masculine Identity in the Fiction of the Arab East since 1967*. Syracuse, NY: Syracuse Univ. Press.

Agnivesh, Swami. 2005. "Missing: 50 Million Indian Girls." *New York Times*, Nov. 25. Online edition.

al-Akbari, Ibn Batta. N.d. *Al-Ibanah al-Kubra*. 123/1. http://www.alsunnah.com.

Alf Layla wa-Layla. 1252 AH. 2 vols. Cairo: Matba'at Bulaq.

Allen, Roger. 2000. *An Introduction to Arabic Literature*. Cambridge, UK: Cambridge Univ. Press.

Amin, Dina. 2010. "Disorientation and the Metropolis in Huda Barakat's *Harith al-miyah*." *Journal of Arabic Literature* 41, no. 1/2:108–20.

Amyuni, Mona Takieddine. 1999. "A Panorama of Lebanese Women Writers, 1975–1995." In *Women and War in Lebanon*, edited by Lamia Rustum She-hadeh, 89–111. Gainesville: Univ. Press of Florida.

Anderson, Benedict. 1983. *Imagined Communities: Reflections on the Origin and Spread of Nationalism*. London: Verso.

Anderson, Linda. 2007. "Diaspora." In *Theories of Memory: A Reader*, edited by Michael Rossington and Anne Whitehead. Baltimore, MD: Johns Hopkins Univ. Press.

Anzaldúa, Gloria. 1987. *Borderlands/la Frontera: The New Mestiza*. San Francisco: Aunt Lute Books.

al-Ashtar, 'Abd al-Karim, ed. 1965. *Funun al-Nathir al-Mahjari*. Lebanon: Dar al-Fikr al-Hadith.

Aslan, Ibrahim. 2008. "Burhan al-'Asal." *Al-'Adala*, Feb. 10. Accessed Jan. 10, 2010. http://www.aladalanews.net/index.php?show=news&action=article&id =36894.

'Azzam, Muhammad. 1994. *Al-Khayal al-'Ilmi fi al-Adab*. Damascus: Dar Tlas.

Babayan, Kathryn, and Afsaneh Najmabadi, eds. 2008. *Islamicate Sexualities: Translations across Temporal Geographies of Desire*. Cambridge, MA: Center for Middle East Studies, Harvard Univ. Press.

Badr, Liana. 1991. *'Ayn al-Mir'ah: Riwayah*. Dar al-Bayda': Dar Tubqal lil-Nashr.

———. 1994. *The Eye of the Mirror*. Translated by Samira Kawar. London: Garnet Publishing.

Baker, Francis, Peter Hulme, and Margaret Iverson, eds. 1992. *Postmodernism and the Re-reading of Modernity*. Manchester, UK: Manchester Univ. Press.

Bakhtin, Mikhail. 1981. *The Dialogic Imagination*, edited by Michael Holquist. Austin: Univ. of Texas Press.

Barakat, Halim. 1985. "The Arab Family and the Challenge of Social Transformation." In *Women and the Family in the Middle East*, edited by Elizabeth Fernea, 25–48. Austin: Univ. of Texas Press.

———. 1993. *The Arab World: Society, Culture, and State*. Berkeley: Univ. of California Press.

Barakat, Hoda. 1990. *Hajar al-Dhahik*. London: Dar Riyadh al-Rayyes.

———. 1993. *Ahl al-Hawa*. Beirut: Dar al-Nahar.

———. 1995. *The Stone of Laughter*. Translated by Sophie Bennett. New York: Interlink Books. Reading, UK: Garnet Publishing.

————. 1998a. "I Write against My Hand." In *In the House of Silence: Autobiographical Essays by Arab Women Writers*, edited by Fadia Faqir, 43–47. Translated by Shirley Eber and Fadia Faqir. Reading, UK: Garnet Publishing.

————. 1998b. *Harith al-Miyah*. Beirut: Dar al-Nahar.

————. 2001. *The Tiller of Waters*. Translated by Marilyn Booth. Cairo: American Univ. in Cairo Press.

————. 2004a. *Rasa'il al-Ghariba*. Beirut: Dar al-Nahar.

————. 2004b. *Sayyidi wa-Habibi* (My Master and My Lover). Beirut: Dar al-Nahar.

————. 2005. *Disciples of Passion*. Translated by Marilyn Booth. Syracuse, NY: Syracuse Univ. Press.

————. 2010. *Viva La Diva*. Beirut: Dar al-Nahar.

Baron, Beth. 2005. *Egypt as a Woman: Nationalism, Gender and Politics*. Berkeley: Univ. of California Press.

Barth, John. 1972. *Chimera*. New York: Fawcett Crest.

Barthes, Roland. 1993. *Camera Lucida: Reflections on Photography*. Translated by Richard Howard. London: Vintage.

————. 2012. *Mythologies*. Translated by Richard Howard and Annette Lavers. New York: Hill and Wang.

al-Bayati, 'Abd al-Wahhab. 1968. *Al-Mawt fi al-Hayat*. Beirut: Dar al-Adab.

Bhabha, Homi K. 1990a. "DissemiNation: Time, Narrative, and the Margins of the Modern Nation." In *Nation and Narration*. Edited by Homi K. Bhabha, 310–11. New York: Routledge.

————. 1990b. "The Third Space." In *Identity Community Culture Difference*. Edited by Jonathon Rutherford, 207–21. London: Lawrence and Wishart.

————. 1994. *The Location of Culture*. London: Routledge.

Bin Hamzah, Husayn. 2009. "Salwa al-Ne'imi: Al-Jins Ihtifalan bi-al Hayat wa-al-Adab." *al-Akhbar*. Feb. 3. http://www.al-akhbar.com/ar/node/116530.

Blanton, Casey. 1997. *Travel Writing: The Self and the World*. New York: Twayne Publishers.

Bloom, Harold. 1973. *The Anxiety of Influence: A Theory of Poetry*. New York: Oxford Univ. Press.

Brah, Avtar. 1996. *Cartographies of Diaspora: Contesting Identities*. London: Routledge.

Braidotti, Rosi. 1994. *Nomadic Subjects: Embodiment and Sexual Difference in Contemporary Feminist Theory*. New York: Columbia Univ. Press.

Brown, Laura. 1995. "Not Outside the Range: One Feminist Perspective on Psychic Trauma." In *Trauma: Explorations in Memory*, edited by Cathy Caruth, 100–112. Baltimore, MD: Johns Hopkins Univ. Press.

Burton, Richard F., trans. N.d. *The Book of the Thousand Nights and a Night*. 10 vols. London: Burton Club for Private Subscribers Only.

Caruth, Cathy, ed. 1995. *Trauma: Explorations in Memory*. Baltimore, MD: Johns Hopkins Univ. Press.

———. 1996. *Unclaimed Experience: Trauma, Narrative, and History*. Baltimore, MD: Johns Hopkins Univ. Press.

Chodorow, Nancy. 1978. *The Reproduction of Mothering: Psychoanalysis and the Sociology of Gender*. Berkeley: Univ. of California Press.

Cixous, Hélène. 1986. "The Laugh of the Medusa." In *Critical Theory since 1965*, edited by Hazard Adams and Leory Searle, 308–20. Tallahassee: Florida State Univ. Press.

Clifford, James. 1997. *Routes: Travel and Translation in the Late Twentieth Century*. Cambridge, MA: Harvard Univ. Press.

Connerton, Paul. 1989. *How Societies Remember*. Cambridge, UK: Cambridge Univ. Press.

cooke, miriam. 1996. *Women and the War Story*. Berkeley: Univ. of California Press.

———. 1999. "Mapping Peace." In *Women and War in Lebanon*, edited by Lamia Rustum Shehadeh, 73–88. Gainesville: Univ. Press of Florida.

———. 2001. *Women Claim Islam: Creating Islamic Feminism through Literature*. New York: Routledge.

———, and Rustomji-Kerns, Roshni, eds. 1994. *Blood into Ink: South Asian and Middle Eastern Women Write War*. Boulder, CO: Westview Press.

Cooper, Brenda. 1998. *Magical Realism in West African Fiction: Seeing with a Third Eye*. London: Routledge.

Dawarah, Jadi'. 2008. "A Father Commits Infanticide." *Syria News* 17 (July). http://www.syrianews.com/readnews.php?sy_seq=79690.

De Capua, Paula. 1992. *Al-Tamarrud wa-al-Iltizam fi Adab Ghada al Samman*. Translated by Nura al-Samman-Winkel. Beirut: Dar al-Tali'ah.

Deleuze, Gilles, and Félix Guattari. 1986. *Nomadology: The War Machine*. Translated by Brian Massumi. New York: Semiotext(e).

———. 1987. *A Thousand Plateaus: Capitalism and Schizophrenia*. Translated by Brian Massumi. Minneapolis: Univ. of Minnesota Press.

Diaconoff, Suellen. 2009. *The Myth of the Silent Woman: Moroccan Women Writers*. Toronto: Univ. of Toronto Press.

Djebar, Assia. 1987a. *Ombre Sultane*. Paris: Editions Jean-Claude Lattès.

————. 1987b. *A Sister to Scheherazade*. Translated by Dorothy Blair. London: Quartet.

————. 1992. *Women of Algiers in Their Apartment*. Translated by Marjolijn de Jager. Charlottesville: Univ. of Virginia Press.

————. 2003. "Writing in the Language of the Other." In *Lives in Translation: Bilingual Writers on Identity and Creativity*, edited by Isabelle de Courtivron, 19–28. New York: Palgrave Macmillan.

Eisen, Arnold. 1986. *Galut: Modern Jewish Reflection on Homelessness and Homecoming*. Bloomington: Indiana Univ. Press.

El Hajj, Onsi. 2007. "Borhan El Assal." *Jetset magazine*.net. Mar. 14. http://www .jetsetmagazine.net/culture/revue,press/livre—borhanel-assal.

El-Rouayheb, Khaled. 2005. *Before Homosexuality in the Arab-Islamic World, 1500–1800*. Chicago: Univ. of Chicago Press.

[El Saadawi, Nawal] al-Saʿdawi, Nawal. 1987. *Suqut al-Imam*. Cairo: Dar al-Mustaqbal al-ʿArabi.

El Saadawi, Nawal. 1988. *The Fall of the Imam*. Translated by Sherif Hetata. London: Methuen.

———— [Al-Saʿdawi, Nawal]. 1995. *Awraqi, Hayati* (My Papers . . . My Life). Cairo: Dar al-Hilal.

The Encyclopedia of Islam. 1986. CD.ROM. Vol. 5:1.0. 2nd ed. Leiden: Brill.

Fadhelallah, Mariam. 2000. "Waʿd al-Banat fi alʿsr al-Jahhili." *Hawaʾ*. Nov. 11. http://www.balagh.com/woman/trbiah/6f0z4e8h.htm.

Faqir, Fadia, ed. 1998. *In the House of Silence: Autobiographical Essays by Arab Women Writers*. Translated by Shirley Eber and Fadia Faqir. Reading UK: Garnet Publishing.

Faris, Wendy. 1995. "Scheherazade's Children: Magical Realism and Postmodern Fiction." In *Magical Realism: Theory, History, Community*, edited by Lois Zamora and Wendy Faris, 163–64. Durham, NC: Duke Univ. Press.

Felman, Shoshana, and Dori Laub, eds. 1992. *Testimony: Crises of Witnessing in Literature, Psychoanalysis, and History*. New York: Routledge.

Fraser, Graham. 2000. "'No More Than Ghosts Make': The Hauntology and Gothic Minimalism of Beckett's Late Work." *Modern Fiction Studies* 46, no. 3:782.

Friedman, Susan. 1988. "The Writing Cure: Transference and Resistance in a Dialogic Analysis." *H. D. Newsletter* 2, no. 2:25–35.

———. 1989. "The Return of the Repressed in Women's Narrative." *Journal of Narrative Technique* 19, no. 1:141–56.

———. 1998. *Mappings: Feminism and the Cultural Geographies of Encounter.* Princeton, NJ: Princeton Univ. Press.

Freud, Sigmund. 1915. *The Interpretation of Dreams.* Translated by A. A. Brill. London: G. Allen and Unwin.

———. 1939. *Moses and Monotheism.* Translated by Katherine Jones. New York: Vintage Books.

———. 1963. *Dora: An Analysis of a Case of Hysteria.* Edited by Philip Rieff. New York: Simon and Schuster.

Galland, Antoine, trans. 1941. *Les Mille et Une Nuits: Contes Arabes.* Edited by Gaston Picard. Paris: Garnier Frères.

Ghanim, David. 2009. *Gender and Violence in the Middle East.* Westport, CT: Praeger.

Giacaman, Rita. 1996. "The Women's Movement of the West Bank." In *Arab Women Between Defiance and Restraint*, edited by Suha Sabbagh, 127–33. New York: Olive Branch Press.

Giladi, Avner. 1990. "Some Observations on Infanticide in Medieval Muslim Society." *International Journal of Middle East Studies* 22, no. 2:185–200.

Gilbert, Sandra M., and Susan Gubar, eds. 1979. *The Madwoman in the Attic: The Woman Writer and the Nineteenth-Century Literary Imagination.* New Haven: Yale Univ. Press.

Gilroy, Paul. 1987. *There Ain't No Black in the Union Jack: The Cultural Politics of Race and Nation.* London: Hutchinson.

Gubar, Susan. 1982. "'The Blank Page' and the Issues of Female Creativity." In *Writing and Sexual Difference*, edited by Elizabeth Abel. Sussex, UK: Harvester Press.

Haddad, Joumana. 2010. *I Killed Scheherazade: Confessions of an Angry Arab Woman.* London: Saqi.

Haddawy, Husain, trans. 1990. *The Arabian Nights.* Based on the text of the fourteenth-century Syrian manuscript edited by Muhsin Mahdi. New York: Everyman's Library.

Hadeed, Khalid. 2013. "Homosexuality and Epistemic Closure in Modern Arabic Literature." In *Queer Affects*, edited by Hanadi Al-Samman and Tarek

El-Ariss, special issue of *International Journal of Middle East Studies* 45, no. 2:271–91.

al-Hakim, Tawfiq. 1974. *Shahrazad*. Cairo: Al-Hay'ah al-Misriyyah al-'Amah lil-Kitab.

Hasan, Khalaf Ali. 2009. "Riwayat al-Shabab Takhtariq al-Tabu al Jinsi: Al-Ta'arri al-Lafzi Yajtahu al-Adab al-Masri." *Al-Jarida* 608, May 2. http://www.al jarida.com/aljarida/Article.aspx?id=108965.

————. 2010. "Ma'a Hanan al-Shaykh Hawla al-Kitabah wa-al-Manfa wa-Adab al-Nisa'." *Al-Rowaee: Arabic Magazine on the Novel*. Mar. 27. http://www .alrowaee.com/article.php?id=586.

al-Hassan Golley, Nawar. "*The Tiller of Waters*." *Association for Middle East Women's Studies* 18: no. 1–2 (2003): 7–8.

Hegel, George W. F. 2001 [1807]. "From *Phenomenology of Spirit*." In *The Norton Anthology of Theory and Criticism*, edited by Vincent Leitch, 630–36. New York: W. W. Norton and Co.

Herman, Judith. 1992. *Trauma and Recovery*. New York: Basic Books.

al-Hibri, Azizah. 2000. "An Introduction to Muslim Women's Rights." In *Windows of Faith: Muslim Women Scholar-Activists in North America*, edited by Gisela Webb, 51–71. Syracuse, NY: Syracuse Univ. Press.

Hill-Collins, Patricia. 1986. "Learning from the Outsider Within: The Social Significance of Black Feminist Thought." *Social Problems* 33, no. 6:14–32.

Hirsch, Marianne. 1997. *Family Frames: Photography, Narrative, and Postmemory*. Cambridge, MA: Harvard Univ. Press.

The Holy Quran. 1984. Revised and edited by the Presidency of Islamic Researchers, IFTA. Al-Madinah al-Munawarrah: King Fahd Holy Quran Printing Complex.

Husayn, Taha. 1951. *Ahlam Shahrazad*. Cairo: Dar al-Ma'arif.

Husayn, Taha, and Tawfiq al-Hakim. 1932. *Al-Qasr al-Mashur*. Cairo: Dar al-Ma'arif.

Ibn Hanbal, Ahmad. 1986. *Ahkam al-Nisa'*. Edited by 'Abd al-Qadir Ahmad 'Ata. Beirut: Dar al-Kutub al-Ilmiyyah.

Ibn Manzur. N.d. *Lisan al-'Arab*. Vol. 6. Cairo: al-Dar al-Misriyyah lil-Ta'lif wa-al-Tarjama.

Irigaray, Luce. 1990. "Women's Exile: Interview with Luce Irigaray." In *The Feminist Critique of Language: A Reader*, edited by Deborah Cameron, 80–96. Translated by Couze Venn. London: Routledge.

al-'Isa, Usama. 2008. "Al-Salafiyyah al-Jinsiyyah Tariq 'ila al Shuhrah al-Adabi-yyah." *Elaph*. June 14. http://www.elaph.com/ElaphWeb/Culture/2008/6/33 9741.htm.

al-Janabi, Hatif. 1995. "Reaching the Light at the End of the Tunnel: Reflections on the Arabic Writing in Exile." *Studia Arabistyczne Islamistyczne*, no. 3:39–42.

Joseph, Suad. 2000. "Civic Myths, Citizenship, and Gender in Lebanon." In *Gender and Citizenship in the Middle East*, edited by Suad Joseph, 107–36. Syracuse, NY: Syracuse Univ. Press.

———. 2001. "Among Brothers: Patriarchal Connective Mirroring and Brotherly Deference in Lebanon." In *The New Arab Family*, edited by Nicholas Hopkins, 24, no. 1–2:165–79.

Jung, Carl. 1966. *Two Essays on Analytical Psychology*. Vol. 7. Princeton, NJ: Princeton Univ. Press.

Kahf, Mohja. 2003. *E-Mails From Scheherazad*. Gainesville: Univ. Press of Florida.

———. 2007. "Lustrous Companions." *Arkansas Times*, Sept. 13.

———. 2008. "Spare Me the Sermon on Muslim Women." *Washington Post*, Mar. 10.

Kaldas, Pauline, and Khaled Mattawa, eds. 2004. *Dinarzad's Children: An Anthology of Contemporary Arab American Fiction*. Fayetteville: Univ. of Arkansas Press.

Kandiyoti, Deniz. 1988. "Bargaining with Patriarchy." *Gender and Society* 2, no. 3:274–90.

Kaplan, Caren. 1996. *Questions of Travel: Postmodern Discourses of Displacement*. Durham, NC: Duke Univ. Press.

Katz, Susan. 1987. "Speaking Out against the 'Talking Cure': Unmarried Women in Freud's Early Case Studies." *Women's Studies* 13:297–324.

Khafaji, Muhammad 'Abd al-Mun'im. N.d. *Qissat al-Adab al-Mahjari*. Cairo: Dar al-Tiba'ah al-Muhammadiyyah.

al-Khal, Yousef. 1979. *Al-'Amal al-Shi'riyyah al-Kamilah*. Beirut: Dar al-'Awdah.

Kilito, Abdelfattah. 2008. *Thou Shalt Not Speak My Language*. Translated by Waïl Hassan. Syracuse, NY: Syracuse Univ. Press.

King, Ynestra. 1989. "The Ecology of Feminism and the Feminism of Ecology." In *Healing the Wounds: The Promise of Ecofeminism*, edited by Judith Plant, 18–28. Philadelphia: New Society Publishers.

Kristeva, Julia. 1986. *The Kristeva Reader*, edited by Toril Moi. New York: Columbia Univ. Press.

———. 1987. "My Memory's Hyperbole." In *The Female Autograph: Theory and Practice of Autobiography from the Tenth to the Twentieth Century*, edited by Domna Stanton, 219–20. Chicago: Univ. of Chicago Press.

Lacan, Jacques. 1977. *Écrits: A Selection*. Translated by Alan Sheridan. London: Tavistock.

Lane, Edward William, trans. 1877. *The Thousand and One Nights*. Edited by Edward Stanley Poole. London: Bickers.

Lavie, Smadar. 2010. "Crossing the Palestine/Israel Border with Gloria Anzaldúa: Sovereignty, Transnationalism, and the Art of Staying Put." In *El Mundo Zurdo*, edited by Norma Cantú, Christina Gutiérrez, Norma Alarcón, and Rita Urquijo-Ruiz, 239–68. San Francisco: Aunt Lute.

Leeuwen, Richard van. 1998. "Autobiography, Travelogue and Identity." In *Writing the Self: Autobiographical Writing in Modern Arabic Literature*, edited by Robin Ostle, Ed de Moor, and Stefan Wild, 27–29. London: Saqi Books.

Lejeune, Philippe. 1988. *On Autobiography*. Edited by Paul John Eakin. Translated by Katherine Leary. Minneapolis: Univ. of Minnesota Press.

Malti-Douglas, Fedwa. 1991. *Woman's Body, Woman's Word: Gender and Discourse in Arabo-Islamic Writing*. Princeton, NJ: Princeton Univ. Press.

———. 1994. "Dangerous Crossings: Gender and Criticism in Arabic Literary Studies." In *Borderwork: Feminist Engagements with Comparative Literature*, edited by Margaret R. Higonnet, 224–29. Ithaca, NY: Cornell Univ. Press.

———. 1995. "Writing Nawal El Saadawi." In *Feminism Beside Itself*, edited by Diane Elam and Robyn Wiegman, 283–96. New York: Routledge.

———. 2006. "Shahrazad Feminist." In *The Arabian Nights Reader*, edited by Ulrich Marzolph, 347–64. Detroit, MI: Wayne State Univ. Press.

Manganaro, Elise Salem. 1999. "Lebanon Mythologized or Lebanon Deconstructed: Two Narratives of National Consciousness." In *Women and War in Lebanon*, edited by Lamia Rustum Shehadeh, 112–28. Gainesville: Univ. Press of Florida.

"Al-Mar'ah al-'Arabiyyah wa-al-Jins min al-Haramlik ila al-Ibahiyyah." 2007. *Maktoobblog*.com. Oct. 4. http://www.Maktoobblog.com.

Massad, Joseph. 2007. *Desiring Arabs*. Chicago: Univ. of Chicago Press.

Massey, Doreen. 1994. "Double Articulation: A Place in the World." In *Displacements: Cultural Identities in Question*, edited by Angelika Bammer, 110–21. Bloomington: Indiana Univ. Press

Mehta, Brinda. 2007. *Rituals of Memory in Contemporary Arab Women's Writing*. Syracuse, NY: Syracuse Univ. Press.

Mernissi, Fatima. 1996. *Women's Rebellion and Islamic Memory*. London: Zed Books.

———. 2001. *Scheherazad Goes West: Different Cultures, Different Harems*. New York: Washington Press.

Merrihew, Kristin. 2009. "The Proof of the Honey." *Mostly Fiction Book Reviews*. Aug. 8. http://bookreview.mostlyfiction.com/2009/proof-of-the-honey-by-salwa-al-neimi/.

Mina, Hanna. 1993. *Fragments of Memory: A Story of a Syrian Family*. Translated by Olive Kenny and Lorne Kenny. Austin: Univ. of Texas Press.

———. 2002. *Baqaya Suwar*. Beirut: Dar al-Adab.

Mitchell, W. J. T. 1994. *Picture Theory: Essays on Verbal and Visual Representation*. Chicago: Univ. of Chicago Press.

Muhaisin, Inas. 2009. "Hoda Barakat: Al-Kutab al-'Arab 'Yatama'." *Imarat al-Yaoum*. Mar. 22. http://www.emaratalyoum.com/life/cutlrue/2009-03-22-1.128270.

Mungello, D. E. 2008. *Drowning Girls in China: Female Infanticide in China since 1650*. Lanham, MD: Rowman and Littlefield.

al-Musawi, Muhsin Jassim. 1981. *Scheherazade in England: A Study of Nineteenth-Century English Criticism of the Arabian Nights*. Washington, DC: Three Continents Press.

———. 2003. *The Postcolonial Arabic Novel: Debating Ambivalence*. Leiden: Brill.

Na'na', Hamida. 1979. *Al-Watan fi al-'Aynayn*. Beirut: Dar al-Adab.

———. 1990. *Hiwarat ma'a Mufakkiri al-Gharb*. Baghdad: Dar al-Shu'un al-Thaqafiyyah al-'Amah.

———. 1995. *The Homeland*. Translated by Martin Asser. Reading, UK: Garnet Publishing.

———. 1998. "Writing Away the Prison." In *In the House of Silence: Autobiographical Essays by Arab Women Writers*, edited by Fadia Faqir, 91–103. Translated by Shirley Eber and Fadia Faqir. Reading, UK: Garnet Publishing.

al-Na'uri, 'Isa. 1976. *Adab al-Mahjar*. Dar al-Ma'arif.

———. 1977. *Mahjariyat*. Libya: al-Dar al 'Arabiyyah lil-Kitab.

Nedjma. 2005. *The Almond*. Translated by C. Jane Hunter. New York: Grove Press.

al-Neimi, Salwa. 1994. *Kitab al-Asrar* (The Book of Secrets). Cairo: Dar al-Thaqafa al-Jadidah.

———. 1999. *Dhahaba Alladhina Uhibbuhum* (Gone Are the Ones I Love). Cairo: Dar Sharqiyyat.

———. 2001. *Ajdadi al-Qatalah* (My Murderous Ancestors). Cairo: Dar Sharqiyyat.

———. 2004. *Inna 'Ataynaka* (We Bequeathed unto You). Damascus: Qadmas lil-Nashir wa al-Tawzi'.

———. 2007. *Burhan al-'Asal*. Beirut: Riyyad El-Rayyes Books.

———. 2009. *The Proof of the Honey*. Translated by Carol Perkins. New York: Europa Editions.

———. 2012. *Shibh al-Jazirah al-'Arabiyyah*. Beirut: Riyyad El-Rayyes Books.

Nourallah, Riad. 2006. *Beyond the Arab Disease: New Perspectives in Politics and Culture*. London: Routledge.

Nujaim, Ahmad. 2009. "Salwa al-Neimi: Al-'Arabiyyah Lughat al-Jins Tuba-lilluni, Tuhaiujjuni." *Manfa Watan*. Feb. 23. http://www.mwatan.net/fm/showthread.php?t=828.

Ofeish, Sami, and Sabah Ghandour. 2002. "Transgressive Subjects: Gender, War, and Colonialism in Etel Adnan's *Sitt Marie Rose*." In *Etel Adnan: Critical Essays on the Arab-American Writer and Artist*, edited by Lisa Suhair Majaj and Amal Amireh, 122–36. Jefferson, NC: McFarland and Co.

Omar, 'Abd al-Rahim. 1989. *Al-A'mal al-Shi'riyyah*. 'Aman: Maktabat 'Aman.

Ortner, Sherry B. 1974. "Is Female to Male as Nature Is to Culture?" In *Women, Culture, and Society*, edited by Michelle Zimbalist Rosaldo and Louise Lamphere, 67–87. Stanford, CA: Stanford Univ. Press.

Ouyang, Wen-Chin. "Metamorphoses of Scheherazade in Literature and Film." *School of Oriental and African Studies*, 66, no. 3 (2003): 402–18.

Payne, John, trans. 1901. *The Book of the Thousand Nights and One Night*. 9 vols. London: Printed for Subscribers Only.

Phelps, Ethel Johnston. 1981. "Scheherazade Retold." In *The Maid of the North: Feminist Folk Tales from Around the World*. New York: Henry Holt.

Poe, Edgar Allan. 1981. "The Thousand-and-Second Tale of Scheherazade." In *Edgar Allan Poe, Greenwich Unabridged Library Classics*. New York: Chatham River Press.

Prasad, Madhava. 1992. "On the Question of a Theory of (Third World) Literature." *Social Text*, no. 31/32:57–83.

Probyn, Elspeth. 1990. "Travels in the Postmodern: Making Sense of the Local." In *Feminism/Postmodernism*, edited by Linda J. Nicholson, 176–89. New York: Routledge.

Qabbani, Nizar. 1999. *Al-A'mal al-Siyasiyah al-Kamilah*. Vol. 6. Beirut: Manshurat Nizar Qabbani.

al-Qurtubi. N.d. *Al-Jami' li-ahkam al-Quran.* Vol. 7. N.p: N.p.

Renan, Ernest. 1990. "What Is a Nation?" In *Nation and Narration*, edited by Homi K. Bhabha, 8–22. Translated by Martin Thom. New York: Routledge.

Richardson, Matt. 2013. *The Queer Limit of Black Memory: Black Lesbian Literature and Irresolution.* Columbus: Ohio State Univ. Press.

al-Sa'dawi, Nawal. 1987. *Suqut al-Imam.* Cairo: Dar al-Mustaqbal al-'Arabi.

al-Saboul, Tayseer. 1998. *Al-A'mal al-Kamilah.* Vol. 2. 'Aman: Azminah lil-Nashr wa-al-Tawzi'.

Said, Edward. 1994. *Representations of the Intellectual.* New York: Vintage Books.

———. 2000. *Reflections on Exile and Other Essays.* Cambridge, MA: Harvard Univ. Press.

Saidah, George. 1956. *Adabuna wa-Udaba'una fi al-Mahajir al-Amrikiyyah.* Cairo: Jami'at al-Duwal al-'Arabiyyah.

Sa'igh, Salma. 1964. *Suwar wa-Dhikrayat.* Beirut: Dar al-Hadharah.

Sakakini, Widad. 1989 [1950]. *Insaf al-Mar'ah.* Cairo. Reprint, Damascus: Dar Tlas.

al-Samman, Ghada. 1975. *Beirut '75.* Beirut: Manshurat Ghada al-Samman.

———. 1976. *Kawabis Bayrut.* Beirut: Dar al-Adab.

———. 1979. *I'tiqal Lahzza Hariba.* Beirut: Manshurat Ghada al-Samman.

———. 1986a. *Ghurbah Tahta al-Sifr.* Beirut: Manshurat Ghada al-Samman.

———. 1986b. *Laylat al-Milyar.* Beirut: Manshurat Ghada al-Samman.

———. 1988. *Tasku' Dakhil Jurh.* Beirut: Manshurat Ghada al-Samman.

———. 1990. *Al-Qabilah Tastajwib al-Qatilah.* Beirut: Manshurat Ghada al-Samman.

———. 1992. *Al-Bahr Yuhakim Samakah.* Beirut: Manshurat Ghada al-Samman.

———. 1994. *Al-Qamar al-Murabba': Qisas Gharai'ibiyyah.* Beirut: Manshurat Ghada al-Samman.

———. 1995. *Beirut '75.* Translated by Nancy N. Roberts. Fayetteville: Univ. of Arkansas Press.

———. 1997a. *Al-Riwayah al-Mustahilah: Fusifusa' Dimashqiyyah* (The Impossible Novel: A Damascene Mosaic). Beirut: Manshurat Ghada al-Samman.

———. 1997b. *Beirut Nightmares.* Translated by Nancy N. Roberts. London: Quartet Books.

———. 1998. *The Square Moon: Supernatural Tales.* Translated by Issa J. Boullata. Fayetteville: Univ. of Arkansas Press.

———. 2003a. *Ra'shat al-Hurriyah.* Beirut: Manshurat Ghada al-Samman.

———. 2003b. *Sahra Tanakuriyyah lil-Mawta* (A Masquerade for the Dead). Beirut: Manshurat Ghada al-Samman.

————. 2005. *The Night of the Billion*. Translated by Nancy Roberts. Syracuse, NY: Syracuse Univ. Press.

al-Samman, Hanadi. 2008. "Out of the Closet: Representation of Homosexuals and Lesbians in Modern Arabic Literature." *Journal of Arabic Literature* 39, no. 2:270–310.

Schlote, Christine. 2003. "An Interview with Hanan al-Shaykh." *Literary London: Interdisciplinary Studies in the Representations of London* 1, no. 2. http://www.literarylondon.org/londonjournal/september2003/Schlote.html.

Scott, Jonathan, trans. 1811. *The Arabian Nights Entertainment*. 6 vols. London: Pickering and Chatto.

Sebbar, Leïla. 1982. *Shérazade: 17 Ans, Brune, Frisée, les Yeux Verts*. Paris: Editions Stock.

————. 1991. *Sherazade: Missing, Aged 17, Dark Curly Hair, Green Eyes*. Translated by Dorothy Blair. London: Quartet Books.

Sedgwick, Eve Kosofsky. 1985. *Between Men: English Literature and Male Homosocial Desire*. New York: Columbia Univ. Press.

Shammas, Anton. 2003. "The Drowned Library (Reflections on Found, Lost, and Translated Books and Languages)." In *Lives in Translation: Bilingual Writers on Identity and Creativity*, edited by Isabelle de Courtivron, 124–25. New York: Palgrave MacMillan.

Sharabi, Hisham. 1977. *Muqadimat li-Dirasat al-Mujtama' al-'Arabi*. Beirut: Al-'Ahliyyah lil-Nashir wa-al-Tawzi'.

————. 1988. *Neopatriarchy: A Theory of Distorted Change in Arab Society*. New York: Oxford Univ. Press.

Sha'rawi, Huda. 1981. *Mudhakkirati*. Cairo: Dar al-Hilal.

————. 1986. *Harem Years: The Memoirs of an Egyptian Feminist (1879–1924)*. Edited and translated by Margot Badran. London: Virago.

al-Shawaf, Rayyan. 2010. "Breaking Taboos in Middle Eastern Fiction." *Globe and Mail*, Jan. 2.

al-Shaykh, Hanan. 1992. *Barid Bayrut*. Beirut: Dar al-Adab.

————. 1995a. *Beirut Blues: A Novel*. Translated by Catherine Cobham. New York: Anchor Books.

————. 1995b. *The Story of Zahra*. Translated by Peter Ford. New York: Anchor Books.

————. 2001. *Innaha London ya 'Azizi*. Beirut: Dar al-Adab.

————. 2002. *Only in London: A Novel*. Translated by Catherine Cobham. New York: Anchor Books.

————. 2005. *Hikayati Sharhun Yatul.* Beirut: Dar al-Adab.

————. 2008. "Hanan al-Shaykh Takshuf Basha'at 'al-Ha'it al-Isminti fi Masra-hiyat *Dhubaba 'ala al-Jidar.*" *Shurufat.* May 13, 2008. http://palwriters.net/news.php?action=view&id=470.

————. 2009. *The Locust and the Bird: My Mother's Story.* Translated by Roger Allen. New York: Pantheon Books.

————. 2011. "Falling under the Spell of Shahrazad." *luminato*.com. June 10–19. http://www.luminato.com/My%20Files/_2011/Misc%20and%20Contests/Hanan%20HP%20article.pdf.

————, and Tim Supple. 2011. *One Thousand and One Nights: Modern Plays.* London: Methuen Drama.

Sheehi, Stephen. 1997. "Failure, Modernity, and the Works of Hisham Sharabi: Towards a Post-colonial Critique of Arab Subjectivity." *Middle East Critique* 6, no. 10:39–54.

Showalter, Elaine. 1990. *Sexual Anarchy: Gender and Culture at the Fin de Siècle.* New York: Penguin Books.

Shukri, Muhammad. 1973. *For Bread Alone.* Translated by Paul Bowles. London: P. Owen.

————. 1982. *Al-Khubz al-Hafi.* London: Dar al-Saqi.

Spivack, Charlotte. 1987. *Merlin's Daughters: Contemporary Women Writers of Fantasy.* New York: Greenwood Press.

Spivak, Gayatri Chakravorty. 2003. *Death of a Discipline.* New York: Columbia Univ. Press.

————. 2009. "Four Women's Texts and a Critique of Imperialism." In *Feminisms Redux: An Anthology of Literary Theory and Criticism*, edited by Robyn Warhol-Down and Diane Price Herndl, 365–89. New Brunswick, NJ: Rutgers Univ. Press.

Suleiman, Nabil. 2006. "Al-Riwayah al-'Arabiyyah wa-al-Turath al-Sardi." *Al-Thawrah.* Aug. 22. http://thawra.alwehda.gov.sy/_print_view.asp?FileName=263664620060822132357.

Suyoufie, Fadia. 2009. "Magical Realism in Ghadah al-Samman's *The Square Moon.*" *Journal of Arabic Literature* 40, no. 2:182–207.

Terdiman, Richard. 1985. *Discourse/Counter-Discourse: The Theory and Practice of Symbolic Resistance in Nineteenth-Century France.* Ithaca, NY: Cornell Univ. Press.

Todorov, Tzvetan. 1973. *The Fantastic: A Structural Approach to a Literary Genre.* Translated by Richard Howard. Ithaca, NY: Cornell Univ. Press.

Tuqan, Fadwa. 1985. *Rihla Jabaliyya, Rihla Saʿba*. Amman: Dar al-Shurouq.

————. 1990. *Mountainous Journey, Difficult Journey*. Translated by Olive Kenny and Naomi Shihab Nye. London: Women's Press.

Vees-Gulani, Susanne. 2003. *Trauma and Guilt: Literature of Wartime Bombing in Germany*. Berlin: W. de Gruyter.

Wild, Stefan. 1998. "Searching for Beginnings in Modern Arabic Autobiography." In *Writing the Self: Autobiographical Writing in Modern Arabic Literature*, edited by Robin Ostle, Ed de Moor, and Stefan Wild, 82–99. London: Saqi Books.

Woolf, Virginia. 1927. *To the Lighthouse*. New York: Harcourt, Brace and Co.

————. 1981. *A Room of One's Own*. San Diego: Harvest Books.

Woolfork, Lisa. 2008. *Embodying American Slavery in Contemporary Culture*. Champaign: Univ. of Illinois Press.

Yazbek, Samar. 2011. *Taqatuʿ Niran: Min Yawmiyat al-Intifadah al-Suriyyah*. Beirut: Dar al-Adab.

————. 2012. *A Woman in the Crossfire: Diaries of the Syrian Revolution*. Translated by Max Weiss. London: Haus Publishing.

al-Zabidi, *Taj al-ʿArus*. N.d. Vol. 13. Beirut: Dar Sadir.

Al-Zayyat, Latifa. 1992. *Hamlat Taftish: Awraq Shakhsiyya*. Cairo: al-Hay'ah al-ʿAmah lil-Kitab.

————. 1996. *The Search: Personal Papers*. Translated by Sophie Bennett. London: Quartet Books.

Zimra, Clarisse. 1992. "Interview with Assia Djebar." In *Women of Algiers in Their Apartment*. Translated by Marjolijn de Jager. Charlottesville: Univ. of Virginia Press.

Index

Hanadi Al-Samman is an associate professor of Arabic Language and Literature in the Department of Middle Eastern and South Asian Languages and Cultures at the University of Virginia. Her research focuses on contemporary Arabic literature, diaspora and sexuality studies, and transnational and Islamic feminisms. She is the author of several journal articles on these topics, and co-editor of an *International Journal of Middle East Studies* special issue titled "Queer Affects."